The Library of
Irish Studies

II. Contemporary
Irish Writing

Contemporary Irish Writing

EDITED BY
James D. Brophy
Raymond J. Porter

Iona College Press
Twayne Publishers

Contemporary
Irish Writing

Copyright © 1983
by Iona College Press
All Rights Reserved

Twayne Publishers
A Division of G. K. Hall & Company
70 Lincoln Street
Boston, Massachusetts 02111

Book design and production by Barbara Anderson

This book was typeset in
10 point Times Roman
by Compset, Inc.
of Beverly, MA

PRINTED ON PERMANENT/DURABLE
ACID-FREE PAPER AND BOUND IN
THE UNITED STATES OF AMERICA

Library of Congress Cataloging in Publication Data
Main entry under title:

Contemporary Irish writing.

(The Library of Irish studies)
Sequel to: Modern Irish literature.
Bibliography:
Includes index.
Contents: Landscape as culture / Anthony Bradley—
"To the point of Speech" / Eamon Grennan—That always
raised voice / John Engle—[etc.]
1. English literature—Irish authors—History and
criticism—Addresses, essays, lectures.   2. English
literature—20th century—History and criticism—

Addresses, essays, lectures.   3. Ireland in literature—
Addresses, essays, lectures.   I. Brophy, James D.
II. Porter, Raymond J. III. Series.
PR8754.C66   1983   820'.9'89162   83-113
ISBN 0-8057-9016-0

Contents

Foreword

This volume is a sequel to the editors' earlier collection of essays (*Modern Irish Literature,* 1972) which dealt mainly with writers of the first half of this century, including already acknowledged luminaries like Joyce, Yeats, and Beckett. *Contemporary Irish Writing,* beginning its range approximately where the other left off, assesses younger and more recent Irish writers who are making important contributions to contemporary poetry, prose, and drama. This new collection recognizes the extension of Ireland's literary significance in the twentieth century beyond the early masters down to the present, and, reflecting intellectual currents in Ireland, it includes two essays on writers who write in Irish.

J.D.B.
R.J.P.

Landscape as Culture:
The Poetry of Seamus Heaney

Anthony Bradley

In a poem in his third collection, *Wintering Out,* Seamus Heaney muses on the difference between the Irish and English landscapes.[1] He summons up the presence of Edmund Spenser, author of *The Shepherd's Calendar* (the first significant pastoral poem in English literature), and a colonist in Ireland during the Elizabethan war of conquest:

> . . . mizzling rain
> blurs the far end
> of the cart track.
> The softening ruts
>
> lead back to no
> "oak groves," no
> cutters of mistletoe
> in the green clearings.
>
> Perhaps I just make out
> Edmund Spenser,
> dreaming sunlight,
> encroached upon by
>
> geniuses who creep
> "out of every corner
> of the woodes and glennes"
> towards watercress and carrion.   ("Bog Oak")

The difference between the landscapes is, the poem implies, partly geographic: the Irish landscape and weather seem inimical to the bright pastoral fiction that might have transplanted Arcadia to Ireland as well as to England. Ireland's wet woods (and there are fewer of those since Spenser's time), its glens, bogs, and mountains seem too rugged to accommodate the Mediterranean configurations of landscape that characterize the pastoral.

1

The city-based, literary myth of the classical pastoral, that the life of a shepherd was enviable because of its leisure, that the country was the uncomplicated sphere of natural and simple feelings, that to live in the country was to live in a prelapsarian Golden Age, found new life in the English renaissance poets—in Spenser, Sidney, Raleigh, Drayton, and a host of others. But the famished "geniuses" of Heaney's poem are the tutelary deities of the Irish landscape, the spirits of the place; they are not the shepherds and nymphs of classical and renaissance pastoral, and they most certainly do not inhabit Arcadia.

The difference between the Irish and the English landscapes, then, is not so much a matter of geography as of historical and political allegiances and sharply differing literary sensibilities. Despite his being educated in the English language and the English literary tradition (as well as the Irish), and despite his enjoyment of Spenser's poetry, Heaney, like most other Irish writers, will feel more sympathy for the starving wretches of "Bog Oak" who escaped death at the hands of the Elizabethan soldiers than he will for the misery and homesickness of Spenser in Ireland. Most importantly, perhaps, the Irish literary sensibility, especially as it manifested itself in a tradition of nature poetry in Gaelic going back at least five hundred years before Spenser, is characterized by a considerably more primitive and animistic sense of place than anything in the European literary tradition. The Irish landscape is, in fact, the repository of a radically different culture than the English.

What does a modern Irish poet like Heaney make of the English landscape? Because he understands the English literary tradition as well as the Irish, he is more appreciative of the English landscape than Spenser was of the Irish, but finds it, ultimately, alien:

> I rode down England
> as they fired the crop
> that was the leavings of a crop,
> the smashed tow-coloured barley,
>
> down from Ely's Lady Chapel,
> the sweet tenor latin
> forever banished,
> the sumptuous windows
>
> threshed clear by Thomas Cromwell.   ("Leavings," *Field Work*)

It is not only the Reformation that has made the English landscape one in which the Irish Catholic does not feel at home. There is also the political consciousness of the colonized, in that the poet sees the firing of the crop as "a thatch-deep, freshening / barbarous crimson burn," in that he has a racial memory of other kinds of burning, threshing, and smashing than the purely agricultural. So the poem defines by implication that other landscape in which he is completely at home. And the poem's structure, moreover, by which agriculture is connected with civilization and culture, is precisely the structure of those poems that embody the *Irish* cultural landscape.

In poem after poem Heaney has given us the sense of a landscape that seems magically real and there; the poems seem, in a very physical way, embodiments of place. But like great landscape painting, say the Dutch of the seventeenth century, there is implicit in Heaney's art not only the visual exactness and the precise feel of the light and weather, but also a rich and full summoning-up of a whole way of life, of a culture. In Heaney, the Irish landscape is inseparable from language, from the etymology and music of place names, from work both agricultural and artistic, from history both archeological and contemporary; landscape is inseparable, too, from the present political conflict as well as from an atavistic sense of nature as religion and work as ritual; it is inseparable, finally, from the community as divided and the community as unified.

This evocation of a whole way of life in Heaney's poetry makes it, I would argue, a realistic version of pastoral structurally akin to that written by Hardy or Lawrence (except that it is, of course, rooted in the Irish experience). It has little to do with shepherds or the conventions of Renaissance pastoral; that genre had lost what vitality it possessed by the eighteenth century. And the emphasis of the Romantic poets (with the partial exception of Wordsworth) on the individual and the sublime had, by and large, separated Nature from the human community of the rural world. In the late nineteenth and early twentieth century, however, Hardy and Lawrence created a new type of pastoral, one that arose initially from their experience and not their reading. This pastoral has strong regional affinities, and uses the rural world as a setting for complex human and social experience. In this strain of pastoral, one has the feeling that social, political, economic, and psychological realities have overtaken the literary convention to make something rich and rare out of the tension between the natural and the cultivated. This version of pastoral is, moreover, an index to what is humane, communal, and renewing, whether in the despairing wasteland that the industrial and technological revolutions have made of our world, or in the context of an island divided by hatred and violence.

Heaney's particular version of pastoral, further, is symbolic in its resonance, primitive and chthonic in its tendency. It is based on the mystery and cult of the earth; as with Antaeus, this is the source of Heaney's strength:

> Down here in my cave
>
> Girdered with root and rock
> I am cradled in the dark that wombed me
> And nurtured in every artery
> Like a small hillock.   ("Antaeus," *North*)

The poems themselves, time after time, give the impression of welling-up, of shouldering-up from the unconscious, however finely crafted each individual poem may ultimately be.

The Language of Landscape

Although Heaney writes in English and the English poetic tradition forms an important part of his consciousness, he is always aware that the cultural freight of the English language is not the same for the Irish as it is for the English. The epigraph to "The Wool Trade" (*Wintering Out*) is taken from Joyce's *A Portrait of the Artist as a Young Man*. In that novel Stephen Dedalus is prompted by a conversation with the English dean of studies at the university to exclaim, "How different are the words 'home,' 'Christ,' 'ale,' 'master,' on his lips and on mine!" In Heaney's poem, when someone (presumably an Englishman) uses the phrase that is the poem's title, it evokes for Heaney the ease and assurance of the English mercantile tradition, and he imagines "square-set men in tunics / Who plied soft names like Bruges / In their talk." But that tradition, although Heaney savors it in the poem, is not something that an Irishman can feel he belongs to; the Irish culture he is part of is harsher, more sanguinary, less comfortable and soft than the English: "And I must talk of tweed, / A stiff cloth with flecks like blood."

In a series of poems in *Wintering Out,* Heaney makes us feel that the identity of a place, its meaning, resides precisely in the linguistic and musical phenomenon of its name. So "Anahorish" (in the poem of the same title) is "soft gradient / of consonant, vowel-meadow," and the Moyola river (in "Gifts of Rain") *is* language and music:

> The tawny guttural water
> spells itself: Moyola
> is its own score and consort,
>
> bedding the locale
> in the utterance,
> reed music, an old chanter
>
> breathing its mists
> through vowels and history.

In "Toome," the place-name suggests burrowing down into the past and the unconscious, and phonetics merges into archeology and psychology: the articulation of the "soft blastings" that form the place-name lead, "under the dislodged / slab of the tongue," into a "souterrain," into an exploration of what lies buried in "alluvial mud." "Broagh" reminds us that Irish place-names are often shibboleths, sharp indicators of cultural difference: the sudden ending of the "low tattoo" of a rain shower is like the ending of the name, "that last / *gh* the strangers found / difficult to manage." Sometimes the one name can indicate two divergent cultural traditions. "Mossbawn," the name of the farm in County Derry where Heaney grew up, according to the Scots and English etymology (Heaney tells us), means "the planter's house on the bog." Yet the local pronunciation suggests, rather, a Gaelic origin meaning "the moss of bog-cotton." Heaney concludes: "In the syllables of my home I see a metaphor of the split culture of Ulster."[2]

Of course, these poems "about" place are also "about" language in their demonstration that the language of poetry is not so much referential as creative. Even if we are familiar with the places referred to in Heaney's poems, in the poems the places have a symbolic function that is independent of their geographical existence. The poems create landscapes of mind, and do not merely refer to some pre-existent, external reality. It is not the actual coastal town of Carrickfergus, County Antrim, for instance, that Heaney depicts, but rather a beautiful and eerie vision inspired by the town's salt mines: "the frosty echo of saltminers' picks," the "chambered and glinting / . . . township built of light" ("The Singer's House," *Field Work*). Similarly, Mossbawn, County Derry and Glanmore, County Wicklow, do not exist for most of us except as landscapes in the poetry of Seamus Heaney. His language creates these places and does not merely describe or reflect them; they are settings for emotions and ideas, not ends in themselves.

Landscape and Community

Although the rural community of Ulster is divided by political and religious differences, and has been since the Plantation of the seventeenth century, there has usually been less tension in the countryside than in the city, just because small farmers are more dependent on each other than city dwellers. There is more cooperation at harvest time or whenever any big job has to be done in a short time. But the rural community is divided, nonetheless, and the particular feel of neighborly differences is sensitively realized in Heaney's poems. In "The Other Side" (the title is a typically oblique way of referring in Ulster to that part of the populace that does not share your religious belief—if a Catholic uses the phrase it refers to the Protestants, and vice-versa), a Protestant farmer casually dismisses the "scraggy acres" of his Catholic neighbor with the thoughtless authority of a Biblical allusion: " 'It's as poor as Lazarus, that ground.' "

The irony of the dismissal is especially piquant because the Plantation of Ulster expropriated the fertile land on behalf of the colonists and left the "scraggy acres" to those Catholics who had been dispossessed. The rationalization for this dispossession in the seventeenth century was based on the planters' conviction that the culture of the natives was inferior. The fact that they were Irish, spoke a different language, observed a different religion, practised a different system of farming, held to different laws, and had a different social organization—all this made them manifestly inferior and unfit to possess the rich arable land of Ulster. The Protestant in the poem is the unconscious heir to this mentality, and so is vaguely disparaging of his Catholic neighbors because their farm is poor, as though their poverty were elective. But the historical irony is almost incidental to the poem's meditative appreciation of the mentality the Protestant farmer expresses, his assurance that he belongs to God's chosen people, and his use of the Bible as a justification for his way of life: "His brain was a whitewashed kitchen / hung with texts, swept tidy / as the body o' the kirk" ("The Other Side," *Wintering Out*).

Yet the other side to the experience shows the Protestant farmer uncomfortable and shut out from his Catholic neighbors whose religion (the rosary in the kitchen "dragging mournfully on") must seem to him as alien and separating as his to them. Heaney's feeling is for the human as opposed to the historical and religious situation, but he makes his readers feel that the historical division of Ulster is a real and conditioning aspect of human relationships in the north of Ireland. The unease, reticence, and wariness that are part of the relationship between Catholic and Protestant, even at the best of times in Northern Ireland, are at war with the purely communal response. So, as the farmer stands in his Catholic neighbor's yard, embarrassed by "the moan of prayers," the poet asks himself whether he should "slip away," or approach him and talk about what the two sides have in common, "the weather / or the price of grass-seed."

The complication of everyday life by the nagging awareness that one is somehow always suspect, always regarded as subversive by the authorities as well as one's Protestant neighbors, is reflected in "A Constable Calls" (North). The child in the poem feels a vague sense of fear and guilt as the policeman records the amount of land under cultivation, and the crops being grown:

> He had unstrapped
> The heavy ledger, and my father
> Was making tillage returns
> In acres, roods, and perches.
>
> Arithmetic and fear.
> I sat staring at the polished holster
> With its buttoned flap, the braid cord
> Looped into the revolver butt.

The policeman is fulfilling a merely clerical task assigned him by the department of agriculture, but despite this, his uniform of the Royal Ulster Constabulary, his "domesday book," the ominous ticking of the gears on his bicycle when he leaves, are all felt by the child to be the outward signs of an inimical authority.

Landscape and Work

There is little sense in earlier Irish poetry of the reality of the "tillage returns" and "root crops" of "A Constable Calls," little sense of the Irish landscape as agricultural as well as emblematic. Only Kavanagh precedes Heaney in creating this new sensibility and social consciousness in Irish poetry. These two poets depict from the inside the way of life of ordinary country people on small farms in the north of Ireland. Their poetry celebrates the unidealized beauty of the familiar, the commonplace, and the unspectacular in a way that recalls Dutch landscape and genre painting. And there is an emphasis on work, whether in the fields or the farmhouse, as ritual, as satisfyingly in touch with the life of nature. The titles of Heaney's poems, especially his earlier ones, are reminiscent of Kavanagh's in directing the reader to the ritual of rural work—"Digging," "Churning Day," "Thatcher," "Rite of Spring," and so on.

"The Wife's Tale" and "The Seed Cutters" have a Breughelesque flavor, especially in the images of the linen cloth laid under the hedge, and the laborers after their meal "Spread out, unbuttoned, grateful, under the trees" ("The Wife's Tale," *Door Into the Dark*). In "The Seed Cutters" (*North*), the laborers "kneel under the hedge in a half circle," their knives

> Lazily halving each root that falls apart
> In the palm of the hand: a milky gleam,
> And, at the centre, a dark watermark.

The companion piece to "The Seed Cutters" is a portrait of a countrywoman in her farmhouse kitchen that is reminiscent in its technique of the intimism

of Dutch interiors and their loving celebration of humble and commonplace
people and things:

> So, her hands scuffled
> over the bakeboard,
> the reddening stove
>
> sent its plaque of heat
> against her where she stood
> in a floury apron
> by the window.
>
> Now she dusts the board
> with a goose's wing,
> now sits, broad-lapped,
> with whitened nails
>
> and measling shins   ("Sunlight")

The ambiance of the dairy is also well-done in "Churning Day" (*Death of a Naturalist*), a poem that radiates a sense of ritual cleansing, of the textures of wood, earthenware, and stone, of coolness and tranquillity.

But agricultural labor (and this is one significant area where Heaney differs from Kavanagh) is frequently not merely itself in Heaney, but is inseparable from another kind of labor, the making of verse. The first poem in Heaney's first collection makes the equation explicit. When Yeats summoned up his ancestors in the dedicatory poem affixed to *Responsibilities,* "Pardon, Old Fathers," he proclaimed that only his books proved his kinship with these illustrious forebears. Heaney's poem makes a similar kind of point, but his metaphor insists that writing, too, is labor, insists on the fusion (in his verse, at least) of the earthy and the intellectual. Like his father and grandfather who dug into the earth and peat of the family farm, Heaney resolves to dig:

> . . . I've no spade to follow men like them.
>
> Between my finger and my thumb
> The squat pen rests.
> I'll dig with it.   ("Digging," *Death of a Naturalist*)

This connection of work with poetry, of the illiterate with the literate world, of the pagan and unconscious with the civilized and conscious, is something that is at the core of Heaney's gift.

In *Field Work,* Heaney's most recent collection, the notion of an activity so cultivated as writing poetry being in fact dependent on the earth is gracefully sustained in a number of poems in the sequences called "Field

Work'' (the title would seem to refer to both literary and agricultural work) and ''Glanmore Sonnets.'' In ''Field Work IV,'' when the poet presses a leaf of flowering currant on the back of someone's hand, and rubs it with brown earth, it leaves a pattern of the leaf's veins. The poem suggests, allegorically, that art is a making palpable of the design inherent in nature. And in an inversion of the ceremony of Ash Wednesday, in which the priest's thumb rubs ashes on the foreheads of the faithful, to humble them by this reminder of their mortality, the poet, in bringing out the leaf's design on the woman's hand, celebrates her life and fruitfulness as part of the wider pattern of nature's fecundity:

> I lick my thumb
> and dip it in mould,
> I anoint the anointed
> leaf-shape. Mould
> blooms and pigments
> the back of your hand
> like a birthmark—
> my umber one,
> you are stained, stained
> to perfection.

By describing Glanmore as a ''hedge school,'' and connecting the plough with verse, Heaney neatly combines the natural with the cultivated. (The term also suggests the kinship the poet feels with the Irish during the penal days, when education was forbidden to Catholics, and they pursued learning illicitly, in the shelter of a hedge):

> Then I landed in the hedge-school of Glanmore
> And from the backs of ditches hoped to raise
> A voice caught back off slug-horn and slow chanter
> That might continue, hold, dispel, appease:
> Vowels ploughed into other, opened ground,
> Each verse returning like the plough turned round.

In ''The Makings of a Music,'' Heaney suggests how Wordsworth's habit of composing aloud, ''to-ing and fro-ing like a ploughman up and down a field . . . unites the old walking meaning of '*versus*' with newer, talking sense of verse . . . 'Verse' comes from the Latin *versus* which could mean a line of poetry but could also mean the turn that a ploughman made at the head of the field as he finished one furrow and faced back into another.''[3] This etymological connection is illuminating in a very precise way: the basis for Heaney's poetry, I think, lies in its marriage or fusion of those two meanings of "versus." Heaney might have gone on to explain the etymology of "cultus," another Latin word which underpins the connection of agriculture with poetry in its range of associated meanings—which include the plough, work, farming, veneration, and civilization. The important point is that like "versus," "cultus" presumes an organic link between husbandry and more refined ideas of cultivation.

"The Memory of Landscape": The Bog Poems

The bog has been an enduring preoccupation of Heaney's poetry: in "Digging" he described his grandfather cutting fuel on a bog, "Nicking and slicing neatly, heaving sods / Over his shoulder, going down and down / for the good turf." In providing fuel the bog plays a significant part in the rural economy of Ireland, perhaps as much as wood does in the countryside of New England. It has other, less practical attributes, though. It is the only land in Ireland that is not fenced or walled in, so that its properties are felt to be different from those of farmland. It has miraculous preserving qualities: "Bogland" (*Door Into the Dark*) tells us that "Butter sunk under / More than a hundred years / Was recovered salty and white;" and many of the Celtic artifacts that comprise Ireland's national treasures were found in bogs. There is, then, a communal sense of the bog as a preserver of the past, of secret knowledge.

The phenomenology of the bog, as Heaney gradually explores it, leads him from the name of his family's farm ("the moss of bog cotton") to an awareness of Ireland's geographical and psychic kinship with other northern European countries that also have large stretches of bogland, especially Denmark. This association of Ireland with the Scandinavian countries has an historical basis in the Viking invasions of Ireland that (though they took much away) gave the country its earliest townships and stamped such names as Dublin, Waterford, Wexford, Strangford, and Carlingford, on the landscape of Ireland. To evoke these associations, as Heaney does in *North*, is, arguably, to place the Irish landscape at a more realistic latitude than the one it is generally reckoned to inhabit; certainly it suggests a bleaker and more northerly place than we might have thought Ireland to be.

But Heaney is, of course, no mere amateur archeologist—it is the psyche of the landscape he is primarily interested in, the human revelations of the geography. So the bog becomes, very naturally, "the memory of the landscape," a metaphor for the personal and racial unconscious, for the earth-goddess, for mother Ireland, becomes a revelation of the tribal feelings that fuel the violence in the North of Ireland.[4]

The most shocking and fascinating finds in the bogs of northern Europe have been not artifacts but corpses, preserved, frequently since the Iron Age, by the peculiar chemistry of the bogs. In "The Tollund Man" (*Wintering Out*) and a series of poems in *North,* Heaney captures the "beauty and atrocity" ("The Grauballe Man") of these preserved bodies. Interestingly enough, the first circumstantial account of the recovery of one of these ancient corpses from the bogland dates from 1780, when a farm laborer on the Moira estate in County Down found the body of a young woman, probably a Viking. "Bog Queen" is inspired by this account. The other bog poems are based on finds in Denmark, but the connection with Ireland is an integral part of each poem's structure of feeling. The Tollund Man was evidently a ritual sacrifice to the earth goddess, part of a fertility ritual that Heaney connects with the apparently endless sacrifice of human life to the female deity of Ireland. So the dream-like landscape of Denmark is only superficially strange, for the juxtaposition of "parishes" with "man-killing" suggests the combination of a civilized Christian organization of communities with a barbaric, cultic religion of violence that is dreadfully familiar to the Ulsterman:

> Out there in Jutland
> In the old man-killing parishes
> I will feel lost,
> Unhappy and at home.   ("The Tollund Man")

Similarly, in "The Grauballe Man," the slashed throat of the victim pre-served in a Danish bog leads us from Northern Europe's past to Northern Ireland's present and the victims of political murder; the physical realization of the victim is so palpable and vivid as to make us feel the dead weight of those other corpses, "the actual weight / of each hooded victim, / slashed and dumped." In "Punishment," the shaved head of a young woman drowned in the bog for her adultery, brings to mind the humiliation of young women in Ireland who were punished by the nationalist community for being too friendly with British soldiers. The complex of emotions in this poem especially, but also in the other bog poems, involves sympathy and identifi-cation with the victim, and at the same time an acknowledgement of the primitive justice of such savage rituals, of the "exact / and tribal, intimate revenge."

Landscape and the Present

The urgent question that is implicit in Heaney's most recent collection is, What is the use of writing poetry in a time when one's country seems torn

apart by such urgent and grave problems as bedevil the North of Ireland? In
Field Work, Heaney adopts a different technique from that of his earlier bog
poems to find "images and symbols adequate to our predicament."[5] In the
main the poems of *Field Work* are a more direct and open treatment of the
troubles than those of *North;* they don't begin in Denmark and circle back to
Ireland, though I think that connection is one that is fully earned by each of
the bog poems.

In *Field Work,* the poet is a more active and conscious presence; he speaks
authoritatively in his own persona, and does not mingle his identity with that
of the victims in the bog poems. Also, the poems set off the earth and its
regenerative potential from the violence and death associated with politics,
makes it the basis of life (whereas the bog, though earth-mother, was
destructive and possessive as well as the source of life and fertility). The
technique is most obvious, perhaps, in a poem like "The Toome Road,"
where the persona encounters

> armoured cars
> In convoy, warbling along on powerful tyres,
> All camouflaged, with broken alder branches,
> And headphoned soldiers standing up in turrets.

The earth, mysterious and renovating, is still the basis of life and beauty, the
center that holds despite soldiers and strife, ancient and modern wars:

> O charioteers, above your dormant guns,
> It stands here still, stands vibrant as you pass,
> The invisible, untoppled omphalos.

In "After a Killing," the first panel of "Triptych," we encounter the two
antinomies of Irish life. The opening image of "Two young men with rifles
on the hill, / Profane and bracing as their instruments," reminds us that the
Irish republic was founded by armed struggle, that its leaders were "terrorists" and that the Irish political identity, for better or worse, is based on
violence. The concluding stanza, in opposition to the opening one, is a bright
image of unspectacular peace, fertility, and domesticity:

> And today a girl walks in home to us
> Carrying a basket full of new potatoes,
> Three tight green cabbages, and carrots
> With the tops and mould still fresh on them.

Heaney's elegies for victims of political murder in this volume are pro-
foundly moving (I find them more so than the elegies for famous people like
Lowell and O'Riada, however excellent these are). While facing squarely

the reality of the victims' death, the elegies enlist images of the natural world to define the meaning of their lives and to convey a healing sense of benediction and resurrection. The title of the elegy for Heaney's cousin, Colum McCartney, an innocent victim of sectarian murder, is "The Strand at Lough Beg," as though the landscape ("The lowland clays and waters of Lough Beg, / Church Island's spire, its soft treeline of yew") were the most significant thing about this man's existence. It is the landscape that offers the sacramental process of healing and cleansing, and it is the poet who is the priest, who ministers to the dead man. The elegy's ending is inspired, as the epigraph indicates, by the beginning of the *Purgatorio*. Having just emerged from Hell, Dante is besmeared with filth and grime. Virgil washes his face with dew and girds his body with rushes. But the emotional impact of Heaney's poem does not depend on its allusiveness. The reference to Dante has been thoroughly assimilated and domesticated, made part of the particular Irish landscape at Lough Beg, its dew and drizzle, moss and rushes. The images of resurrection are images of the green world renewing itself, and while not conventionally religious, their effect is of a comforting absolution and spiritual renewal. The poem's calm acceptance of the murdered man's existence after his death and of his need for consolation is very moving. And there is something heartbreaking and yet exalting about the image of the green rushes (like the barley growing out of the graves of the rebels in "Requiem for the Croppies"):

> I turn because the sweeping of your feet
> Has stopped behind me, to find you on your knees
> With blood and roadside muck in your hair and eyes,
> Then kneel in front of you in brimming grass
> And gather up cold handfuls of the dew
> To wash you, cousin. I dab you clean with moss
> Fine as the drizzle out of a low cloud.
> I lift you under the arms and lay you flat.
> With rushes that shoot green again, I plait
> Green scapulars to wear over your shroud.   ("The Strand at Lough Beg")

The strategy of this and the other elegies, "Casualty" and "A Postcard from North Antrim," is essentially that of the collection, which is to juxtapose the beauty and value and unselfconscious dignity of ordinary people's lives, expressed as a function of the natural world, with violence, hatred and sudden death.

While I have focused mainly on the way Heaney's poetry takes us from the simple to the complex, from the natural to the cultivated, there is an undertow in his poetry that also takes us in the opposite direction. And a particular and emphatic value lies in that direction for people living in our industrial and technological age, when we have, generally speaking, lost touch with feelings that come from intimacy with nature and the rural world. Indeed, as Raymond Williams points out, the more the actual country has diminished in its economic function in modern society, the more the feelings and ideas associated with the country have become urgent and significant: "There is almost an inverse proportion, in the twentieth century, between the relative importance of the working rural economy and the cultural importance of rural ideas."[6]

What Heaney has given us in his poetry is a profound and resonant portrait of the cultural landscape of Ireland, centered in Ulster. Heaney's distinction as a poet depends, I feel, on his marvellous ability to unify, in his portrayal of this landscape, the two apparently antithetical connotations of culture—the earth and the intellect. The essence of his technique is to evoke the life of nature as a way of generating aspects of culture that might seem at first sight to have little to do with nature—to charge the landscape with a political or historical or linguistic or psychological significance, so that the connection seems natural and right. In this regard his poetry should be conceived of as Heaney intends, "as restoration of the culture to itself."[7]

Notes

1. Seamus Heaney, *Wintering Out* (London: Faber and Faber, 1972). The other collections of poems referred to in the text are also published by Faber: *Death of a Naturalist* (1966), *Door Into the Dark* (1969), *North* (1975), and *Field Work* (1979).

2. Seamus Heaney, "Belfast," in *Preoccupations: Selected Prose 1968-1978* (New York: Farrar, Straus, Giroux, 1980), p. 35.

3. Heaney, "The Makings of a Music," in *Preoccupations,* p. 65.

4. Heaney, "Feeling into Words," in *Preoccupations,* p. 54.

5. Ibid., p. 56.

6. Raymond Williams, *The Country and the City* (New York: Oxford University Press, 1973), p. 248.

7. Heaney, "Feeling into Words," in *Preoccupations,* p. 41.

"To the Point of Speech":
The Poetry of Derek Mahon

Eamon Grennan

The publication of *Poems 1962–1978* confirmed Derek Mahon's reputation as one of the most important voices in contemporary Irish poetry.[1] Unlike Seamus Heaney, Thomas Kinsella, and John Montague, however, Mahon is scarcely known on this side of the Atlantic. Reviews of his work have occasionally appeared, but these have, for all their commendations, done little to make him a felt presence.[2] Yet Mahon's compelling independence of voice and vision; the elegant mastery of craft that marks everything he writes; a range of imaginative commitments that link him not only to major Irish poets of the preceding generation like Louis MacNeice and Patrick Kavanagh but also with Auden, with Robert Lowell, with Matthew Arnold of "Dover Beach," and the Wallace Stevens of "The Idea of Order at Key West"—all these and other excellences have made him indispensable to any comprehensive understanding of Irish poetry at the present time. And although there is probably a need for a general introduction to his work, I have chosen in this essay to meditate instead upon what I take to be the single most important element of his poetry. By doing this, I hope to illuminate the value of the work as a whole, and to suggest some ways in which we may as readers bring to it a measure of the attention it deserves.

The strongest impression made on me when I read any poem by Derek Mahon is the sense that I have been spoken to: that the poem has established its presence in the world as a kind of speech. In addition, I am aware that its status as speech is an important value in itself, carrying and confirming those other, more explicit values which the poem endorses as part of its overt 'meaning.' What I hear in these poems is a firm commitment to speech itself, to the act of civil communication enlivened, in this case, by poetic craft. Listen, for example, to a few lines of the elegy for MacNeice, "In Carrowdore Churchyard":

> Maguire, I believe, suggested a blackbird
> And over your grave a phrase from Euripides.

15

> Which suits you down to the ground, like this churchyard
> With its play of shadow, its humane perspective.

The mannerly plainness of this makes the speech itself a tribute to MacNeice as well as a revelation of Mahon's chosen way as a poet of being in the world. Here is wit in the delicate, inventive animation of the cliché, modesty in those self-effacing hesitations. Intimate and polite, such speech is a gesture of admiration and reconciliation, its perfect pitch and balance denying the excesses of feeling and form which would jeopardize the whole enterprise:

> All we may ask of you we have. The rest
> Is not for publication, will not be heard.

I hear in this speech (some of the qualities of which are probably derived from the influential practice of MacNeice himself) a tenacious commitment to what is private in experience. Intimacy is the desired end of such poetry—with the dead poet (an intimacy of shared idiom, gratitude for the gift of speech) and with the reader—but such an intimacy as permits the experience to have a "public" expression without losing its essentially private nature. This kind of skater's balance, this decency of deportment, locates Mahon's deepest instinct for form, an instinct which makes its presence felt in the actual body and pressure of his poetic speech.

Mahon's belief in speech as value and as an epitome of identity is extremely clear in those poems in which he invents another speaker. In "Van Gogh in the Borinage," "Bruce Ismay's Soliloquy," and "The Forger," he gives each of these outsiders a voice of his own: in speech, he seems to be saying, human identity finds itself. These poems act out of and act out the pressing need to be articulate in difficult straits. By converting distress into a distinct clarity of utterance, each speaker raises his speech to a value in itself, a civil declaration of independence against the forces of disastrous circumstance. The general model might be Van Gogh, tempering the ugliness of "pits, slag heaps, beetroot fields" with a vividness of perception that illuminates the ordinary and communicates it in a speech possessing its own tough grace:

> A meteor of golden light
> On chairs, faces and old boots,
> Setting fierce fire to the eyes
> Of sunflowers and fishing boats,
> Each one a miner in disguise.

For Mahon, then, poetry is speech, an act—perhaps the fundamental act—of true communication between one human being and another (or others: Van Gogh speaks to his brother; Bruce Ismay and the forger, Jan Van Meghrem, deliver their distraught yet dignified confessions to the world). Even in love poems (like "Preface to a Love Poem" or "Bird Sanctuary") love itself is a search for a way of speaking to the other, who is "the soul of silence," a way

> To say 'I love you' out of indolence,
> As one might speak at sea without forethought,
> Drifting inconsequently among islands.

Love poem, elegy ("The Death of Marilyn Monroe," "The Poets of the Nineties," "Homage to Malcolm Lowry"), translation (Villon's "The Condensed Shorter Testament," Jaccottet), autobiographical vignette ("My Wicked Uncle"), and extended verse letter ("Beyond Howth Head," "The Sea in Winter")—all these poems seem informed by the same belief in poetry as speech. This belief also determines the nature of those poems which emerge from what I see as the central dilemma in Mahon's poetic consciousness. To simplify, it is a dilemma that manifests itself as a struggle with the difficult exigencies of historical circumstance, a struggle which ends in the rejection of history itself and those values it urges upon us.

As one moves through the collection, one can see how Mahon's growing disenchantment with historical circumstance is grounded in his vexed and complex relationship with the North of Ireland. In poems like "Glengormley," "The Spring Vacation," and "Ecclesiastes," the complicated nature of the relationship is effectively accommodated by the speech of the poem. He is compelled to acknowledge the fact that he belongs to this place. "By / Necessity, if not choice," he admits in "Glengormley," "I live here too," and in "The Spring Vacation" (original title: "In Belfast") he advances from astute criticism to uneasy acceptance:

> One part of my mind must learn to know its place.
> The things that happen in the kitchen houses
> And echoing back-streets of this desperate city
> Should engage more than my casual interest,
> Exact more interest than my casual pity.

Speech here seems like Mahon's own way of making himself honest. Its peculiar forthrightness of presence makes it the proper medium for communicating difficult truth. It is speech that negotiates the strain in the poet's complicated response, just as it is the vigorously ironic cadences of his speech in "Ecclesiastes" that actively disengages him from his native place. Significantly enough, this separation itself is perceived in terms of speech—a refusal to surrender to historical circumstances which would require a certain constriction of expression:

> Your people await you, their heavy washing
>   flaps for you in the housing estates—
> a credulous people. God you could do it, God
>   help you, stand on a corner stiff
> with rhetoric, promising nothing under the sun.

Freedom of speech (the opposite to "rhetoric") is what Mahon craves. In later poems, such freedom of speech becomes part of that value for which he undertakes inner and outer exile: the speech of the poems themselves becomes a space emancipated from the destructive environment of history.[3]

This release from history is central to the most important poems in the collection. In contrast to history's clamorous demands, Mahon offers the subdued affirmations of a civil speech. Whether these poems have an invented persona or speak in the voice of the poet himself, their speech is consistently a value opposed to those of historical circumstance. In careful, polite tones, the speaker in "The Last of the Fire Kings" informs us he is "through with history." He would pass to a new world, "Not knowing a word of the language." In its deliberate patience, its poise and lucidity of syntax, his speech opposes that noisy world of "Sirens, bin-lids / And bricked-up windows" from which he turns. His speech has the cadences of reasonable conversation, a kind of communion impossible inside the din created by "the fire-loving people":

> Five years I have reigned
> During which time
> I have lain awake each night
>
> And prowled by day
> In the sacred grove
> For fear of the usurper,
>
> Perfecting my cold dream
> Of a place out of time
> A palace of porcelain
>
> Where the frugivorous
> Inheritors recline
> In their rich fabrics
> Far from the sea.

Such a poem obviously contains an indirect reflection on Mahon's own relationship as poet with the North. In a comment he once made on another poem ("The Studio"), he mentioned "the oblique, and possibly escapist, relationship of the Artist to his historical circumstances, particularly where these circumstances include a violent and complex political upheaval.''[4] The lines quoted above give in their speech a fullness of life to this complicated relationship. Escape from history is, in part, into the secure composure of such a style of speech, with its direct tone, its frankness, its fluency of movement between plainness and unusual eloquence.

What might be called the ritual of such expression achieves an even more vivid existence in "The Snow Party," the details of which establish in summary form the two opposing forces in Mahon's extended meditation on history. Speaking this poem, the poet stands on a border between barbarous violence and civil peace, his unhurried, precise speech an attempt to endorse the value of the latter:

> Bashō, coming
> To the city of Nagoya,
> Is asked to a snow party.
>
> There is a tinkling of china
> And tea into china;
> There are introductions.
>
> Then everyone
> Crowds to the window
> To watch the falling snow.

Here it is as if the urge for quiet, plain utterance itself enacts the poem's theme. Politeness of tone and indicative simplicity of grammar reflect the sanity and ceremony of the occasion. Verbs are almost invisible: the strongest one is "crowding" and this, in the present context, conveys a sense of courteous community rather than jostling disorder. Ritual discovers the shining at the heart of ordinary events, redeeming the infections of the violent world that surrounds this oasis of peace with its uproar, though even this uproar is communicated in the same modest, polite tones of infinite courtesy:

> Elsewhere they are burning
> Witches and heretics
> In the boiling squares,
>
> Thousands have died since dawn
> In the service
> Of barbarous kings.

The quietness of this communication graduates naturally to an emblematic silence, the falling snow bringing man and nature into civil accord: "there is silence / In the houses of Nagoya / And the hills of Ise." The speaker need do no more than tell us: further assertion would do violence to the delicate fabric of the poem. In such speech you can hear the poet turning away from the unspeakable chaos of history toward the besieged but peaceful retreats of his own imagination. Inside these quiet stanzas beats a desire for peace which, in the honest intensity of its expression, achieves the status of a moral value. In its reasonable politeness and unsentimental exactitude such speech is at once a withdrawal from history and a calm, unflinching meditation upon it.

Like other refugees and exiles from history, the mushrooms in "A Disused Shed in Co. Wexford" have learnt "patience and silence." Rich, casual, beautifully specific, the speech of this splendid poem first accommodates their silence, then provides them with a voice of their own with which to make a special claim upon our attention. The poem inscribes a journey from silence to speech, that entry of imagination into an object which in Mahon's poetry almost always culminates in the object itself achieving a kind of speech. Through gestures of controlled eloquence ("What should they do there but desire? / So many days beyond the rhododendrons / With the world waltzing in its bowl of cloud") the poem moves discreetly to the realization that the poet is in fact being addressed, is being asked to speak for these victims of historical amnesia, these forgotten creatures:

> They are begging us, you see, in their wordless way,
> To do something, to speak on their behalf
> Or at least not to close the door again.
> Lost people of Treblinka and Pompeii!

Here, as elsewhere, Mahon's authoritative use of the first person plural (the very icon of true speech) enhances my sense of the poem as immediate address, an immediacy confirmed by that mannerly "you see." Such civil softspokenness not only gives vivid dramatic life to the exclamatory surprise of the last line; it also allows us to endorse its dangerously expansive gesture. The precise allusion has been earned. The poem ends, then, by transforming the speaker into a listener. The speech which the poet allows to the mushrooms and all their corollary creatures confirms our sense of his imaginative engagement with the world as a species of conversation. It is, I might say, a condition of sustained desire that balances, in a way at once nervous and reassuring, the act of speech with that of listening. These castaways of history are connected with us by the plangent urgency of their address. Its unaffected simplicity reveals the depth of their distress and the intensity with which they are present to the poet. We enter a circle of sympathy as we listen:

> 'Save us, save us,' they seem to say,
> 'Let the god not abandon us
> Who have come so far in darkness and in pain.
> We too had our lives to live.
> You with your light meter and relaxed itinerary,
> Let not our naive labours have been in vain!'

Such a speech holds our attention by its spare intensity, its refusal to sentimentalize its subject. In this poem, Mahon converts the whole relationship between history and the individual into a part of speech, which it is the poet's business to parse and make present in the world.

Silence is a necessary element in this retreat from history. The fact that history may be understood as contaminated speech must be one source of Mahon's recurrent preoccupation with silence. So, in "Beyond Howth Head" he refers to political jargon (especially, according to himself, that of the Vietnam War)[5] in the following terms:

> And everywhere the ground is thick
> With the dead sparrows rhetoric
> Demands as fictive sacrifice
> To prove its substance in our eyes.

Silence, then, becomes a salient gesture against a world diseased in its capacity for honest communication. The extravagant "destruction of all things" in "Matthew V 29–30" ends "in that silence without bound" where no offence will remain. In "The Antigone Riddle," man is opposed by the silence of the natural world, where

> the windfall waits
> In silence for his departure
> Before it drops in
> Silence to the long grass.

The bleak speakers of "Going Home" have given up "Inventing names for things / To propitiate silence. / It is silence we hug now." And in the curiously tranquil apocalypse of "The Golden Bough," silence marks a new beginning: "There will be silence, then / A sigh of waking / As from a long dream."

The speech of these poems reaches out of this regenerative silence toward some act of tactile worship, an engagement with objects for their own sake. It cannot escape notice, indeed, that, for Mahon, the withdrawal from historical circumstance stimulates an intense attachment to the world of simple objects. So "The Banished Gods" "sit out the centuries / In stone, water / And the hearts of trees." Here, close to elemental things, they dream

> Of zero-growth economics and seasonal change
> In a world without cars, computers
> Or chemical skies,
> Where thought is a fondling of stones
> And wisdom a five-minute silence at moonrise.

Thought becomes simple tactility, the affectionate acknowledgement of the object-world; wisdom is silence. Here is a speech that eschews verbs almost entirely, as if for Mahon the verb itself were an act or instrument of aggression. He will not interfere with the object's simple presence; his speech embodies his desire for a fresh, untroubled beginning in a relationship with such a presence.

Silence and a new speech of continuous accommodation (antithesis of the hectoring rhetorics of historical circumstance) belong to the ideal world of Mahon's imagination. So the hermit who speaks in "The Mayo Tao," having turned from history to the natural world, "lives in a snow-lit silence," spends his days "in conversation / with stags and blackbirds," and is an expert on "the silence of crickets." He makes a fresh beginning out of this silence and its accompanying engagement with primary objects, with "frost crystals" and "stars in the mud." The reason he gives for such an attachment may also be understood as Mahon's own explanation for his commitment to the "mute phenomena" of the world: "There is," he claims,

> an immanence in these things
> which drives me, despite
> my scepticism, almost
> to the point of speech.

The communal voice in "The Apotheosis of Tins" must be heard as a projection of this same commitment. These creatures too have been exiled from history:

> Deprived of use, we are safe now
> from the historical nightmare
> and may give our attention at last
> to things of the spirit.

Voice here is simply the occasion of the objects' presence: it is how this presence registers in the world, under the peaceful light of the verb "to be": "This is the terminal democracy / of hatbox and crab / of hock and Window-lene." This speech is itself an act of surrender to the comically various world of humble phenomena, animating them with that witty linguistic dexterity characteristic of all Mahon's work.

As I have said, then, the retreat from "history" pushes the poet toward a deep commitment to "object." And the speech of the poems is at once the expression of this commitment and its confirmation. Such speech celebrates presence, turning away from those "meanings" which history asks the poet to espouse. His affection for the phenomenological world makes itself felt in an almost neutral lyricism of naming. Making no harsh demands of us, his speech claims our attention by the simple luminosity of that which it names. Such a love for the object grows more intense as the surrounding circumstantial life grows bleaker. In "Consolations of Philosophy" and in "An Image from Beckett," it is the extremity of death itself which gives the loved particular sheen to objects. In the perspective provided by the grave, ordinary objects shine with a startling vividness. The subdued voice that utters them allows them an unmediated presence in our sight:

> Oh, then a few will remember with delight
> The dust gyrating in a shaft of light;
> The integrity of pebbles; a sheep's skull
> Grinning its patience on a wintry sill.

Love in such a context is unsentimentally direct, enlivened by the unobtrusive arrangements of rhyme, unhesitating in its simple indicative speech. Here, as in the following lines from "An Image from Beckett," warmth and exactitude purify to toughness this lyrical nostalgia: identity is a tone of voice:

> In that instant
> There was a sea, far off,
> As bright as lettuce,
>
> A northern landscape
> And a huddle
> Of houses along the shore.
>
> Also, I think, a white
> Flicker of gulls
> And washing hung to dry.

This voice expends itself in naming ("Naming these things is the love-act and its pledge," says Patrick Kavanagh);[6] the speaker is there only in the delicate pressure exerted by that qualifying "I think." Emotion is a quality of cadence, a tone, the way the objects press into the world as words, impress themselves upon the air. On this illuminated border between life and death, speech is a careful negotiation between hopelessness and belief, a belief— even when the worst is admitted—in some residual abiding value:

It was good while it lasted,
And if it only lasted
The biblical span

Required to drop six feet
Through a glitter of wintry light,
There is No one to blame.

Calm, plainspoken, unobtrusively eloquent: it is truly in the poet's speech we find the affectionate stoicism the poem urges, with infinite tact, upon our attention.

That vivid existence of objects which Mahon opposes to the conventional values of history is in itself the dramatized subject of "Lives." As elsewhere, the object is granted a voice to recount its various incarnations. The "I" of the poem is the metamorphic essence of "object," its speech the persistent current of being that animates its lives:

First time out
I was a torc of gold
And wept tears of the sun.

That was fun
But they buried me
In the earth two thousand years

Till a labourer
Turned me up with a pick
In eighteen fifty-four

And sold me
For tea and sugar
In Newmarket-on-Fergus.

Buoyantly independent of history, the life of this object comes to us as pliable speech—colloquial, well-mannered, with its own excitement and its own melancholy. The concrete simplicity of speech itself becomes an analogue for the presence of the object, and this conjunction achieves an authentic release from the anxiety of historical circumstance, even from geographical fixity: "I was a stone in Tibet, / A tongue of bark / At the heart of Africa." Speech here is not so much about the object as it is the object's actual mode of being. This may be seen in an even more radical way in "Deaths," where the very breath of the poem is composed of the objects desperately named:

Who died nails, key-rings,
Sword hilts and lunulae,

> Rose hash, bog-paper
> And deciduous forests,
> Died again these things,
>
> Rose kites, wolves,
> Piranha fish . . .

Commitment to the object is a commitment to a certain sort of speech, a speech that in its intense accommodation of the world of objects enacts a gesture against historical circumstance that would simply use, abuse, or cast out the object. Imaginative existence-as-speech, that is, enables Mahon to move beyond his struggle with history toward a condition where the object is its own justification. His poetic speech is simply, then, an acknowledgement of this discovery, his way of endorsing that which he takes to be authenticity of being in the world.

By getting rid of even the last vestiges of voice, some of the poems in the final section of *Poems 1962–1978* try to achieve an even closer association between word and object. Speech in a poem like "Light Music," for example, is almost transparent, surrendering its identity to the simple acknowledged presence of the object:

> A stone at the roadside
> watches snow fall
> on the silent gate-lodge.

At their best, the brief poems of "Light Music" have a sort of luminous neutrality, verbless inhabitants of space rather than time, objects of eye rather than voice: "Gulls in a rain-dark cornfield / crows on a sunlit sea." Mahon has described this language as a deliberate choice, a sort of "tabula rasa on which careful plain words might be placed."[7] Such plainness informs "Autobiographies," "The Return" ("And often thought if I lived / Long enough in this house / I would turn into a tree"), or "The Attic":

> At work in your attic
> Up here under the roof—
> Listen, can you hear me
> Turning over a new leaf?

Speech here starts again from the very center of the self, as an appeal for a listener. Such speech seems to be the agent of a newly created self, as if the poems represented a fresh phase of Mahon's experience of the world: beyond the struggle with history and his discovery of the object lies the struggle with and discovery or rediscovery of the self. The speech of these poems is "self"-centered in a painfully unmediated way. Here Mahon stands outside the complexities and civil strategies of the earlier work, simply exposing the self in a speech that neither affects nor allows itself any protection:

> I lie here in a riot of sunlight
> watching the day break and the clouds flying.
> Everything is going to be all right.

In this later work, poems dealing with his life in Surrey are, again, suggestive of someone starting over, leaving behind some of that debonair wit and verbal elasticity which marked the earlier work. Although this retreat into Surrey (from London) realizes in fact some of the ideals posed fictionally in earlier poems, the poet's condition, curiously enough, is that of one looking for speech, trying to establish conversation (as in "Dry Hill"). In "The Return" there is a courageous plainness, agent of a confessional instinct that realizes the dangers inherent in its own impluses:

> I have watched girls walking
> And children playing under
> Lilac and rhododendron,
> And me flicking my ash
> Into the rose bushes
> As if I owned the place.

Inside this speech I hear the poet's own discovery of *himself* beyond the violent circle of history. The tone, as I've said, is suggestive of a fresh start, a beginning which permits his re-engagement with the world and through a renewed speech, an affirmation of older values. So, even in a context of impossible violence (beyond Surrey and back in Northern Ireland), speech can be a commitment to the immanent loveliness of the world. "The Chinese Restaurant in Portrush," for example, offers an image of peace in spite of the vulgar and violent actualities of the North. Its straightforward speech embodies the reconciled consciousness of one who has learned to locate what can be loved *inside* the actual, the way immanent beauty resides inside ordinary objects. His speech here is one of celebration, of alertness to the actual, of honest elegy, and of the acceptance of all these as elements in a single consciousness of the world:

> While I sit with my paper and prawn chow-mein
> Under a framed photograph of Hong Kong
> The proprietor of the Chinese restaurant
> Stands at the door as if the world were young
> Watching the first yacht hoist a sail—

> An ideogram on sea-cloud—and the light
> Of heaven upon the mountains of Donegal;
> And whistles a little tune, dreaming of home.

In these last poems of the collection, Mahon shows us an identity revising itself toward a fresh alignment with the world, and registering this transformation in a speech of experimental plainness. Speech itself, that is, as it has been throughout the volume, is both identity and philosophical disposition; a total mode of being in the world. It is at once the means of carrying the struggle with history to a reasonable conclusion, and it is itself the redemption from that engagement.

It is what I have called a single consciousness of the world that informs many of the poems in Mahon's most recent collection, *Courtyards in Delft.* The struggle with history can still be a present concern, but as an object of meditation now, in a speech calmed by this condition, and not as a dramatic urgency prodding the poet's own psyche into action. So, in "Rathlin Island" the poet repeats a phrase of "The Last of the Fire Kings," but as an observer, as someone for whom this struggle is over: "Bombs doze in the housing estates / But here they are through with history." The island is a silence "slowly broken / By the shearwater, by the sporadic / Conversation of crickets." As in other poems, this natural silence, this no-man's-land beyond the violent borders of history and its "unspeakable violence," is imagined as "the infancy of the race." What such a meditative posture and answerable style convey, however, is a sense of the poet's present acceptance of things as they are, a natural outcome of his almost programmatic commitment to the phenomenological presence of ordinary objects in the ordinary world. In its fluent, unruffled mingling of plain and lyrical elements, one shining inside the other, as it were, the speech embodying such acceptance perfectly realizes the vision that recognizes, in spite of all circumstantial opposition, the immanent, desirable beauty of the world. A renewed, unabashed commitment to rhyme and stanza pattern gives further buoyancy to such speech. Awareness is all, and it can light up even the grimly circumstantial shades of a "Derry Morning":

> Here it began, and here at least
> It fades into the finite past
> Or seems to; clattering shadows whop
> Mechanically over pub and shop.
> A strangely pastoral silence rules
> The shining roofs and murmuring schools;
> For this is how the centuries work—
> Two steps forward, one step back.

In its supple range, speech here seems released into self-possession, beyond the claims of any external commitment except to the minutiae of the speaker's own enlightened awareness of the world. In such speech I detect the actuality of that new beginning which so many of the earlier poems had made a speculative possibility. Here—tutored by the plainness of those poems in the last part of *Poems*—is a tougher, more experienced version of that civil elegance informing the earlier work. Here is a strengthening of the capacity for speech as the enabling means of poetic communication between the speaker and those who choose to listen. The accepting energy of such speech appears in the epigraph to "North Wind" from Nadine Gordimer's *The Late Bourgeois World*: ("'If I had gone to live elsewhere in the world, I should never have known that this particular morning . . . continues, will always continue, to exist.'"). And this poem itself finds in plain speech the beauty of things, even inside a context of disaster:

> Yet there are mornings when,
> Even in midwinter, sunlight
> Flares, and a rare stillness
> Lies upon roof and garden,
> Each object eldritch-bright,
> The sea scarred but at peace.

In its quiet reasonableness, its fastidious care to pick the right word, its assertive modesty, such speech seems the perfect agent of the kind of complex reconciliation to be found here.

The title poem of this volume, a poem in praise of a painting by Pieter de Hooch, might stand as a summary and model of this condition. The qualities Mahon chooses to admire in the painter tell us of what he values in his own work: "Oblique light on the trite, on brick and tile—Immaculate masonry . . . scrubbed yards, modest but adequate . . . the trim composure of those trees." Speech here is the agent of meditation, both on the things of the world and on the art that best construes them. It is a speech that resists the verb and embraces the adjective and noun—the locations of being, presence. Here, in Mahon's precise utterance itself, is "the chaste / Precision of the thing and the thing made," where "Nothing is random, nothing goes to waste." By admitting that such a vision is exclusive of the shadier complexities of experience, the speaker manages to make his own meditation an inclusive act. For he knows that "This is life too, and the cracked / Outhouse door a verifiable fact." Spare, exact, lyrical, engaging, this speech becomes a capacious version of the world. As such, it is capable of including the self, along with a consideration of the relationship between self and history that provides an emblematic source for that struggle with historical circumstance marking the earlier poems. In addition, it is a celebratory assertion of the immanent loveliness in the everyday objects of the world. Possessed of that ''elegiac clarity'' that Huizing attributed to Dutch painting, the speech perfectly echoes the poet's way of being inside his whole existence:

> I lived there as a boy and know the coal
> Glittering in its shed, late-afternoon
> Lambency informing the deal table,
> The ceiling cradled in a radiant spoon.
> I must be lying low in a room there,
> A strange child with a taste for verse,
> While my hard-nosed companions dream of war
> On parched veldt and fields of rain-swept gorse.

Finally, in ''Table Talk,'' Mahon allows his commitment to the ''mute phenomena'' of the world be itself the object of scrutiny and comment. His own work-table speaks to him, turning him into a listener (as in ''Disused Shed''), a condition that is implicit in a commitment such as his. Direct speech is the mode he chooses for this deliberate reflection upon his work and his progress in it. The object posits its identity in a voice of its own, a speech of its own. The poet is someone who is spoken to. Such a condition seems infinitely satisfying to an imagination which has constantly discovered and renewed its own body and its own covenant with the world as a style of speech, speech as being and speech as value. The following quotation is, I believe, a fitting illustration and confirmation of what I have attempted to show about Mahon's work in the course of this essay. ''And yet I love you,'' says the table, ''even in your ignorance,''

> Perhaps because at last you are making sense—
> Talking to me, not through me, recognizing
> That it is I alone who let you sing
> Wood music. Hitherto shadowy and dumb,
> I speak to you now as your indispensable medium.

To grasp Mahon's work as speech is, I have been arguing, a necessary first step toward its proper understanding and appreciation. For while so much of its content deals with a withdrawal from history, especially from that complex and violent socio-political variety of it unhappily indigenous to the North of Ireland, the form of the poetry, in its acute urge to make and sustain civil communication, is a radically political statement. Both in form and content, moreover, his commitment keeps us in touch with what truly matters: the importance of the object in its own unique life, and the desire to speak to one another in tones that are those of simple exchange, not confrontation. I hear such speech as one of the most profound responses it is possible to make to the embattled conditions of border living, where, whatever idiom you choose, you have defined yourself as someone's enemy. (It is a context in which it is almost imperative to believe, as the title of one of Seamus Heaney's poems exhorts us to: "Whatever you say, say nothing.") I receive Mahon's poetry, his poetic speech, as a persistent (even if unconscious) attempt to negotiate his own way through these impossible and unspeakable conditions, and by so doing to show us how we might move beyond them. His poetry is a constant reminder (as is that of another poet animated by the need for delicate balances, Andrew Marvell) that civility is still possible, that the world awaits our attention and speaks to us in its own way, that "vodka and talking / Are ceremonies," that facts, and a speech that adequately makes them a part of our world, have their own redemptive possibility. These poems, and those acts of speech that they comprise, are grounds for a condition that is one of Mahon's most definitive characteristics—a sort of battered optimism that finds one of its more moving expressions in "The Sea in Winter":

> One day, the day each one conceives—
> The day the Dying Gaul revives,
> The day the girl among the trees
> Strides through our wrecked technologies,
> The stones speak out, the rainbow ends,
> The wine goes round among the friends,
> The lost are found, the parted lovers
> Lie at peace beneath the covers.

His despatches from the embattled regions where he's been are, however, no facile reassurances that all is well with the world. It is, he says in "Girls on the Bridge," "an insane / And monstrous age, . . . / And we have come / Despite ourselves, to no / True notion of our proper work." This is a world where, as his two verse-letters especially show (their very existence emblematic of his will for immediate communication, communion), a world where the individual is perpetually at risk. And yet, in spite of all this, a true buoyancy of spirit remains possible, its telling sign the undefeated urge to speak, and the truly civil presence this speech realizes in the world. In his wish to speak to us, and sometimes for us (the authority of his use of the first person plural is notable among contemporary poets), he manages to have his work embody a kind of optimism that is only guaranteed by the authentic desperation of its circumstances and the unflinching honesty with which he confronts them. His poems, without sentimentality, make that offering of the self that is true speech, that entering into genuine relationship—with an object (which lives in his way of speaking about it) and with an audience of fellow-creatures who become, in their listening, a community. He brings us in every sense "to the point of speech," and we should have no choice but to hear him out.

Notes

1. Published by Oxford in 1979, it contains Mahon's three earlier Oxford volumes—*Night Crossing* (1968), *Lives* (1972), and *The Snow Party* (1975)—as well as more recent work. My references and quotations will all be to and from the collected volume. Such revisions as appear there, and they are numerous and various enough, are not my concern in the present essay. See Blake Morrison's review of *Poems 1962–1978* in *TLS*, February 15, 1980, p. 168, for a brisk treatment of the range and nature of these revisions.

2. I would refer the reader especially to the extensive review of *The Snow Party* by Michael Berryhill, in *Eire-Ireland* 12, no. 1 (1976):144–52, and to Brian Donnelly, "From Nineveh to the Harbour Bar," *Ploughshares*, 6, no. 1 (1981):131–37.

3. Exile: he is from Belfast and has lived in Dublin, Paris, Toronto, Cambridge (Massachusetts), London, Surrey, Coleraine, and, at present, in London again.

4. In *Choice*, Desmond Egan and Michael Hartnett, eds. (Dublin: Goldsmith Press, 1979), p. 80. If one were to do a study of Mahon's influences the names of Joyce and Beckett, as well as that of Andrew Marvell, would have to be mentioned, all of whom have had a share, I would say, in tutoring Mahon's own encounter with history.

5. In conversation with the author of this essay.

6. *Collected Poems* (London: Martin Brian & O'Keefe, 1972), p. 153.

7. In a letter to the author of this essay.

That Always Raised Voice:
Seán O Riada and Irish Poetry

John Engle

During his lifetime Irish composer Seán O Riada acted as a lightning rod for the cultural energy of a people. By the time of his death, as a young man who looked sixty, in 1971, he had come to represent both radical innovation and a humbling, fundamental return to pure traditionalism. Those who knew his Masses, his film music, and his work with the Ceoltóirí Chualann saw him as a mediator with the past—one who helped tradition live, not molder as a tourist curiosity or museum piece. Those who knew *him* were left with a legacy of more ambivalent feelings. Intimate with his vision and his presence, they knew a charming friend of large, flamboyant gifts; yet they could be granted an audience with another O Riada, the mean avenger or the unfulfilled talent intent on squandering his incandescent creativity. Both private and public "readings" of O Riada agree on one thing: that, in Maurice Harmon's words, it was he "who did the most in our time to popularize and purify the form of the native musical tradition."[1] What complicates and enriches the story is O Riada's own mystical intimacy with this native tradition, its pre-rational responses and nether-worlds. He worked by listening to the cuckoo, and, like a true descendent of a first-century hero cult, he had an appetite for vengeance and the curse as well as for love; on the first anniversary of his death, it is said that he returned to visit at least one friend.

Among the people O Riada touched were the best Irish poets of his generation, the three men who, with Austin Clarke and Patrick Kavanagh, represent the most resonant voices since Yeats. In the several years following O Riada's death, Thomas Kinsella, John Montague, and Seamus Heaney wrote a remarkable series of elegies that reviewed their relationship with this difficult, dramatic blend of private and public man. That all three would elegize O Riada seems at first surprising, and then inevitable—for, scanning their work, one finds the same nervous, exhilarating play between the personal and the national that marked O Riada's career; the same longing to heal the "great rift" in Ireland's broken culture and the same knowledge that every artist "has to make the imaginative grasp for identity himself."[2] The O Riada we get in the elegies has been smelted down and forged anew. His life and work have been, wrote Auden of Yeats, "'modified in the guts of the living"; as Auden's great elegy, or Tennyson's, or Whitman's shows, it is this chemical reaction which makes the elegy as much "about" its author as its subject. An emotional and intellectual engagement with O Riada encouraged Kinsella, Montague, and Heaney to front their own basic assumptions about race, the individual, and the function and practice of art. The result is four poems which, almost of necessity, stand at the broad center of recent Irish poetry.

But who, again, was the subject of these poems? In the best biographical source, an eloquent prose commentary published with his two elegies to O Riada,[3] Kinsella memorializes a career and a friendship that stretched from the composer's early twenties through (and perhaps beyond) his death at forty. Though O Riada, né John Reidy, was "Ireland's foremost composer and musician," his greatest achievement may have been an escape from "traditional 'European' relationship between the composer and a select audience." It came about, continues Kinsella, "through his revival of the old native relationship between Irish traditional music and the Irish community, and his renovation of it for the twentieth century." Paradoxically, modern mass communication aided O Riada in this task, but more important were his selection of material—traditional songs and dance tunes surviving "in relative purity" in certain parts of the gaeltacht—and "his great personal gift for presentation."

"Measured by orthodox standards," Kinsella writes, "his achievement is small: half a dozen works for full orchestra, of varying scope, in advanced modern idiom and of striking quality; also a group of songs and some early piano pieces." To O Riada, though, music was means as well as end, "a means toward cultural integration; language, song and music fitted into, and fulfilling, a way of life." Drawing together the finest traditional musicians in Ireland, he founded the Ceoltóirí Chualann (and, indirectly, The Chieftains); later he reached his widest audience with the film score for *Mise Eire* (I am Ireland), a documentary on the Irish battle for political freedom. Toward the end of his life, as he worked to adapt a traditional melodic line for a series of Masses, he could say in an interview that "the European tradition can struggle along without me for the time being."[4] Yet was O Riada's true metier the so-called "art music" he neglected in the latter part of his life? To many people his choice represented a frustrating decision to work in an honorable but minor scale, a refusal to fulfill great potential; O Riada could argue the point vigorously.

In evaluating O Riada's effect on his contemporaries, Charles Acton once drew a comparison between the composer and George Russell (AE), the Irish poet and painter whose work seemed to diminish in critical stature as his friends passed away. Acton wondered whether O Riada's contemporaries too "saw his achievements through the magnifying lens of what they knew to be his oustanding personality and influence upon them."[5] This remains conjecture, but the magnetic personal appeal of O Riada does not. It is clear, for example, that the vivid friendship he offered figured highly in the decisions of the three poets to elegize the composer; on that rainy October day in Coolea, after all, Montague and Kinsella were among the pallbearers. Yet these poems came to be written for other reasons as well—reasons more directly pertinent to an understanding of Irish poetry.

Take the problem of nationalism. Montague's worry when O Riada "became identified with the national consciousness and lost his personal identity"[6] points to perhaps the central preoccupation of his poetic genera- tion. As Seamus Deane has written, theirs is a poetry "related to nationalism—the need to join with it or escape from it; with Ireland, and the need to create identity on its terms or to dictate identity on the poet's own. All through there is a fluctuation between . . . the sense of the self as definitely Irish and the sense of the self as free from any such category."[7] This balance has held throughout Montague's career; it is manifest in as simple a comparison as that between the loosely "public" intent of *The Rough Field* (1972) and the intimacies of Montague's later sequence of betrayal and redemption, *The Great Cloak* (1978). So too with Kinsella, whose 1968 "Nightwalker" pictured a lone consciousness at large in the sour Irish night. Since that time a long sequence of poems has followed him along parallel paths down into self and back into race. Though Seamus Heaney is best known for tapping the landscape's memory in the bog or in the word, his recent *Field Work* (1979) justifies the claim that he is also out "to redraft the emotional geography . . . in terms, not of history and politics, but of the free personality."[8]

O Riada's identification with the nation was reciprocal. As a composer, he was faced daily with any artist's fundamental creative and practical challenges, one of which is audience. With his enviably wide common audience, he could be seen as reviving the ancient bard's broad, assured role in cultural and national life (or perhaps our idealized conception of that role). Yet he too knew the lonely quest of all artists for a precise personal voice. Addressing this point, Heaney makes a distinction relevant equally to the composer and the poet. Craft, the "skill of making," differs from technique, a more complex matter that partakes in "a definition of [the artist's] own reality."[9] At a windlass you may take up bucket after bucket of air, then "one day the chair draws unexpectedly tight, and you have dipped into waters that will continue to entice you back. You'll have broken the skin on the pool of yourself." For O Riada, who had the craft already, that moment seems to have come during a trip to Dingle in the late 1950s. Kinsella remembers his sudden impetus toward Irish music at the time in terms similar to Heaney's: "He was rapidly setting something free in himself." At Smerwyck, looking into waters that would entice him back, O Riada said, "I feel as if I have never done anything else in my life."

Heaney's elegy twines quietly about this faith in the gift. The scene is again water, the speaker O Riada:

> 'How do you work?
> Sometimes I just lie out
> like ballast in the bottom of the boat
> listening to the cuckoo.'
>
> The gunwale's lifting ear—
> trusting the gift,
> risking gift's undertow—
> is unmanned now
>
> but one whole afternoon
> it was deep in both our weights.[10]

Hear the dead weight *b*'s of the third line or the assonance of a dozy afternoon. Beneath the surface of this affectionate glance, though, the poem roils with a hint of subdued, caged violence. O Riada is a "black stiletto trembling in its mark" and "more falconer than fisherman, I'd say, / Unhooding a sceptic eye." This division of attention should key one's understanding of the poem and Heaney's reading of O Riada. Like most commentary on the composer, it seems to accept its own ambivalence as the proper response to a deeply ambiguous personality. Though the elegy is finally a tribute to O Riada, its praise is hard won and leavened with reservation.

An earlier version sounds even more equivocal. Like many of Heaney's poems, "In Memoriam Sean O'Riada" appeared first in one guise, then as a revised, shorter poem in a later volume. The important changes occur at the opening. The early version begins descriptively and accelerates into judgement:

> O'Riada's white head was Easter snow,
> the silver knob on a swordstick.
> . . .

> He had a cornered energy.
> He was in a fallow hell,
> a snowball that would neither
> thaw nor flow.[11]

The elegy later published in *Field Work* alters the opening sentence (blandly, to "a quickened, whitened head") and skips the final two. The result is a considerably kinder poem but one bled of some passion and, though less ambivalent, slightly shaky in its focus. The omitted imagery encourages a properly complex reading of the remaining quatrains. "Cornered energy" sharpens the talons on the imagery of birds of prey that rules the conclusion. With his picture of a fallow field and snow which cannot melt into life-giving water, even in spring, Heaney evokes an artist's special hell; O Riada's later remark about lying like ballast in the bottom of the boat then comes tinged with the nagging complaint that he had misused his abundant genius. "I'd like to do what I want to do. I may feel differently in a week's time," O Riada once said. "A potential Sibelius who is mucking about in a boat on the Kenmare River because he wants to do it," his interviewer called him.[12] Trusting the gift, risking its undertow—the Janus-face of Romantic instinct.

This calculated double vision should not surprise. Yeats said we make poetry out of the quarrel with ourselves. If I have accentuated the reservations and distinctions which mark Heaney's engagement with O Riada, it is to focus upon the way such a quarrel was inherent in his choice for subject matter of an artist at once so similar and dissimilar. On the one hand, he and O Riada seem made for each other—both as "concerned with reclaiming old ground," with art "as restoration of the culture to itself."[13] Heaney acknowledges this comradeship; his metaphor for O Riada at work, "a quill flourishing itself," allies the conductor's slim figure and his baton with an image of the poet's instrument. He completes the identification of music with the word in the direct address final line of the elegy: "Wader of assonance." The music of the Irish language is assonance. Here Heaney is praising the composer's first, leading steps toward the culture's reimmersion in itself and again asserting their consanguinity as artists. Music—especially the muscular, natural expression of a live tradition—bears cultural and historical weight in the same way as language. O Riada's preoccupation with the native musical tradition runs roughly parallel to Heaney's romance with the native word. *Wintering Out,* the poet's third volume, savors the pre-plantation past alive in the music of place names. Digging in their "vowel meadows" was a crucial stage in Heaney's progress from the darkness of personal memory and a Northern childhood to the echoing darkness of his best book, *North.*

Yet the poet "concerned with reclaiming old ground" had his differences
with O Riada as well. One need only read Heaney's poems to hear the
workings of a different heart. In the broadest sense of terms, Heaney's
largely romantic transactions with the physical world have a clean classical
edge to them—possessed, despite their aural and imaginative richness, of a
tight-mouthed Ulster austerity born in self-discipline and imposed limits.
His is a poetry of restraint and quiet witnessing, a circumscribed art of inner
expansiveness. Instinct for Heaney is the dowser's gift; "circling the terrain,
hunting the pluck / Of water," he detects what is buried and gives it public
life, all with love for traditional craft and little fuss. Contrast this with
O Riada's pendulum swings of personality and the wilder tang of what he
knew as his "instinctive side": "No matter what I say to you now today, I do
not know what my instinct is going to make me do next week, or even
tomorrow."[14] The difference is less one of intent than of tone and color. In
revising toward the more generous later version of the elegy, Heaney
necessarily chose for his opening lines the image of O Riada most compati-
ble with his own poetic temperament: "He conducted the Ulster orchestra /
like a drover with an ashplant / herding them south." He begins with a
snapshot not of the self-indulgent, erratic composer, but of the conductor
charged with bringing the composition to ordered expression. Conductor,
then drover, the image epitomizes Heaney's own work—the relatively
conservative formal principles of its presentation yoked to its homing
instinct.

Even as revised, "In Memoriam Sean O'Riada" does not violate the
ambivalence of Heaney's feelings. Simply stated, it reads like the work of
someone drawn to O Riada "thematically" but not personally. John
Montague's elegy has a wholly different air—like the troubled intimacy it
describes, it is muggy and unventilated. Montague too finds his emotions
mixed, but he is writing from a position considerably closer to O Riada. He
accepts the whole of his friend, then tempers a deep, genuine empathy with
worry, anger, fear, and some posthumous scolding—the toughness that
lends human density to affection. "O Riada's Farewell"[15] (titled after
O Riada's last Claddagh record, which Montague named) is a dark, nervy
performance in eight sections, as cryptic in parts as its subject. Yet, though it
places O Riada the *man* in the foreground, the poem is as much about its
author and his art as Heaney's. In Montague's response to the private plight
of Seán O Riada lay troubling questions which few Irish artists have answered without stress: Where does the nation end, and where do I begin?

The elegy needs a frame. Throughout his career Montague has gone home
poetically, but always unblinkered, the global-regionalist. Like William

Carlos Williams he knows that the local is the only universal, and that this is only true if one grants the local its honest, provocative complexity. *The Rough Field* does this for Ulster, steadfastly denying the easy point of rest in its search for the meaning of home—a difficult, responsible feat in a field sown with the dragon's teeth of sectarian hysteria. The eighth of its ten sections, "Patriotic Suite,"[16] is a disquieting meditation which strips away the cobwebs of much comfortable thought by juxtaposing the South's national dream with certain stopping realities. Dedicated to O Riada, the poems read like a warning to the artist who had just settled down in the *gaeltacht*. Unsentimentally, even cynically, they examine "that point / where folk and art meet": the Revolutionists and Revivalists set the tone with their artificial, expedient relationship to the past; now, when a "symbolic depth charge of music / Releases a national dream," Montague listens skeptically. Aware that Ireland is as much its present and its future as its past, he asks whether tin whistle and *bodhrán* are summoning a fertile tradition alive to the people or sounding a parochial, timorous retreat to a country long unwilling to take its place among the modern nations of the world:

> The gloomy images of a provincial catholicism
>
> (in a thousand schoolrooms
> children work quietly while
> Christ bleeds on the wall)
>
> wound in a native music
> curlew echoing tin whistle
> to eye-swimming melancholy
>
> is that our offering?
>
> While all Europe seeks
> new versions of old ways,
> the hammer of Boulez swing-
> ing to Eastern harmonies.

There is more here than cool, distanced concern. Montague is referring pointedly to what he calls in the elegy O Riada's "two gifts"—his astonishing, equal talents in the native and European traditions. The ruling theme of "O Riada's Farewell" is Montague's anxiety over his friend's headlong, exclusive rush back into the native musical tradition and its old versions of old ways. During the last years of O Riada's life (as Gael-Linn was producing the film music and concerts but not *his* "art music," as O Riada was enjoying celebrity less for composing than for taking Irish music seriously), Montague and others sensed that he had had to give up a large part of himself to assume the consciousness of the nation: the credo *Mise Eire* had its

rewards and its painful, if stoically unacknowledged, costs. "O Riada's
Farewell" dramatizes the lure of this dark lady, the national muse. The
elegy's lure is that it does this while remaining true to the warty inconsistencies of O Riada's character. Montague's O Riada is neither victim nor
suicide, but something of both.

And a good deal more. In fact, only sections five and seven, "Samhain"
and "The Two Gifts," specifically concern the national dream as personal
nightmare. Montague would understand O Riada's bottomless soul, probe
the spirit behind the mask. In the rest of the poem, he recounts a tense,
feverish tale of rivalry and malediction that brings O Riada back in full body
heat. By section four, when the cursed, tearstained beloved enters the room,
he had established an edgy, spooky climate that dares the rational mind to see
beyond the world of appearance. The poem is marked by the imagery of
masks, roles, and deceptive surfaces. In such terms Montague's evaluation
of O Riada hits at what a personal cult of "instinct" and "personality" may
come to:

> Instinct wrung and run
> awry all day, powers idled
> to self-defeat, the vacuum
> behind the catalyst's gift.
>
> Beyond the flourish
> of personality, peacock
> pride of music or language:
> a constant, piercing torment!

Again instinct gone to seed, wasted powers—the "great danger" hidden
within. Like Heaney, but more acutely, Montague regrets the self-defeat he
finds intrinsic in the artist's resolve to exchange creativity and its rigors for
catalysis. His O Riada strikes a bargain like that of Mann's Faustus—yet, in
"fatal confusion of the powers / of the upper and lower air," he barters *away*
a magnificent creativity.

The background of the elegy is country Ireland, the dead man's "chosen
earth" where such deals can be struck, old ways still hold, and the night is
full of presences. There O Riada wields his mysticism like a club whose heft
he comes to like: "a stranger / made to stumble at a bar door . . . a playing
with fire, leading / you, finally, tempting you / to a malevolence, the /
calling of death for another." Montague sees the conjurer's gift as a focus for
his friend's smoldering frustrations, a glass that could turn the "failing" or
"dying" fire into a volcanic core, ready to erupt. This hotly inward realm
also provides Montague with the perfect stage on which to perform the

haunted central act of his drama. The introductory story ends on the sound of splashed acid: *"How pretty you look, / Miss Death."* Then it is Samhain, when the gates between the living and the dead fly open.

As the composer moves to meet the temptress, his own Miss Death, the music changes, becomes gay and melancholy at once, a fiddler's or a piper's tune: "Sing a song / for the mistress / of the bones. . . ." Montague's ironic metaphor is the *aisling,* or vision poem, in which the poet comes upon a maiden who foresees some vague relief for Ireland. The setting here is not an Edenic meadow but jagged, wintry rocks and the sea. Montague specifically recalls Egan O Rahilly's *"Gile no Gile,"* or "Brightness of Brightness"— seeing it as a kind of lure.[17] The "seaweed stained sorceress" offers no brightness, just a chiaroscuro "marshlight of defeat," "slowly failing fire," and finally the tragic counter to O Rahilly's vision, "Darkness of Darkness." Elsewhere, as in parts of *The Rough Field* or in the rich elegiac strains of "The Two Gifts," Montague can communicate sympathetic understanding for a traditional art. But when the artist was a friend who "couldn't see that his national phase was over and return to composing,"[18] the wound was personal. The feelings of "a lonelier lady" must be considered, "the muse of a man's particular gift, / Mozart's impossible marriage of fire & ice / . . . the harsh blood pulse of Stravinsky, / the hammer of Boulez / which you will never lift."

In "O Riada's Farewell" Montague crafted a miniature of his most vigorous and distinctive work. Like *The Great Cloak, The Rough Field,* and several briefer pieces, it is a sequence of poems loosely unified by a thread of music, image, and plot. Wedding the fleeing intensity of the lyric with the epic's ambition to complete, the sequence encourages the implication of the general and abstract through the specific and personal. Montague's experiments with the form base themselves upon a modern attitude toward human vision and understanding: something as large as a culture or a marriage or a life cannot be comprehended in one long look. One must understand piecemeal, agilely shift perspectives; and the effort must be made, says the "completed" sequence, though the whole can never be fully grasped. To explain a complex, impossible man, Montague offers a series of variously angled and lighted photos: the hairy night in the Big House, a mytho-dramatic seductress, inner beasts of prey circling for the kill, the nation mourning "the blind horseman." A similarly labile sense of form results in the macabre reel of "Samhain" or the generous dirge of "The Two Gifts," music gauged to each vignette's atmospheric pressure.

In the end "O Riada's Farewell" does not put its subject's "roving, unsatisfied ghost" to rest, coming determinedly, like *The Great Cloak,* to poetic closure that does not close. The last section, a brief lyric that may try too hard, presents a song which is a curious distillation of O Riada's bottled-up talent and torment. The voice rises directly "out of the threatened beat / of the heart & the brain cells"—lost; abstracted; stripped of body, family, and country; no longer "for the broken people"—in other words, O Riada's own as Montague knew it on the last record, an echo of the tortured last months after the unheard warnings, when alcohol, the pressures of an abused gift, and the stress of a semi-public life focused their effects. The conclusion is free of end punctuation, open and multivalent—and the best moment in the lyric for the way it cuts loose of earth orbit at the last halting second:

> a lament so total
> it mourns no one
> but the globe itself
> turning in the endless halls
>
> of space, populated
> with passionless stars
>
> and that always raised voice.

Elsewhere Montague calls this the sound of "the only true madness . . . loneliness / the monotonous voice in the skull / that never stops / because never heard."[19] Yet one man's stranded personal hymn "in empty church of the world" is also beyond time and place, a universal cry. Isolating the last line and according it the only unconditional affirmatives in the poem, Montague sings of the voice in the void, the song which keeps on affirming itself.

The poem profits from such an ending, if only as a reminder that its author's impatience, exasperation, and cosmopolitan wariness were planted in a bed of affectionate empathy. Montague's poetic relationship with O Riada stands midway between Heaney's and Kinsella's. Heaney keeps his distance; Montague is considerably warmer, though he knows O Riada can scald; Kinsella's elegies are charged with a lived sense of an almost total personal and artistic kinship. Kinsella was one of O Riada's oldest friends, a Finance bureaucrat who put him up for a week of flat-hunting in 1951. The two shared stout, Sibelius, the raising of two young families, and a 1959 journey to Ballyferriter in West Kerry for John Reidy's awakening into the world of traditional music. Their "minds shared an odd blend of rigour and squallor."

Reservations held by Heaney and Montague seem not to worry Kinsella. Noting the way O Riada startled "the heart of a whole people," he does admit that the composer's own was "soon beating to a coarse pulse / to glut fantasy and sentiment."[20] Yet immediately Kinsella alters the direction of his gaze to O Riada's, any artist's "next beginning"; he is disposed to sympathize and to discover in his friend's errors and achievements those things which chime with his own notions that are about personal growth, the past, order and disorder. When, like Heaney and Montague, he envisions O Riada as "a beast of prey," he is writing not about vengeance but the "predatory energy" of a mind which ingested experience whole and an art which channeled primitive hungers. So too with the artist who heard the cuckoo of his instinct in a drifting boat. In recent years Kinsella has found himself more comfortable with the artistic equivalent of "squallor." Since *Nightwalker* he has edged progressively further from the traditional preroga- tive of the artist to trap experience in a network of order; in 1978 when he advises the poet to "move, if you move, like water,"[21] he is recalling the Taoist parable of the stream and reflecting a long-held trust in the virtue of receptive passivity. This is an artist constitutionally more sympathetic than most to the O Riada who lay about like ballast.

These attitudes form the background for two elegies of deeply personal grief and appreciation. Aside from the lines quoted above, the poems make little attempt to assess O Riada's public life, content instead to communicate the flavor of private gestures and reflections. The three numbered sections of "A Selected Life"[22] (1972) offer a vision of O Riada alive, running forward as out of the past while "cruelly" striking the *bodhrán,* and accounts of the day and evening of his burial. "Vertical Man" (1973) eerily celebrates the first anniversary of O Riada's death: I thought "that you had been directed toward / crumbling silence . . . / It seems it is hard to keep / a vertical man down." Kinsella has since spliced the poems, a canny artistic move for, alone, "Vertical Man" comes nearly as disembodied as its subject—its core is abstract musing, incompletely illuminated private memory, and a ghostly visitation. The element of "A Selected Life" is not air but earth, a heap of vividly observed details alongside "that hole waiting in the next valley"; it provides an emotional locale for the later poem, where its vapor can con- dense into something more recognizable and human.

"A Selected Life" sticks resolutely to description, as though at the time of writing the day's events were not yet fully digested. Holding his emotions in check, or trying to, the speaker glances about at a physical universe that offers some security, inventories it, finds himself rummaging desultorily for significance. When the funeral bell begins to beat, Kinsella even provides a catalog of "your" few forgotten essentials: "a standard array of dependent beings, / small, smaller, pale, paler, in black," "a piercing / sweet consort of whistles crying,'' ''a lurid cabinet'' of friends (''hugger mugger / and murder; collapsing back in laughter''), ''a workroom askew.'' The whole poem is a ledger of dull emotional pains resident in such items and gone over absent-mindedly, the way one fingers a bruise. Occasionally the ache heightens, as when a rat is sighted, back torn open, and Kinsella calls it ''devil-martyr; / your sad, mad meat.'' O Riada the predator-victim—the point is made in a raw, high-proof way that burns the throat. The quiet numbness of the day requests instead that emotion whisper from within the imagery, not interject itself:

> The gate creaked in the dusk. The trampled grass,
> soaked and still, was disentangling
> among the standing stones
> after the day's excess.

Kinsella's fidelity to the way things look enfolds a precisely expressive music: evenly measured as sad, tired feet, with sibilants that disentangle slowly from a thicket of nasal *n*'s and *g*'s. No tricks here, only bleary eyes noting things that might matter. Or consider this bit of scene-setting. Its simplicity is both chiseled and numinous:

> A fine drizzle blew
> softly across the tattered valley
> onto my glasses, and covered
> my mourning suit with tiny drops.

Kinsella frames the burial scene with equally resonant images of two O Riadas, the artist-performer and the man whose ''genius was life and not works.''[23] In the stanza following the latter picture, the flamboyant rail in black overcoat and beret then gives way, as bodies will: ''swallowed back; animus / brewed in clay, uttered / in brief meat and brains, flattened / back under our flowers.'' With this juxtaposition of the corpse decomposing and the man deathless in memory, Kinsella alludes cryptically to a central tension throughout his work. As far back as *Downstream* (1962), he has viewed his life as a helpless cascade toward oblivion—while all the time shyly treasuring a counter-vision, that of certain barely-understood lines of connection which offer a species of redemption. These ''gossamers'' that ''grope for function''[24] touch variously upon a faith in the preserving power of memory and bequeathed customs, a belief in the virtue of distanced perspectives from which chaos seems to resolve itself into pattern, and Kinsella's increasingly Jungian view of the self's transactions with the race. The latter has found expression particularly in *Notes from the Land of the*

Dead (1973) and *One* (1974). Exploring the personal and Irish past in himself, he has come increasingly upon bits of the dark common shadow which each person bears about through life and which he returns to the common store on death. This "ghost-companionship"[25] does not defeat mortality; however, it does offer primitive, pre-rational consolations, a degree of human solidarity at the level of some basic, common, continuous substance.

These ideas find a striking metaphor in the literal ghost-companionship of "Vertical Man." As Kinsella says in a prose commentary that fills in its sketchy outlines, the genesis of the elegy "was the strangest of any poem I have written." The scene was Kinsella's Philadelphia apartment, where he uncrated books, records, and the strange components of a little altar: his friend's death mask, a photo, a cast of his left hand. He poured a drink, proposed a toast to the picture, and there came "a sudden terrifying amplified screaming"—only the fire station. "I relaxed and drank, and then O Riada's presence was in the room; for an extraordinary moment we drank together. Then the presence went off into the darkness. It was a definite farewell . . . and it occurred on the first anniversary of O Riada's death."

The poetic context of the elegy and Kinsella's humor-shaded directness help make this otherwordly material into the unnerving "real thing." "A Selected Life" had painted the backdrop, a landscape somberly shaded by Celtic mysticism yet warmed by the boozy amber of a long, multilingual toast to the master. Here the shared drink becomes a sacramental rite of friendship. Leave memory's hangover for later, now is the time for swift, intelligent talk between friends. First about problems of the craft, the nagging worry "that for all you have done, the next beginning / is as lonely, as random" as the first, all in a voice which anticipates *A Technical Supplement* (1976) and its link between the creative process and the imperatives of biology. Kinsella broods over his own work, the "self-devouring prayer" and how, in the old miracle, each night "the notes come crawling to life again"—just as "pools of idea" coalesced in O Riada's workroom. He then presents a tight plot summary of his current project, the sequence that would begin with *Notes from the Land of the Dead.* Searching "the dark beyond our first father,"[26] the poems cross the great rift in the Irish past and the modern self to end up among childhood's garden walls and Gaelic dolmens. The first strange cast and props are assembled: the scaly woman of young nightmares, a blind drop back and down, the "packed star" dividing and redividing. This is an act of propitiation to a demanding spirit who, in his own life and music, had explored some of the same territory—who, in the enigmatic emblem that closes the poem, leans over into murky depths to net

"shrimp ghosts" and drop them "in the crawling biscuit-tin." The O Riada
Kinsella knew followed a homing instinct as infallibly as the first settlers
from Finisterre—not only into Irish music and the *gaeltacht,* but into a hazy
psychic territory where it is hard to make out the individual from the
common body. "If the eye could follow that, accustomed to / that dark
. . . ," he trails off; then adds, with something like envy, "But that is your
domain."

So O Riada's voice flickers and rises "from palatal darkness," his domain living and dead, in the eerie anecdotal quatrains that conclude the
poem. Lifted from an earlier elegy to a common friend, a Dingle fisherman
named Jerry Flaherty, the image casts back to the dateless traditional world
that O Riada returned to and found he could never leave. Being captured by
the past was his friend's "sudden liberation," wrote Kinsella. To certain
other friends, though, the past more resembled a prison. Montague warned
that an Irish inheritance might carry a heavy tax. He and Heaney feared that
tradition had frozen O Riada's true gift to Easter snow, always *about* to
melt. In the end, implies the imagery of Heaney's elegy, O Riada may have
been only the cuckoo, a bird which refuses to hatch its own eggs—which,
confined by instinct, cannot bring what it starts to fruition.

O Riada was silly like us, yet the slim, exquisite body of original work
and the catalyst's gift to the nation will survive, and something smaller and,
to a few, more precious. On the day after O Riada's death, Charles Acton
remembered what he gave in such abundance to his friends: a blood-sense
that life itself was "a process of artistic, imaginative creation."[27] Com-
memorating that life, Heaney, Kinsella, and Montague have done the
inverse with their art. In the often rarefied air of modern poetry, their elegies
stand as reminders that the poem and the song traditionally have been, and
must remain, rituals central to lived life—that art must muddy its feet
carrying the coffin. The O Riada elegies embrace life's ecstatic and tragic
possibilities, the flux between the communal and personal, the complex
interweaving of impulse and responsibility, malice and affection. The poets
know that, in the shadow of life's brevity, what Kinsella says about
O Riada's successes is true of their own: "These achievements, despite their
communal aspect, were truly individual; like all art they stemmed from one
tragically perishable talent." To grasp this, they had only to rely on their
ears, to hear the chords of O Riada's art and life, their unfinished strains.

Notes

1. Maurice Harmon, "By Memory Inspired: Themes and Forces in Recent Irish
Writing," *Eire-Ireland* 8, no. 2 (Summer, 1973):13.

2. Thomas Kinsella, "The Irish Writer," in *Davis, Mangan, Ferguson?*, ed. Roger McHugh (Dublin: Dolmen Press, 1970), pp. 59, 66.

3. Thomas Kinsella, *Peppercanister Poems 1972–1978* (Winston-Salem, N.C.: Wake Forest University Press, 1979), pp. 143–58. I use this commentary throughout the essay; any other biographical or critical sources are footnoted.

4. Charles Acton, "Interview with Seán O Riada," *Eire-Ireland* 6, no. 1 (Spring, 1971):113.

5. Ibid., p. 114.

6. John Montague, letter to John Engle, March 17, 1980.

7. Seamus Deane, "Irish Poetry and Irish Nationalism," in *Irish Writing: A Critical Survey,* ed. Douglas Dunn (London: Dufour Editions, 1975), p. 17.

8. Ibid., p. 17.

9. Seamus Heaney, "Feeling into Words," in *The Poet's Work: Twenty-nine Masters of 20th Century Poetry on the Origins and Practice of Their Art,* ed. Reginald Gibbons (Boston: Houghton Mifflin, 1979), pp. 269–70.

10. Seamus Heaney, "In Memoriam Sean O'Riada," *Field Work* (London: Faber and Faber, 1979), pp. 29–30.

11. Seamus Heaney, "In Memoriam: Sean O'Riada," *Poetry Review* 68; 4–5.

12. Acton, "Interview with Seán O Riada," p. 112.

13. Heaney, "Feeling into Words," p. 263.

14. Acton, "Interview with Seán O Riada," p. 111.

15. John Montague, "O Riada's Farewell," *A Slow Dance* (Winston-Salem, N.C.: Wake Forest University Press, 1975), pp. 57–63. Originally published in slightly different form as a 1974 Golden Stone (Cork) pamphlet.

16. John Montague, "Patriotic Suite," *The Rough Field* (Dublin: Dolmen Press, 1972), pp. 65–72.

17. See also the opening poem of "Patriotic Suite," first published in *A Chosen Light* in 1967 as "The Lure."

18. Montague, letter, March 17, 1980.

19. Montague, "The Wild Dog Rose," *The Rough Field,* p. 81.

20. An example of the inconsistencies in attitude that O Riada seemed to encourage. In his commentary, Kinsella notes that O Riada made the whole nation his audience "without abandoning musical standards."

21. Kinsella, "Tao and Unfitness at Inistiogue on the River Nore," *Peppercanister Poems 1972–1978,* p. 107.

22. Kinsella, *Peppercanister Poems 1972–1978,* pp. 21–33. The elegies, joined here in a sequence, were originally published as 1972 and 1973 Peppercanister (Dublin) pamphlets.

23. Charles Acton, "I Gcuimhne Sheáin Uí Riada," *Eire-Ireland* 6, no. 3 (Fall 1971):3.

24. Thomas Kinsella, "Cover Her Face," *Peppercanister Poems 1956–1973* (Winston-Salem, N.C.: Wake Forest University Press, 1979), p. 49.

25. Kinsella, "One," *Peppercanister Poems 1972–1978,* p. 72.

26. Kinsella, "One," *Peppercanister Poems 1972–1978,* p. 60.

27. Charles Acton, "Sean O Riada: Changed sound of Irish traditional music," *The Irish Times,* October 4, 1971.

Richard Murphy:
Poet of Nostalgia or *Pietas*?

James D. Brophy

The question raised by the title of this essay derives most recently from
Seamus Heaney's essay in Maurice Harmon's *Richard Murphy: Poet of Two
Traditions*.[1] It also has a provenance in Donald Davie's 1975 review of
Murphy's *High Island*.[2] The question, which might be stated more familiarly and polemically as "Can an Anglo-Irishman possess a genuine Irish
commitment?," is important to consider because its skeptical prejudgement
(more obviously implied in the latter formulation) seriously depreciates
Richard Murphy's poetry. In my estimate the position that Murphy adopts a
superficial posture toward the Irish sources and material of his poetry is
unsupportable. And it will be the work of this paper to demonstrate that
Murphy is not a poet of "nostalgia" with its overtones of insincerity, but is
indeed a poet who reveals a genuine commitment to his country—a commitment that might usefully be defined by the Latin term, *pietas.*

There is, of course, no question about Murphy's English heritage. The
grandson of two Church of Ireland bishops, the son of the Mayor of Colombo
(Ceylon) and Governor General of the Bahamas, Murphy was educated by
an English nanny in Ceylon and schools in England (including the Canter-
bury Cathedral Choir School) and finally at Magdalen College, Oxford
(where he had C. S. Lewis as a tutor). Murphy's "Anglo" background is
public and formidable. Moreover, it is acknowledged by the poet: "Techni-
cally," he has said, "there is no one writing who could be more strictly
defined as Anglo-Irish."[3] At the same time, however, he claims for himself
another essential part of his being, the "Irish" side of the hyphen. Murphy
speaks of himself as a "complicated person," and, indeed, there is, as part
of the complexity, a thoroughly Irish dimension, private and unimposing in
credentials but nonetheless genuine. Born in Galway, he speaks with feeling
about his Irish heritage:

My father's father came out of the dark poverty of rural Ireland where nothing was written down—it was handed down in oral tradition. I don't know at what period his father or grandfather became Protestants, but I suspect, because there is no record of it, that during one of the many famines one of them couldn't afford to get to America or Liverpool and became a Protestant, as vast numbers did in the 19th century in order to survive—it was one of the ways of surviving.

He remembers this grandfather, although a Protestant rector, being on excellent terms with his Catholic father-in-law, and he speaks of his grandmother, a Mulvaney of Dublin whose sister Isabella was one of the first Irish women to get a university degree, and who saw to it that the poet's father received a good education. Murphy further recalls with pride his grandfather's refusing the living of Clifden because part of the salary was paid by the Irish Church Missions, and he would have nothing to do with that body's direct proselytizing of Irish Catholics. When later he did take the position it was without that tainted support. With this background and a family tradition of respect for the Irish Catholic it is not surprising that the poet has raised his daughter as a Roman Catholic.

In 1946, while at Oxford, Murphy returned to the West of Ireland, renting a cottage on Lough Fee, and in 1951, having won the AE prize of £100, he again returned to Ireland, renting for two years (at £20 a year, furnished) the Coast Guard cottage built by his grandfather in Rosroe. While living there, Murphy discovered accidently that the philosopher Ludwig Wittgenstein had previously occupied the cottage while recovering from illness. (Essentially, Murphy's residence was also for a recuperative purpose—from disillusionment with the world of London.) After these two years Murphy frequently returned to Ireland, and since 1961 has permanently resided in the seaside village of Cleggan. In 1969 he purchased High Island, the tiny island site of St. Fechin's seventh-century monastery, and began the restoration of its ruins. Since 1946, as he became more introspective and meditative about his life, Ireland has become more and more important to him, so much so in fact that by 1975 he could tell me (when I asked him what he was currently writing during his academic year as Poet-in-Residence at Bard College) that "I now find I cannot write outside of Ireland." He accepts offers of writer-in-residence in the United States, he told me, in order to support his life and poetry in Ireland.

Given this background of Murphy's extending back to the "dark poverty of rural" and Catholic Ireland, it is difficult to account for Donald Davie's remark about Murphy's "The Battle of Aughrim" that "if I read the case aright, all of Murphy's forebears would have been on the other, the winning side, and the way of life which they then built up for themselves, a way of life which conditioned Murphy himself, was made possible only by that victory.''[4] The answer, obviously, is that Davie has not "read the case aright,'' that a considerable part of the poet's heritage was on the losing side, and, indeed, Murphy has never lost sight of that.

It is instructive to observe that Murphy on one hand states that "there is no one who could be more strictly defined as Anglo-Irish'' and yet also admits to being "embarrassed'' by the term. This embarrassment is important, because it reveals his feelings as one genuinely tied to Ireland. The Anglo-Irishman of Ascendancy preference is not at all embarrassed by this double term: it keeps his priorities right, the English first, the Irish on the other side of the pale or hyphen.

Like Davie's, Seamus Heaney's evaluation of Murphy's poetry is largely depreciative, but, based on the poet's language and style rather than Davie's procrustean sociology, it is more acceptable as literary criticism, although, ultimately, it too has a sociological bias. For example, in a typical passage of analysis Heaney notes (about "The Battle of Aughrim'') that

The whole poem is a tessellation of deliberately shaped lyrics, just in their long views, solid in their crafted shapes, occasionally rich in their violent content—as in the account of the death of the traitor Luttrell—or entranced by the satisfactions of their language, as in the evocations of rapparees who materialize before the battle 'Out of the earth, out of the air, out of the water.' Yet in this lovely section there is symptomatic unease between the manner and the matter of the poetry:

> . . . At the whirr of a snipe each can disappear
> Terrified as a bird in a gorse-bush fire,
> To delve like a mole or mingle like a nightjar
> Into the earth, into the air, into the water.

Moles are not to be found in Ireland, and nightjars have to my ear an indelibly English literary ring to them, so that at a moment when the tutelar presences of the Irish ground are being summoned, they are subtly debilitated by the idiom in which they surface. It is not that Murphy wishes to rob them of their proper force: it is more that his language retains its ancestral bias in spite of his intention to exorcise ancestry as a determining limit of vision.[5]

This sophisticated analysis is, unfortunately, ultimately unconvincing as literary criticism. I say "unfortunately,'' because Heaney, apart from being a first-rate poet, is usually a perceptive and resourceful critic. His error here is falling into the organic fallacy that the form must mirror the content in every way. The logical conclusion of this thesis is that one must write about Ireland in Irish, which, of course, is not what Heaney himself does. In fact, he has elsewhere written of how, although his own poetry has been criticized for not sounding "very Celtic,'' he thinks of himself as a poet whose "roots were crossed with his reading'' and who thinks of his ''personal and Irish pieties as vowels, and the literary awareness nourished as English as consonants.''[6] To disallow ''delve like a mole'' as an illustrative simile for a readership that (being in English) would surely extend beyond Ireland is carping of the severest kind. And to make this judgment after the remarks about his own poetic mixture is to compound the issue with hypocrisy. If moles are not to be found in Ireland, the phrase indicts Murphy at most of not being a naturalist. If ''nightjar'' sounds ''English'' to Heaney, I submit that to a reader of modern poetry it also suggests Dylan Thomas (''Fern Hill'') who is Welsh or Celtic rather than English. Or should we disallow Thomas's evocation of a farm in Wales because he uses a word putatively of English allusion? Heaney's acute perception has the considerable merit of dealing with the language of the poem, but surely his demands for something like linguistic purity are unreasonable. If Heaney wishes to establish an *Académie Irlandaise,* it will have to be confined solely to Irish speakers, for the English language by its nature is the most heterogeneous and accommodating of languages.

The basis of Heaney's rejection of Murphy's poetry, however, is that Heaney does not believe that Murphy possesses a genuine sympathy for his Irish subject matter: there is in ''Aughrim,'' for example, according to Heaney, ''a lack of sympathetic imagining.'' And once the critic is armed with this bias the analysis of the language can indeed create supporting evidence. In the opening paragraphs of his essay in Harmon's book, Heaney compares Murphy unfavorably with the Orcadian poet George Mackay Brown:

Whereas Mackay Brown offers his world as the emblem of a desirable culture to which he would be affiliated, Murphy conducts us into a bleak and beautiful environment toward which he is sympathetic but finally ambivalent. Murphy's fidelity to the world of boatmen and tinkers and natural beauties and disasters does not altogether constitute a faith in it because that world is inadequate to his social and cultural recognitions.[7]

This passage is the key to Heaney's approach to Murphy. In his own terms the criticism is ''social and cultural'' rather than literary.

One wonders (looking for objective corroboration of Heaney's thesis) what the boatmen amongst whom Murphy has lived for decades would themselves say to Heaney's estimate. Harmon's book offers an answer. *Poet of Two Traditions,* initially published as the Richard Murphy issue of the *Irish University Review,*[8] was, in Harmon's words, ''launched on the island of Inishbofin in April, 1977.''[9] Murphy was present as guest of honor at the

Island's Art Festival, and gave a reading of his poems in the presence of many from the island, including "his old friend, Pat Concannon, to whom he dedicated the reading." The poet read "superbly, with a keen sense of occasion," according to Harmon, "only poems that had their origins in the life of the region and among its people. When some of them actually wept during his narration of 'The Cleggan Disaster,' their feelings seemed to confirm the validity and integrity of his relationship with them as man and poet." Harmon further records that Concannon (the survivor of the "Disaster") remarked, "What you've said is true."[10] In his "Preface" Harmon emphasizes that Murphy represents a remarkable accomplishment as a poet of two traditions:

His deep attraction to the people of the western seaboard does not involve a denial of his own Ascendancy background. He aims to explore both the Irish and the Anglo-Irish traditions. To these he responds through a sense of history and of ancestry, with an awareness of place, and a feeling for event.

One notes the interesting difference between the editor and his contributing critic's views. In support of Harmon it would seem that if Heaney moves his criticism to the plane of the poet's relationship with Irish culture, then the responses and feelings of the Inishbofin and Cleggan boatmen are valid testimony in Murphy's favor.

Heaney, in a passage characteristic of the depreciative tone of his essay, states that "The constricted space Murphy moves in and writes out of is a march between his Anglo-Irish Protestant background and his Irish Catholic surroundings, a space at once as neutral and torn as the battlefield at Aughrim, as problematic and personal as the house he builds for himself from ruined famine cottages, sometimes invaded by nostalgia for the imperial, patrician past, sometimes hospitable to deprivations and disasters which somehow rebuke that heritage."[11] Reading here the deliberate distinction which he makes between Protestant "background" and Irish Catholic "surroundings," one might wonder if Heaney knows (as Davie did not) about Murphy's Irish Catholic background as distinct from more accidental and superficial "surroundings." Since he notes later in his essay concerning the opposing forces at Aughrim that Murphy can "trace affiliations with both sides,"[12] one is indeed curious as to why affiliations that go back to 1691 do not qualify as "background" rather than "surroundings." It would seem that a valid case can be made for considering Richard Murphy a poet of *pietas*[13] rather than nostalgia.

The basic, interrelated themes of Richard Murphy's poetry from the poems of his first collection, *Sailing to an Island* (1963), to his most recent edition, *High Island* (1974),[14] are the need for a homeland or home and the requisite search for it. (Since one implies the other, this may be a single theme.) In "Sailing to an Island," the stark, compelling opening poem of his first book, the presence of a relentless drive is acknowledged:

> The boom above my knees lifts, and the boat
> Drops, and the surge departs, departs. . . .
> . . . and the mast draws eight and eight across
> Measureless blue.

The boat labors "all day for our chosen island," and typically for Murphy the choice is an Irish one, "Clare, with its crags purpled by legend," where the poet hopes to "locate in sea, earth and stone / The myth of a shrewd and brutal swordswoman / Who piously endowed an abbey." In a very real sense his third and latest book, *High Island,* demonstrates the completion of that earlier unsuccessful voyage which ended in turning back to Inishbofin for refuge. The poem "High Island" does indeed describe the location of "An older calm" amid "the kiss of rock and grass." The sense of certitude in the midst of flux is conveyed in the final lines of the later poem:

> Round the wrecked laura
> Needles flicker
> Tacking air, quicker and quicker
> To rock, sea and star.

Murphy's highly symbolic voyage is difficult, and, finally thwarted by the wind and tide, the *pookhaun* which had earlier in its history been the instrument of drowning in the Cleggan "disaster" is turned around toward a safe harbor. But that refuge, Inishbofin, of course, is equally Irish, and it is important to note that the poem ends with partial and tentative solution:

> Later, I reach a room, where the moon stares
> Cobwebbed through the window. The tide has ebbed,
> Boats are careened in the harbour. Here is a bed.

There is at least the possibility of temporary haven after struggle, although it is to be noted that the poet's vision of an elemental fact (the moon) is "cobwebbed" and not yet clear. And things are not yet "on an even keel" ("boats are careened"). Nor is the "bed" of the final statement ultimately satisfying; at best it is a respite till morning, when presumably the voyage will continue, perhaps with another attempt at reaching Clare.

That the experience of heroic return to historical Irish origins is neither easy nor concluded is further embodied in the poem by the presence of another searcher on the island, one who has come or returned from America in retirement:

> . . . . An old man grips my arm,
> His shot eyes twitch, quietly dissatisfied.
> He has lost his watch, an American gold
> From Boston gas-works. He treats the company
> To the secretive surge, the sea of his sadness.

If this old man is an American of Irish descent (it is not clear) the point is that he is striving to find a superficial peace apart from his real roots. If he is an Irishman who is returning to the land of his birth, then the implication is different, yet similar: that finding or rediscovering the source of peace or happiness is not easy, especially if one remains attached to "American gold." Is the loss of this watch a symbol of the necessity to cut off ties to America if life in Inishbofin is to be meaningful? Is there irony in this loss that the old man does not yet understand? Thinking of Murphy's embarrassment by the term "Anglo-Irish," is unease intended for the old man until he forgets about the symbolic watch, because until then he is a hyphenated Irish-American?

The theme of disappointment in search with concomitant instruction about the nature of finding a fulfilling refuge is even more the central theme of "The Poet on the Island," another poem from his first collection, about the visit of the American poet Theodore Roethke to Inishbofin. But the poem emphasizes that Roethke is not Irish: he is "one of the Yanks." He is "stumbling under the burden of himself," which situation is to be an American "looking for a refuge" on an Irish island. It is only natural, in Murphy's universe, for Roethke's words to "weirdly take off inwards," since only within the poet could he find himself amidst the alien externality of Inishbofin. "Doctors were called, and he agreed to sail," the only possible solution within the logic of Murphy's poetry.

"The Poet on the Island" is a curious work from the standpoint of this reading, because the poem is dedicated to Roethke. It would seem to be less than an act of friendship to document, as I believe the poem does, the failure of Roethke to achieve the "refuge" he sought on the island. Yet, considering Murphy's recognition of his own difficulty in finding his "chosen island" (Clare) and the resultant failure or partial failure in being diverted, defeated by the sea to Inishbofin, there is a kind of honor conferred on Roethke for his attempt. Murphy does not deride those who fail in the central struggle of life, most obviously portrayed by Murphy in the arduous lives of the Connemara seamen who seek to make the sea their own. Even those men, as in "The Cleggan Disaster" (from *Sailing to an Island*), who meet death through misjudgment of the storm, are portrayed as heroes in an epic situation. Roethke's faults are instructive: he is lost as a stranger on an island that is nameless in the title and throughout the poem. Symbolically, Inishbofin is nameless to "one of the Yanks." But Roethke's failure is an under-standable error, perhaps a necessary one to make, in learning how indeed to find a refuge of fulfillment. This poem, then, in the final analysis, extends to Roethke the kind of commendation given to the wounded soldier who partook of but did not complete the heroic sortie.

Murphy's "The Philosopher and the Birds," dedicated "In memory of Wittgenstein at Rosroe," is another poem from *Sailing to an Island* that honors a kind of heroic search for wisdom and refuge. It also, as the poem described above, qualifies the achievement in instructive parable. The eminent philosopher had gone to the west coast of Ireland to recuperate, and in large measure the poem honors the "solitary invalid" (Man in general?) who faced a kind of struggle "on this savage promontory":

> . . . Old, in fieldfares
> Fantasies rebelled though annihilated.
>
> He was haunted by gulls beyond omega shade,
> His nerve tormented by terrified knots
> In pin-feathered flesh.

While there, in action especially appealing to a poet, Wittgenstein "at last tamed, by talking, wild birds," and as his "wisdom widens: he becomes worlds / where thoughts have wings." Down to the concluding two lines of the poem there is unqualified praise of the philosopher. The ending, how-ever, seems to be a strange reversal: the philosopher departs,

> But at Rosroe hordes
> Of village cats have massacred his birds.

This conclusion colors our estimate of Wittgenstein; the massacre is a blot on an otherwise positive remembrance. What is Murphy demonstrating? Not surprisingly in a poem called "complex" by the author, this conclusion is not simple or straightforward. Although it qualifies our opinion of Wittgen-stein, it does not completely nullify the admiring tone of the rest of the poem. Wittgenstein emerges flawed in that he abandoned his birds to a fate which he did not foresee but should have. (There is irony in "His wisdom widens.") And yet this is forgivable, because after all he was not Irish, or a native of Rosroe, and there was no reason why, after his recuperation, he should have remained. And therein is Murphy's subtle point: The good of a place can only be fully served by those who are committed to it. The birds at Rosroe suffered from Wittgenstein's commitment elsewhere, and, con-versely, to the extent that we feel some betrayal of Rosroe, Wittgenstein's character is diminished. This moving poem is one of the poet's most effective parables. The terrible concluding irony moves us to hope that Wittgenstein's widening wisdom will enable him to make a more benign commitment elsewhere: in short, that he may come to realize what Murphy is continuously evoking in his poetry—*pietas*.

Although "The Poet on the Island" and "The Philosopher and the Birds" are moving and successful poems, the theme of the self needing to find its own place is most powerfully conveyed—perhaps because it does not specifically pertain to the poet or philosopher—in Murphy's "The God Who Eats Corn."[15] The God in this poem (in the language of the African Matabele) is the white man in general, and, in particular, Murphy's father, who after retiring from his career in the British Foreign Service chose to settle in Rhodesia. This very description introduces the disabling ironies that Murphy deals with in his poetry: "Foreign Service," in the ethos we see Richard Murphy developing, is a contradiction in terms. We have seen what ensues from Roethke's and Wittgenstein's "foreign service." And the father's service in Ceylon (before going on to become Governor General of the Bahamas and retiring to Rhodesia) indeed affected the poet as a young boy. Five poems of *High Island* recollect his sense of dislocation in a strange land.

In "The Fall" the sense of alienation abounds for the boy: his kitten is called "Marmalade," but "Appu's cooking curry for lunch," the calls of the bird in the temple tree in their garden "were spoken in a language I never understood." And the temple tree itself was known "by no other name" as if to the boy it should have had another; that is, English name. In "Traveler's Palm," recounting the young boy's trip to a temple with his nanny, the poet compellingly conveys the ironies of the situation. As the boy takes off his "new balanced shoes at the temple door" Nanny

> . . . wraps them in tissue paper
> Humming her favourite bar of *Pomp and Circumstance*

and when he begins to slide on the marble floor, he is admonished to "remember where you are." The boy, dismayed and becoming thirstier in the heat by the display of devil-dancers / pleads, "Nan, I'm thirsty. Can't we go home?" And again, as a symbolic refrain, after "A monk hangs a lei of temple flowers" around his neck, he asks, "Can we go home soon?" Finally, on the way home, to alleviate the boy's painful thirst, his nanny shows him a Traveler's Palm and the place to sink his pen-knife in to locate water. Knowing the hesitancy to taste the liquid, and posing the question, "If you die, can you be reborn?," the poet recognizes the paramount need and urges "Try: Even if the water of the tree is poison, drink." The implication is that no risk should be avoided to enable the traveler's return home and all that it symbolizes.

One notes that in the British edition of *High Island* "Traveler's Palm" is the penultimate poem before "Stormpetrel," a poem which evokes the sea and cliffs of Connemara, Murphy's home. In the American edition the poem is in the same position preceding "High Island," the poet's abiding symbol of rebirth ("Flowers in the dead place") and the substantiality of homeland. The petrels of "High Island," evoking this,

> . . . slip down to nest
> Under altar-stone or grave.

The island is described in the poem as "A fisherman's mark," but certainly it is an even more important mark to the poet.

More important than these poems of Ceylon, "The God Who Eats Corn" is essentially an extension of the Ceylon poems in that it describes the life of an Anglo-Irishman in a foreign setting. It is a remarkable poem for its achieved balance of tenderness toward his father and revulsion for the colonial experience. The poet's uneasiness about his father's well-intentioned endeavor to establish a farm and later a school for African children as part of his "duty to improve the earth," is evident from the ironies of the opening lines,

> In his loyal garden, like Horace's farm,
> He asks his visitors to plant a tree.
> The black shadow of the African msasa
> Squats among the lawn's colonial company.

The Queen Mother has given a cypress to preside in honour "over cool English rosebeds / Handweeded by a pink-soled piccanin." A chairman of mines gave a copper beech, a silver oak was planted by the governor, and his father himself has brought seed for a plane tree from Cos "From shade where Hippocrates swore his oath." But the plane tree "Wilts in the voodoo climate," and the gums which "The trekkers imported have sapped the earth." Only two indigenous trees are planted: one a wild fig, given by Livingstone's heir "From the burnt-out forest of Africa," and the other, "the native candelabra," by the poet "as a son." The force of "as a son" emphasizes the principle of generation and heritage that the whole project ironically betrays. "Under these trees," mostly foreign, the father believes that *indaba,* the native parlay, will "heal the blood-feud." The poet's comment is allusive and mordant: "Bullfrogs crackle in the lily-pond."

"Tall in his garden, shaded and brick-walled," Murphy's father "upholds the manners of a lost empire." And although for the old man "Time has confused dead honour with dead guilt,'' the son's poem distinguishes and illuminates both. There was indeed the goal of Livingstone's prayer, ''to do some good for this poor Africa,'' but that was not Rhodesia's founder's dream of ''gold and diamonds.'' In the colonial era there is more food grown and fever cured, but nonetheless there are shocking contrasts:

> To each black, his ten acres for millet;
> To each white, his three thousand of grass.
> The gospel of peace preached from the pulpit;
> From the hungry fields the gospel of force.

And, inevitably, as with Wittgenstein, the strangers depart or die leaving an unhappy legacy:

> The concrete cracks and the brown rivers bleed,
> Cattle die of rinderpest, dogs with rabies
> Bite their masters, the half-freed slaves are freed
> But not into a garden that anyone remembers.

Whether the colonials stay or leave, ''the old mopani forest is felled,'' and the present is flawed. The new club-room for the school that his father plans will not cure his boredom which the poem implies has deeper sources. Murphy the poet has indeed compassion for the colonized and subdued Africans, and he prophetically observes that ''Thunder is pent in the drums of the compound,'' but his main purpose in the poem is to illuminate the terrible toll on his father that his wrongheaded mission takes. Never is his memory or mind free of memories of his Irish past:

> Last thing at night he checks the rain-gauge
> Remembering his father on a rectory lawn.

And the concluding line of the poem is a compelling, compassionate statement that

> He feels too old to love the rising moon.

By separating himself from the ties of his birthplace, he has, ironically, in his efforts to reclaim a new land, alienated himself from the elemental forces of nature. (In ''Sailing to an Island'' the moon was symbolically obscured rather than rejected.) The poem clarifies both the poet's devotion to his father and the perverse nature of the father's abandonment of his West of Ireland culture. The ironic conjunction of remembering the Irish homestead with its ''rectory lawn'' and consulting the rain-gauge in Rhodesia with its ''dry indaba trees'' suggests how disregarded the hereditary ties have become. In context, one does not imagine the Irish rector father alienated, like the transplanted son, from "the rising moon." Remembering *his* father, Richard Murphy manifestly rejects the colonial world's ironies and aliena- tion. For the reader of "The God Who Eats Corn" the poet's own chosen return to settle in the West of Ireland is not a capricious or nostalgic act.

"To settle" in Ireland is, of course, not the right phrase. It suggests an overtone of colonial propriety, which, to the author of "The God Who Eats Corn," would be anathema. Moreover, it also suggests a kind of repose or bourgeois self-containment that is not the life that Murphy has made for himself and others. And "others" are indeed important to him. Consonant with the sense of duty to one's patrimony implicit in the concept of *pietas,* Murphy has actively sought to restore a sense of value to the people and culture of the West of Ireland. His poems abound with images of reconstruc- tion and life supplanting death: the cleaning out of Brian Boru's well on High Island "seven times a year," the rebuilding of the well, the recurring reference to birds nesting in a skull, the "flowers in the dead place" that inspirit him in "High Island." It is in this spirit that I interpret "Little Hunger"[16] which Seamus Heaney sees as a poem of colonial exploitation. It is possible, but distorting, to read the isolated poem as a statement of personal aggrandizement at the expense of others:

> I drove to Little Hunger promontory
>   Looking for pink stone
> In roofless houses huddled by the sea
>   To buy to build my own.
>
> Hovels to live in, ruins to admire
>   From a car cruising by,
> The weathered face caught in a sunset fire
>   Hollowed with exility.

Murphy is not admiring the ruins from a passing car; the irony of the lines indicates that he is not pleased to see the ruins now hovels. He will accept their "gradual fall" which will enable him to rebuild the seven cabins as one ("to make it integral"). But surely, the "gradual" clearance of these "hovels" is more beneficial than perpetuating the "roofless" hovels in what might be thought of indeed as "nostalgia" instead of a more clear-headed resolve to do something positive with the ruins. The situation obviously indicates that no one else besides Murphy had sought to do anything with these hovels or ruins except to let them stand picturesquely for the tourist's camera. The crux, for me, in the tone of the poem is whether the poet's acquisition involves the eviction of the wretched poor who live there. I read, however, a deep sense of the poet's outrage in the line "hollowed with exility,'' and I see in the emphatic ''gradual'' an assurance to the reader that the speaker is not about to add further exile to that ''weathered face.'' The ''dismemberment'' of the ruins and the construction of a new house, in my reading, will not contribute to the misery of others. If one type of Irishman would prefer to preserve the symbols of poverty and ruin, another who would make some resolution of decay should not be considered any less Irish for that disposition.

Aside from his purchase and care of High Island, one of Murphy's most interesting Irish concerns has been his generous and symbolic rehabilitation of a family of tinkers. In 1972 he learned of an itinerant family in which the parents were estranged and the seven children put into an industrial school and an orphanage. Working to get the family back together, Murphy accepted responsibility for them, and obtained a house for them in Cleggan. Endeavoring literally to domesticate them, he discovered that the children liked keeping goats, and he bought pasture land for that occupation on nearby Omey Island (accessible at low tide). When I met him at Bard College in 1974, he told me that he had brought the two boys of the family with him to America, so that when they returned to Ireland they would be looked up to for that distinction, and given a much-needed ''leg-up'' in their lives.

Murphy's poem ''The Reading Lesson''[17] conveys some of the problems of this rehabilitation of the tinkers, and most importantly, the reason for his work on their behalf. The problems include the tinker's own unregenerate attitude, resisting the difficult business of learning to read:

> He looks at a page as a mule balks at a gap
> From which a goat may hobble out and bleat.
> His eyes jink from a sentence like flushed snipe
> Escaping shot. A sharp word, and he'll mooch
> Back to his piebald mare and bantam cock.
> Our purpose is as tricky to retrieve
> As mercury from a smashed thermometer.

The boy complains, ''I'll be the same man whatever I do,'' and protests, ''I'll not read anymore.'' The poet asks ''Should I give up?'' and in this is confronted by another problem for the tinkers, the attitude of other Irish toward them: ''A neighbor chuckles, 'You can never tame / The wild duck: when his wings grow, he'll fly off.' '' But the poet perseveres, because he sees the tinker boy with ''hands, longfingered as a Celtic scribe's,'' and he believes that the tinkers of modern Ireland are the descendants of the Celtic bards who were turned out of their positions by the British invaders to find

their lives in the lanes and hedges. Thus, the tinkers are highly and importantly symbolic to Murphy; in helping them he is restoring a rightful Irish
patrimony. Regardless of whether Murphy's hypothesis about the tinkers'
origin is correct or not, what matters is his commitment to the Irish past and
the sense of duty it generates. The arduous task of bringing two boys, one
nine and one fourteen, to America for a year is not explained adequately by
Heaney's "nostalgia." It is more understandable as an action informed by a
sincere sense of justice and duty, the qualities that define *pietas*.

It is this commitment to justice that shapes "The Battle of Aughrim" as it
begins with "Who owns the land . . . ?" One notes that only a few stanzas
later we read that "a tinker woman hired to stoop / Is thinning turnips by
hand." Irony is Murphy's central technique in "Aughrim," and its opera-
tion here in this passage is clear. Those who are closest to the earth do not
indeed own it, and with the case of the tinkers that fact is even more ironic or
distressing. But the role of tinkers in "Aughrim" is incidental to the larger,
overriding theme of the betrayal of Ireland and the Irish by foreign powers.
The force of Murphy's irony is mostly directed at the British planter
hegemony, but he demonstrates other ways in which alien powers work
against Ireland's ultimate good: the battle itself was directed not by Irishmen
but by Germans (on the British side) and French (on the Irish side). Murphy
has said that "Aughrim" is his attempt to reconcile the division of Ireland in
poetry. And his chief method is to dramatize the injustice of the Irish not
controlling their own destiny and lives. Mainly the Irish are the victims of the
colonial ethos as when (in the "Orange March" section)

> On Belfast silk, Victoria gives
> Bibles to kneeling Zulu chiefs.

But they also show some evidence of self-betrayal as alluded to by the
woman who brings as a souvenir from Knock shrine "John Kennedy's head
on a china dish." Kennedy's presence suggests the Irish dispersion, the
"wild geese" who, for whatever good reasons, nonetheless depart and
disconnect. The conclusion of "Aughrim" makes very clear the irony of
Irish rejection of Ireland. And that is an important connection between
"Aughrim" and "The God Who Eats Corn" which documents the father's
distance from "the rectory lawn" of Connemara. Murphy depicts the
descendants of the Irish who died at Aughrim returning to view the
battlefield. They are "strangers." "They know by instinct," he writes,
"this cool creek of traitors."

This is sharp indictment indeed, and may be especially rankling to some
readers coming from one who can be "Strictly defined as Anglo-Irish." The

final line of this powerful poem describes the visitors of Irish heritage as they "turn in time to catch a plane for France." Conquest, abandonment, betrayal—all are shown by Murphy in "Aughrim" to be Ireland's burden and trouble, past and present. And what informs the eloquent ironies of their manifestation in "The Battle of Aughrim" is the poet's own devotion to Ireland. "Who owns the land?" Ironically, it has not been those of similar devotion, and this has been dire for Ireland and the Irish. For as Murphy consistently shows in his poetry from first to last, from *Sailing to an Island* to *High Island,* an individual's fulfillment is to be found within his own heritage, in the realization of homeland and home. The theme as well as the source of this poetry is *pietas.*

Notes

1. Seamus Heaney, "The Poetry of Richard Murphy," in *Richard Murphy: Poet of Two Traditions,* ed. Maurice Harmon (Dublin: Wolfhound Press, 1978), pp. 18–30.

2. Donald Davie, "Cards of Identity," *The New York Review of Books* (March 6, 1975):10–11.

3. Interview with the author at Rhinebeck, N.Y., May 13, 1974. All further references below to statements by Richard Murphy are from this interview unless otherwise cited.

4. Davie, "Cards of Identity," p. 11.

5. Heaney, "The Poetry of Richard Murphy," p. 26.

6. Heaney, "1972" in *Preoccupations: Selected Prose, 1968–1978* (New York: Farrar, Straus, and Giroux, 1980), pp. 36–37.

7. Heaney, "The Poetry of Richard Murphy," p. 18.

8. *Irish University Review* 7, no. 1 (Spring 1977).

9. Harmon, *Richard Murphy: Poet of Two Traditions,* p. 6. See note 1. Further references in this paragraph are to this same page of the Editor's "Preface" unless otherwise cited.

10. Ibid., p. 15.

11. Heaney, "The Poetry of Richard Murphy," p. 19.

12. Ibid., p. 25.

13. It is noteworthy that Heaney also uses the term *pietas* but only to describe Murphy's feelings toward Ascendancy heritage in "The Woman of the House."

14. Murphy's books are: *Sailing to an Island* (London: Faber and Faber, 1963); *The Battle of Aughrim* (London: Faber and Faber, 1968); *High Island* (London: Faber and Faber, 1974). The American edition of *High Island* published by Harper and Row in 1974 is a collected edition including all but two poems of *Sailing to an Island,*

all of *The Battle of Aughrim,* and all of *High Island* (British edition) plus two added poems.

15. Published together with ''The Battle of Aughrim'' to constitute the volume, *The Battle of Aughrim.*

16. Murphy, *High Island,* p. 89.

17. Murphy, *High Island,* p. 107.

Appropriate Performance:
Thomas Kinsella and the Ordeal of Understanding

Daniel O'Hara

The act of understanding . . . ends in an understanding of what lies in wait for unreasonable hope.[1]

The Poetic Impulse

Traditionally, one important motive for poetry has been to achieve the sublime, and so to secure for one's self a significant place among the literary giants of the past. As Helen Vendler succinctly describes the sublime in a recent essay, the poet aims in his work for "vastness and grandeur of conception, nobility of diction and a vehemence of passion," so as to evoke in the reader "a sizable awe and a posture of ecstatic reverence."[2] In this way, the poet establishes an identity of his own which can withstand the onslaughts of time, since he has impressed his way of looking at things on the psyches of his readers, and so, in a sense, continues to live on in them. Not only does the poet thereby gain a measure of symbolic immortality, but he also helps to educate his readers to a nobler vision of existence than that which they can otherwise afford to entertain, a vision which they need, as a community, if they are to go on at all. In short, the desire of the self to make something stand still amidst the flux of time becomes transformed, in the greatest poetry, into what Yeats called "a superhuman /Mirror-resembling dream,"[3] which, given the right light, can drive men happily to their knees if not into the madhouse.

This motive for metaphor became generalized and exclusive, the sole motive for poetic expression, with the Romantics. And, despite the modernist poets' revolt against the Romantic inheritance, this conception of poetry and of the poet's function still haunts the academy. Its unquestioned status explains why many critics today have such a hard time figuring out what is going on in contemporary poetry, or, if partially successful in that effort, why they rush generally to negative judgments about the various poetic projects under survey. For it should be abundantly clear by now—after the examples of Auden and Larkin in England, of Williams and Lowell in America—that poets nowadays no longer aspire to the sublime; in fact, they look on such aspiration as suspect, old-fashioned and out of touch, silly: rather like reciting Virgil in the supermarket. Instead of aspiring to sublimity, contemporary poets quest for understanding of their significant experience, for a stance of openness that takes experience on its own terms, amidst all its rigors and wastes, and elicits order from its complexities, an order that testifies to "the actuality of response" on the poet's part. As Thomas Kinsella puts it in a recent interview: "If an artistic response is called into existence, that itself modifies the situation: it's a positive response even if we never solve anything. It colours reality in a way that makes it more acceptable."[4] The ordeal of understanding, unlike the passion for sublimity, requires an honest recognition of the essentially unfinished nature of experience and a refusal to gloss over this fact in the interests of the aesthetics of perfection.

The rift between what academic critics expect and what contemporary poets supply accounts for the curious reception, especially lately, that Thomas Kinsella's poetry has received. Hugh Kenner is a case in point. In a recent piece, he accurately describes the major strategy of Kinsella's poetry as the affording of "focal moments when a quality isolates itself." But then Kenner characterizes this quality in a strangely narrow manner, as "Nightmare glowing, fading, glowing, amid the equable pace of metered discourse." The pervasive effect of the poetry, according to Kenner, is a perverse subversion of the reader's every expectation:

it [Kinsella's poetry] treats [the reader] as an element in the poem's strategy: not someone addressed, but someone to be deceived, by various devices of rhetoric and typography, into expecting what will not be provided. For that is how it is in the world of these poems: nothing we might expect will be provided.[5]

Rather than impressing the reader, as Yeats had done, with "some single emblem backed by a whole literature and culture," which would function to define the community—Major Robert Gregory as "our Sidney and our perfect man"—Kinsella, according to Kenner, claims a license to tell private nightmares" in an "intensely solipsistic verse" that turns its back on our public world.[6]

Clearly, what Kenner expects from poetry, for all his immersion in the ironies of modernist poetry, is the sublime effects of transport to a purely aesthetic world of luminous details and balanced tensions desired by the persona of Yeats's "Sailing to Byzantium." But to come to contemporary poetry with such an expectation is to ignore the last thirty years of literary history, to say the least. What Kenner desires appears to be uplift; aesthetic illusion. But what Kinsella is willing to provide are possibilities of understanding, self-knowledge. What Kinsella calls that "ethic of suffering" for art's sake of Yeats, which influenced much of the willed rhetoric of his own early poetry, has been replaced in his mature verse with a scrupulous attention to those open-ended moments of nearly mute communication that sometimes occur between radically different minds, each in search of understanding: "I don't believe the creative response has anything to do with making people behave better; it has to do with understanding them— however they behave."[7] What all this means in practice can best be seen by turning to "Ely Place," a poem representative of much in Kinsella's later poetry.

"Ely Place" occupies a central position in the final section of poems entitled "Nightnothing" that climaxes the suite "Notes From the Land of the Dead," itself part of a larger sequence of poems that begins with "Phoenix Park" and includes *Notes* (1973), *One* (1974), *A Technical Supplement* (1976), *Song of the Night* and *The Messenger* (both 1978). In addition, "Ely Place" represents in an explicitly contemporary, nonmythical form the nadir of isolation, murderously impotent rage, and self-destructive irony that the evolving consciousness of the sequence must face in the course of its development. Like the rest of the sequence, the aim of "Ely Place" is understanding—understanding those moments of blind dereliction that afflict anyone. For in understanding them one may learn how to distill something positive out of such ordeals that life repeatedly serves up to us. If we can swallow the bitter secretions of experience and transmute them into art, an art of temporality and not of eternity, then we can resume "in candour and doubt the only individual joy—the restored necessity to learn."[8] This is the principle that "Ely Place" would prove upon the pulses.

Certainly, "Ely Place" presents a terrible prospect. The poem's speaker, out of doors on a Sunday at noon, attempts to compose his impressions of George Moore, the Irish novelist and playwright, Yeats's occasional collaborator, and the most famous resident of Ely Place. But the speaker's will to coherence is repeatedly frustrated, first, by the insistent cry of a gull perched on a nearby hospital gutter, then, by the intrusive distraction of a female passerby, next, by George Moore's own randy ghost, and, finally, by a horrific "blood vision" that overwhelms the speaker's will. He succumbs to the forces of disorder that continuously break in on him, overmatching the violence from without with a violence from within that is truly terrible:

Sunday.
    'Such a depth of charm
here always . . .'
                 Doomed in the sun.
In Mortuary Lane a gull
cried on one of the Hospital gutters
—I. I. I . . . harsh
in sadness, on and on,
beak and gullet open
against the blue.
              Down at the corner
a flicker of sex, a white
dress, against the railings.
'This is where George Moore . . .'
                    rasps
his phantom walking-stick
without a sound, toward the Post Office
where her slight body, in white,
has disappeared.
                 (A flustered
perfumy dress—a mothering
shocked smile—live muscle
starling in skin.)
               A blood vision
started out of the brick: the box
of keys in my pocket—I am opening it,
tongue-tied. I unpick the little
pen-knife and dig it in her throat,
her spirting gullet!
              Vanishing . . .

Moving inside grants the speaker no relief. Instead, he suddenly has the sense that the entire visible world of solid matter is being eaten up by the various physical processes at work generally, all of which fuel the ultimate cosmic entropy to come:

Indoors, darkness pours down
through half light stale as the grave
over plates and silver bowls
glimmering on a side table.
Vanishing . . .
             Solid matter
flickering in broad daylight

(and they are on it in a flash,
brief tongues of movement
ravenous, burrowing and feeding,
invisible in blind savagery,
upstreaming through the sunlight with it
until it disappears, buried
in heaven, faint, far off).

And yet, for all the unremitting horror here, out of the wreckage of such experiences something significant emerges:

'. . . with a wicked wit, but self-mocking;
and full of integrity behind it all . . .'

A few beginnings, a few
tentative tired endings over
and over . . .

             Memoirs, maggots.

                         After lunch

a quarter of an hour at most
of empty understanding.[9]

So what are we to make of this curious poem?

"Ely Place" is a poem that interprets itself. The lines describing the oxidation and disintegration of solid matter function also as a reading of all the other flickering, glimmering visions of agonizing dissolution and violent destruction. These lines compose a fable that gathers up earlier portions of the poem and that foreshadows the conclusion. All these disruptive, vanishing visions are part of one universal process of decay, which, in a kind of awful parody of the Pentecostal visitation to the Apostles, appears as devouring "tongues of movement" that would consume and carry off all, "buried in heaven, faint, far off." Yet this ironically apocalyptic vision holds the suggestion of possible order, not a human order, nor, certainly, that of any Divine Logos, but some pattern of experience manifesting itself here that the speaker can come to understand, however "empty" that understanding is said to be.

Earlier in the poem the speaker is seen impotently and inarticulately raging and striking out in a "blood vision." But he achieves here a perception, however terrible, of "brief tongues of movement" articulating precisely, if only momentarily, the structure of experience. The whole point of the sequence of poems beginning with "Phoenix Park" is the overcoming of the temptation to dumb rage or silent despair. And the symbol of the keys, as well as that of the pen-knife and other variations, point to the desire on the speaker's part to master his disorder in words, to understand so as to be able to sing again. Unlike Yeats, who postured heroically, one foot planted in eternity, as he urged on the final consummation of things, Kinsella represses all such urges to posture, with, as in "Ely Place," a wicked wit ("Solid matter /flickering in *broad* daylight"), and, certainly, with an honest self-mockery that enables him to go on to an understanding whose emptiness becomes fruitful.

The poetic impulse in a Kinsella text develops into an open-ended act of understanding that solicits from reality a significant form, a form like that of "Ely Place" which enacts this development in an allegory of its own unique, purely provisional, yet rigorously integral, creativity. To compare the particular poetic act of this poem with any other before attempting to understand its own structure is to leap prematurely to judgment. As Kinsella puts it: "If adequately understood and responded to, poetry should add dynamically to the understanding of the reader. It is a form of significant reality processed in advance for the understanding; it's like a meaningful model for the life lived. I try to use the word 'significant' only to mean that which will bother all of us equally."[10]

Psychic Geography

Rather than pinning his hopes on the star of the sublime, and trying to substitute his personal phantasmagoria for the larger communal forms of the imagination that have gone by the boards—religious myths and rituals, moral values, shared political attitudes—Kinsella, like Lowell, rejects heroic posturing and chooses instead to rely on the minimal general things we all do still share: the coils of the family romance. He builds his mature poetry on this admittedly meager if inescapable basis, tracing in the long sequence of poems inaugurated by "Phoenix Park" the growth of an individual consciousness. Consequently, critics, like Kenner, who go to the poetry expecting the sublime in its modernist variant are in for a shock. In fact, as John Montague recently suggests, Kinsella's real achievement, the finest and strongest of "post-Yeatsian Irish poetry," stems from his progressive shedding of the high modernist manner, that "thickness of language and old-fashioned technique," that balancing of tensions and carving out of poetic wholes, that "willed rhetoric," which affected Kinsella's poetry up to the *Nightwalker* (1968) volume.[11] As Montague also suggests, the "subterranean psychic explorer" of *Notes* and after has been able to develop and to deploy tactfully a remarkable "corrective variety of tones" to wean himself away from a certain "heaviness of diction" and a once apparently unappeasable "appetite for horror."[12]

What Kinsella recognizes, and such critics as Hugh Kenner ignore, is that whether the country is Ireland or America, England or France, Western culture generally no longer possesses a credible public realm. There is no space of rationality and concern in which we can discuss our differences, criticize our poems, and reaffirm our values. Instead, as Kinsella powerfully asserts in "The Irish Writer" (1966), among even the most creative people, we find only "a scattering of incoherent lives. . . . a few madmen and hermits, and nothing more."[13] There are simply no commonly shared standards of any kind. Even the model of the life lived that Kinsella claims good poetry offers to the careful reader is nontransferable. Each individual must work out such a model of creative response for him or her self.

Kinsella has worked out his model by wrestling with the influence of Yeats, the inescapable modern poetic father. He has done so by mediating or handling his influence, first, by imitating Auden's ironic manner and self-deprecating stance. Next, he turned away from Yeats's selective Ascendency ideal erected above the filthy modern tide, and turned to Joyce's comprehensive vision of Irish reality, filth and all. Then, finally, since *Notes,* Kinsella has been adapting the open American voice of William Carlos Williams and the ideogrammatic method of Ezra Pound to his autobiographical project, at the heart of which stands a quest-myth of the contemporary poetic imagination. The goal of the sequence and of the quest is to purify the psyche of that violently insistent "I. I. I . . ." of "Ely Place" and substitute for it an understanding empty of the solely egocentric.

Those excruciating moments of imaginative vision in Kinsella's poems, like that of the consuming tongues in "Ely Place," compose a myth of creative response appropriate for contemporary experience. Kinsella characterizes such response in "Hen Woman," one of the opening poems of "Notes From the Land of the Dead," as a process that involves as much the purgation of the psychic as the concentration of the will. The poem, which centers on the speaker's early memories of his grandmother's failing to catch an egg as it falls from the hen in her arms, rises to provisional generalization near its conclusion:

> I feed upon it still, as you see;
> there is no end to that which,
> not understood, may yet be noted
> and hoarded in the imagination,
> in the yolk of one's being, so to speak,

there to undergo its (quite animal) growth,
dividing blindly,
twitching, packed with will,
searching in its own tissue
for the structure
in which it may wake.
Something that had—clenched
in its cave—not been
now was: an egg of being.
Through what seemed a whole year it fell
—as it still falls, for me,
solid and light, the red gold beating
in its silvery womb,
alive as the yolk and white
of my eye; as it will continue
to fall, probably, until I die,
through the vast indifferent spaces
with which I am empty.[14]

In a typical maneuver, Kinsella expresses here his myth of the imagination in terms, however humble or lacking in traditional decorum, drawn directly from the materials of the poem. A higher principle of decorum is operative, clearly. The ordeal of understanding requires the digestion of much in the filthy modern tide that even the later Yeats, the Yeats of "Among School Children" and "A Dialogue of Self and Soul," reflexively spat out. The poetic impulse, to become an act of understanding, must swallow such Romantic pride and learn most of all to mock itself. The exile of the contemporary Irish writer is as much interior as it may be exterior fate.

The best introduction to the "psychic geography" of Kinsella's later poetry, and especially of the sequence, is "Worker in Mirror, At His Bench." The poem emerges from the materials that make up a longer meditation, "The Good Fight," written for the tenth anniversary of John F. Kennedy's death in 1973. In that poem there is an uneasy identification explored between the assassin who caresses his rifle and the poet who wields his wicked pen, each the other's double and both full of urges to murder and destroy that are directed against the entire range of shabby authority figures in modern society, from alienated father to tyrannical boss, from literary predecessor to President. Yet at the end of the poem the speaker adopts a scaled-down vision of human potential, reminiscent of early Auden, that substitutes the possibility of understanding for the deforming epic ambitions afflicting both assassin and his victim:

> Plump and faithless;
> cut, as it were, in the sinews
> of our souls; each other's worst company;
> it is we, letting things *be,*
> who might come at understanding.
> That is the source of our patience.
> Reliable first in the direction
> and finally in the particulars of our response,
> fumbling from doubt to doubt,
> one day we might knock
> our papers together, and elevate them
> (with a certain self-abasement)
> —their gleaming razors
> mirroring a primary world
> where power also is a source of patience
> for a while before the just flesh
> falls back in black dissolution in its box.[15]

This necessity to restrain unreasonable hope, and the role poetry plays in such an act of self-discipline, are the twin subjects addressed in "Worker in Mirror."

The poem consists of three parts, the first two of which dramatize the Worker's confrontation with some people who, coming into his shop and interrupting his work with their questioning gazes, provide him with an opportunity to interrogate himself concerning the personal and social functions of art. Part One opens with a brief description and a set of rhetorical questions that establish the self-consciously anti-Yeatsian stance:

> Silent rapt surfaces
> assemble glittering
> among themselves.
>
> A few more pieces.
>
> What to call it . . .
> > Bright Assembly?
> Foundations for a Tower?
> Open Trap? Circular-Tending
> Self-Reflecting Abstraction . . .[16]

These questions are formulae that could fairly characterize the aesthetic developments of many of the modernist poets, but certainly Yeats is the figure that comes foremost to mind. The rest of the poem discloses the Worker's answer to these questions concerning the proper name for his creation, and, as well, the end the poetic object serves.

In the poem's last section, the self-reflecting mirror-assembly that the Worker produces does not close self-defeatingly in on itself. Rather, it becomes the basis for a process of communication, and, potentially, self-understanding. Looking into the mirror-work with the speaker, the reader "puts on" the forms of the poet's sensibility and discovers in doing so some hard truths about himself and, of course, about the poet that are necessary to come to terms with. The poet, looking into his own work, must make a similar discovery about himself and any potential reader. He learns something about the psychological genesis of art and, more significantly, gets a prophetic glimpse of what lies in wait for "unreasonable hope." In a recent interview, Kinsella describes the process succinctly as follows:

The idea . . . is that his face is gathered by the mirrors and projected off into a false infinity; it looks back at him from this immense distance, dominating the scene, and passes through various stages: gold, silver, bronze, iron—the ancient Greek "Ages." . . . As realization grows, through different aspects of the face, we come to the full immersion in blood: the wolf muzzle lapping at brother's blood. . . . Looking back at what is actually the foundation of the image, he sees something else out of the Greeks: a stone face half-submerged in silt at the bottom of some lifeless sea. This is the truth towards which we are pushed: the face that is waiting, in fact, for the first, innocent face.[17]

These four distinct faces, with the possibility of a fifth and final face, which dawns on the Worker as he disengages from his "reading," define a "progress" into experience that all of us must necessarily undergo:

> Did I dream another outline
> in the silt of the sea floor?
> Blunt stump of limb—
> a marble carcase
> where no living thing can have crept,
> below the last darkness,
> slowly, as the earth ages,
> blurring with pressure.
> The calm smile of a half-
> buried face: eyeball
> blank, the stare inward
> to the four corners of
> what foul continuum . . .
>
> blackness—all matter
> in one light-devouring
> polished cliff-face
> hurtling rigid

> from zenith to pit
> through dead[18]

The question that arises here, as in the earlier discussion of "Ely Place," concerns the significance of this multi-phase vision of unremitting cosmic horror. Is it all just Kinsella's "personal grouse" against the world, as Eliot characterized his poem *The Waste Land?*

The answer, I think, resides in Part Two of the poem. Although the Worker remains suspicious of his own easy formulation here, the general thrust of the following passage appears absolutely central to any understanding of Kinsella's later poetry:

> No, it has no practical application.
> I am simply trying to understand something
> —states of peace nursed out of wreckage.
> The peace of fullness, not emptiness.
>
> It is tedious, yes.
> The process is elaborate, and wasteful
> —a dangerous litter of lacerating pieces
> collects. Let my rubbish stand witness . . .
> Smile, stirring it idly with a shoe.
> Take, for example, this work in hand:
> out of its waste matter
> it should emerge light and solid.
> One idea, grown with the thing itself,
> should drive it searching inward
> with a sort of life, due to the mirror effect.
> Often, the more I simplify,
> the more a few simplicities go
> burrowing into their own depths,
> until the guardian structure is aroused . . .
>
> Most satisfying, yes.
> Another kind of vigour, I agree
> —unhappy until its actions are more convulsed:
> the 'passionate'—might find it maddening.
> Here the passion is in the putting together.[19]

The emergence of this "guardian structure," the always particular, always provisional, never predictable structure in poem after poem (the structure *of* each poem), promises a possibility of articulation and so understanding that rises lightly above, even as it still rigorously reflects, the most abysmal of prospects:

The act of understanding initiated by the worker, as observer, when he looks into the construct, ends in an understanding of what lies in wait for unreasonable hope. This realization "dawns upon" him. It isn't insisted upon as part of his perception of the thing—he is already looking up away from the structure when that final image dawns on him as a possibility.[20]

The putting together of these always tentative, open-ended poetic acts of understanding constitutes "the passion."

What we have in "Worker in Mirror," then, is, among other things, a poetic credo that serves as a rough map of the "psychic geography," the different phases of experience (each with its own presiding face), explored in the sequence. Throughout *Notes, One, A Technical Supplement, Song of the Night,* and *The Messenger,* there is a loosely Jungian process of individuation being worked out, according to a numerological "plot," with *Notes* representing the zero-opening of consciousness in childhood; *One* representing the first stroke of order; *A Technical Supplement* dramatizing the further "fall" into self-division of the poet-narrator of the sequence; *Song of the Night* recalling the earlier assembling of the self and the beloved into a greater unity that constitutes another facet of the psyche; and *The Messenger* enacting the latest encounter with ancestors and with death, which makes up a full composite picture of the self. As a general guide to the different books in the sequence, this Jungian schema is functional. But I prefer the more traditional poetic outline of "Worker in Mirror"—that of the Greek Ages and the five masks or faces. For such an extra-literary schema, if pursued in a literal-minded way, will result in bringing to the poetry too much extraneous material having to do with the four primary functions of the self—thinking, willing, feeling, imagining—the anima and animus archetypes, and all the rest of the Jungian paraphernalia. It is not that this information could not prove to be an illuminating aid. It is that Kinsella, in "Worker in Mirror," has already provided the simplest thematic and structural gloss on the "psychic geography" of the sequence: a "progress" in experience and understanding, an education in human limitations. His "guardian structure" in this poem acts carefully to direct the alert reader to the most accessible route to the poetic meanings of his later work.

The Guardian Structure

In *The Messenger* (1978), a beautifully moving elegy for his father who died in May 1976, Kinsella again provides us with the most useful gloss on the term "guardian structure":

> Typically, there is a turning away.
> The Self is islanded in fog.
> It is meagre and plagued with wants
>
> but secure. Every positive matter
> that might endanger—but also enrich—
> is banished. The banished matter
>
> (a cyst, in effect, of the subject's aspirations
> painful with his many disappointments)
> absorbs into the psyche, where it sleeps.
>
> Intermittently, when disturbed, it wakes
> as a guardian—or 'patron'—monster
> with characteristic conflicting emotional claims:
>
> appalling, appealing; exacting sympathy
> even as it threatens. (Our verb 'to haunt'
> preserves the ambiguity exactly.)
>
> Somewhere on the island, Cannibal
> lifts his halved head and bellows
> with incompleteness . . . Or better—
>
> a dragon slashes its lizard wings uneasily
> as it looks out and smells the fog
> and itches and hungers in filth and fire.[21]

So the guardian structure, here called the guardian or patron monster, and imaged as a dragon (in "Ely Place" it appeared as both George Moore's ghost that takes possession of the speaker and those devouring tongues of movement), is that portion of the self built up out of one's disappointed aspirations, impossible ideals, and unreasonable hopes. In other words, it is the poetic version of Freudian repression or the Jungian shadow. This "monster" is set off, as it were, by any serious threat to psychic integrity, however potentially enriching that threat, and it comes, of course, between father and son:

> *Often, much too familiar for comfort,*
> *the beast was suddenly there*
> *insinuating between us:*
>
> 'Who'd like to know what *I* know?'
> 'Who has a skeleton in *his* meat cupboard?'
>
> 'Who is inclined to lapse and let
> the bone go with the dog?'
>
> Who flings off in a huff
> and never counts the cost

as long as there's a bitter phrase
to roll around on the tongue?'

When Guess Who polished his pointy shoe
and brushed his brilliantine
to whose admiring gaze
guess who hoodwinked Who?'

Or it would sigh and say:
'Guess who'd love to gobble *you* up. . . !'
Or 'Who'd like to see what *I* have?'

I would . . .[22]

And yet, the very act of self defense discloses the life-long act of mourning
that fuels the poetic project, as one after another abandoned hope falls back
into the unconscious to compose the guardian structure. In addition, such
disclosure makes possible imaginative acts of mutual understanding rising
beyond all but poetic speech:

And have followed
the pewtery heave of hindquarters
into the fog, the wings down at heel,

until back there in the dark
the whole thing
fell on its face.

And blackened . . . And began
melting its details and dripping them away
little by little to reveal

him (supine, jutjawed and
incommunicable, privately
surrendering his tissues and traps).

And have watched my hand reach in under
after something, and felt it
close upon it and ease him of it.

The eggseed Goodness
that is also called
Decency.[23]

In such unexpected ways, the guardian structure functions in both defensive
and exploratory capacities.

Kinsella's vision in *The Messenger* can be taken as part of his myth of the
imagination, a fable of how he handles all kinds of influences poetically, a
fable that, I think, possesses representative status. Unlike Yeats's sublime

allegory of inspiration enacted in "Leda and the Swan," in which a more than human agency takes possession of and forces union upon the merely human (daimon raping the ego, as it were, and leaving in its wake prophetic knowledge commensurate, perhaps, with such awful power); Kinsella's fable is set to a human scale, in which neither party in the exchange of influences, the transference of understanding and "decency," can honestly maintain an inhumanly dominant position for very long without suffering a final disillusionment.

In this respect, Kinsella's poetic practice gives the lie to the most influential version of the Romantic sublime in the academy: the theory of poetry propounded by Harold Bloom.[24] Of all contemporary critics, Bloom is the continuator of Yeats's visionary ideas of poetic creation. For Bloom, poetry is always a luminous creation out of the dark void of anxiety, an "imagining" of "its own origins," the "telling" of "a pervasive lie about itself, to itself," in a generally vain attempt to invent the poetic father one would have liked to have descended from, in order to avoid facing directly one's true indebtedness to the real precursor.[25] Poets, according to this view, engage in revisionary acts of reading, so as to win for themselves living space in the empyrean, and so become "mortal gods" like Homer and Shakespeare, Milton and Yeats.

What this means in more practical terms is that T. S. Eliot, for example, in claiming Jules Laforgue as a precursor, tried (vainly) to evade facing the authentic source of his imaginative power—Tennyson. By repressing self-knowledge, understanding, Eliot was able to achieve a little something of his own—at a great cost. Similarly, in "Leda and the Swan," Yeats "forgets" sublimely that his poem is a misreading of certain portions of Shelley, especially of his "Alastor, or the Spirit of Solitude," and so is able to think of himself as a sublime influence on later readers, much as Shelley had been in relation to Yeats. For Bloom, then, every poem becomes an allegory of the belated poet's oedipal anxieties, an ironic fable of the poet's revisionary strategies for avoiding understanding.

Like Kenner, then, Bloom comes to contemporary poetry with inappropriate critical assumptions. His vision, like Kenner's, could not be further from what Kinsella is doing in his poetry. Clearly, "Ely Place," for example, is not trying to do what Kenner desires. It is not trying to impress on its readers "some single emblem backed by a whole literature and culture." Nor is it out to become the perfect model illustrating Bloom's theory by ironically revising Yeats's vision of universal conflagration from "In Memory of Eva Gore-Booth and Con Markiewicz." In short, neither modernist nor neo-Romantic version of the sublime is appropriate critical equipment to bring to bear on Kinsella's poetry, or on contemporary poetry generally. I stress this point not simply because Kenner and Bloom have misunderstood Kinsella's poetry, but because between them these critics fairly well define the range of opinion and approaches unfortunately now current.

Perhaps, the best commentary on the vision and tactics of Kinsella's mature poetry, representative of much of the best contemporary verse, appears in "The Good Fight." At one point early in the poem, the speaker, in characterizing the style of the late president, provides us with the most fitting embodiment of Kinsella's creative engagement with the ordeal of understanding:

> (It sounds as though it could go on for ever,
> yet there is a shape to it—Appropriate
> Performance. Another almost perfect
> working model . . . But it gets harder.
> The concepts jerk and wrestle, back to back.
> The finer the idea the harder it is
> to assemble lifelike. It adopts hardnesses
> and inflexibilities, knots, impossible joints
> made possible only by stress,
> and good for very little afterward.)[26]

As "Worker in Mirror" makes clear, "the passion" is neither in emblematic outcry, nor in heroic rhetoric, but "in the putting together"—at the very least—of a life for now.

Notes

1. Daniel O'Hara, "An Interview With Thomas Kinsella," *Contemporary Poetry* 4, no. 1 (1981):14.

2. Helen Vendler, "Wallace Stevens: The False and True Sublime," *Part of Nature, Part of Us: Modern American Poets* (Cambridge, Mass.: Harvard University Press, 1980), p. 2.

3. *The Collected Poems of W. B. Yeats* (New York: Macmillan, 1956), p. 197.

4. "Thomas Kinsella," *Viewpoints: Poets in Conversation with John Haffenden* (London and Boston: Faber and Faber, 1981), p. 107.

5. Hugh Kenner, "Thomas Kinsella: An Anecdote and Some Reflections," *Genre* 12, no. 4 (Winter 1979):591, 592, 597.

6. Ibid., p. 596.

7. *Viewpoints,* p. 106.

8. Prose Prologue to *Wormwood* (1966) in *Poems, 1956–1973* (Winston-Salem, N.C.: Wake Forest University Press, 1979), p. 66. It is here that Kinsella introduces the figure of the ordeal as his ruling metaphor for experience: "It is certain that maturity and peace are to be sought through ordeal after ordeal, and it seems that the search continues until we fail."

9. *Poems, 1956–1973,* pp. 166–67.

10. *Viewpoints,* p. 113.

11. John Montague, "Heaney and Kinsella: North and South," *The Irish Times* (1980); the phrase "willed rhetoric" referring to Kinsella's early poetic manner is Haffenden's and comes from *Viewpoints,* p. 107.

12. Ibid.

13. Roger McHugh, ed., *Davis, Mangan, Ferguson? Tradition and the Irish Writer: Writings by W. B. Yeats and by Thomas Kinsella* (Dublin: Dolmen Press, 1970), p. 57.

14. *Poems, 1956–1973,* p. 136.

15. *Peppercanister Poems, 1972–1978* (Winston-Salem, N.C.: Wake Forest University Press, 1979), p. 50.

16. *Poems, 1956–1973,* p. 178.

17. O'Hara, "An Interview With Thomas Kinsella," pp. 13–14. It is in this interview that Kinsella uses the term "psychic geography" to describe the landscape of his later poetry (cf. p. 4). For two related mappings of this territory, see my essay "Love's Architecture: The Poetic Irony of Thomas Kinsella," *Boundary 2* 9, no. 2 (Winter, 1981) and my review-essay of *Song of the Night* and *The Messenger* in *Éire-Ireland* 14, no. 1 (Spring 1979):131–35.

18. *Poems, 1956–1973,* p. 182.

19. *Poems, 1956–1973,* pp. 179–180.

20. O'Hara, "An Interview With Thomas Kinsella," p. 14.

21. *Peppercanister Poems, 1972–1978,* p. 124.

22. Ibid., pp. 124–25.

23. Ibid., pp. 125–26.

24. For the best introduction to Bloom's criticism, see Jonathan Arac, "The Criticism of Harold Bloom: Judgment and History," *Centrum* (Spring 1978), pp. 32–42.

25. Harold Bloom, *Poetry and Repression: Revisionism From Blake to Stevens* (New Haven: Yale University Press, 1980), p. 18.

26. *Peppercanister Poems, 1972–1978,* pp. 39–40. See Kinsella's gloss on these lines in *Viewpoints,* p. 110. For a discussion of Bloom's views on Kinsella, see my essay "Love's Architecture" in *Boundary 2* cited in note 17.

Diarmuid Devine and Ginger Coffey: Entrapment and Escape

Raymond J. Porter

In *The Feast of Lupercal* (1957), Brian Moore remains in the Belfast of his first novel, *The Lonely Passion of Judith Hearne* (1955), and creates a male counterpart of the protagonist of that work. Diarmuid Devine, a thirty-seven-year old master at St. Michan's College, has always led a cautious and circumscribed existence both on and off the job. His family background, his schooling, his society, and his religion have all played a part in making him the man he is: reliable but overly predictable, well-intentioned but hesitant, likable but lonely. During the two weeks or so covered by the novel, Devine has a chance to assert himself rather than conform and to seek love rather than settle for loneliness, but ultimately he fails to do so. Like Pegeen Mike in Synge's *Playboy of the Western World,* he is worse off at the end of the work than at the beginning for, after experiencing that there is more to life than he has had, he settles for less.

Moore's physical description of Devine immediately suggests his lack of identity: "He was a tall man, yet did not seem so; not youthful, yet somehow young; a man whose appearance suggested some painful uncertainty."[1] He is indistinguishable from the educational system of which he is a part and the school at which he was a student and is now a master. Always conscious of being punctual for class, he knows when a session will end without consulting his watch. His students are attentive because he has a knack for anticipating the examiners' questions on upcoming examinations and because, like his colleagues, he uses corporal punishment: "boys respected the cane, the cane was what got results in his day, and still did" (163).

Because Devine does not like confrontation, he is "all things to all men" (189) and prefers to stay "behind the scenes" (65). This behavior pattern elicits varied responses from his colleagues at school, his associates in amateur theatrical circles, and his students. Various masters at St. Michan's consider him "discreet" (5), "a decent fellow" (86), and "that old woman'' (5); the Dean feels he is "very obliging" (96) and a "harmless enough lad" (97). His theatrical companions refer to him as "poor old Dev" (115), his students as "Do-less Dev" (107).

Devine's basement rooms at Mrs. Dempsey's, where he has boarded for ten years, give evidence of a life with no present or future, just a past. The sideboard, gramophone, dresser, and chairs are from his dead parents' home, and the bed in which he sleeps is that of his boyhood. Above the fireplace are photographs from his undergraduate days, class pictures from St. Michan's, and, in a place of honor, his parents' wedding picture. Also present are two religious pictures from his family home: one, the Divine Infant of Prague, which he has kept out of "some vague need for penance" (54); the other, a reproduction of *Ecce Homo*, which hangs in pious but guilty memory of his father.

As for romance, there has been none in Devine's life. After watching dating couples from afar as a teenager, he had some unsuccessful encounters with girls at the university, and then as a master has had to be careful of his public image. Fear of failure has made him like a "flower that had never opened. He had been afraid to open, afraid" (124). As a result, for many years he has contented himself with sinful thoughts. Like Judith Hearne, he'd had "some shocking sinful thoughts in his day. Shocking" (52).

When Una Clarke enters Devine's life, she is an unsettling but stimulating influence. His reaction to her is interesting and revealing from the start. The two meet at a party hosted by Tim Heron, Una's uncle, and Devine's immediate reaction is excited and joyful: ". . . here he was flirting with a girl. It was pleasant, was it not? Very" (27). His enthusiasm is quelled when a colleague comments that the twenty-year-old Una is a Protestant and was "mixed up" with a married man back in Dublin, her home. His immediate inner response is, "It had been a great beginning: it was bound to fail" (31). Dev leaves the party to catch a bus home and, although tempted to turn back, joins the passengers "jerking like marionettes in their seats . . ." (35). A marionette for years, he allows the strings of conventional response to control his movements.

Throughout the book, Moore uses light and dark imagery as a motif in relation to Dev and Una. Living in a basement, a man who "keeps out of the limelight" (33), he is blinded by light when they first meet at Heron's: "A door opened: a bedroom light shone into the corridor, dazzling him with its brightness" (25). Their second meeting, a chance encounter at a coffee shop, finds him "blinking into the white window light" (42) to see Una. In the ensuing interview, she dazzles him with her honest and forthright revelation that Moloney is keeping him "in the dark" (43) about getting her a part in an upcoming play. Dev then makes what is a daring move for him by offering to coach her in preparation for a tryout. His actions of the day so fill him with joy that he gets off at the wrong bus stop on the way home, and when he arrives at his rooms, takes down the pictures of the Infant of Prague and *Ecce Homo*.

Their first date is to a production of Shaw's *Saint Joan*. At the intermission, Una expresses admiration for people who defy others and do what they think is right. Dev is not quite so sure. In fact, when he sees among the theater crowd a clerical member of the St. Michan's faculty, he worries about what the school authorities might think of his dating a twenty-year-old Protestant and how Tim Heron, whom Dev deliberately has not told about the play part or date, would react to these goings-on. When the lights dim for the next act, he is "thankful for the darkness" (58).

As noted above, Una's approach to life is more open and direct. In addition to the revelation about Moloney and her comments at the Shaw play, she later tells Devine about her Dublin love affair, and on another occasion suggests they go to his rooms for a drink. Furthermore, because of her inexperience and integrity, she cannot understand how her married lover was able to sleep with his wife while seeing her. Dev does not know what to make of such openness. At times he admires it, but at other times he attributes it to the fact that she is a Protestant, and thus fast.

Despite misgivings and uncertainty, Dev senses that this girl could be his salvation, and so makes a definite effort to change his image and his ways. He shaves his mustache, buys new clothes, and takes dancing lessons. He misses Sunday Mass waiting for a phone call from Una, takes her dancing to a club he has never entered before, and even shows a willingness to fight a young man who tries to cut in on the dance floor. In fact, at one point, he seems willing to sacrifice his position at St. Michan's if Una will marry him. Moore emphasizes this theme of image and identity by having Devine on a number of occasions observe himself in a mirror.

But any new image, or identity, must be substantiated by deeds and must withstand the pressures to conform and be agreeable. For one thing, Devine must face up to Tim Heron, whose temper he fears, and the possibility that Tim will expose him to the school authorities, who, like Dev, are conscious of appearances.

It was all perfectly innocent, of course, but it would not look innocent to the authorities. Man was born sinful, he must avoid the occasions of sin . . . Occasions of sin must be rigorously guarded against, was that not clear? Then why did he, a teacher of boys, show such bad example? The authorities would say he had courted an occasion of sin; he had risked giving scandal. (78)

Always cautious, Devine does not seek out Heron, but opts to let "sleeping dogs lie." When the older master does confront him, he shifts the blame to Una, with some feelings of guilt, and fails to make a strong stand against Heron's demands and threats. However, he does not agree to take Una out of the play. There is still some hope for Devine, although as this scene closes his eyes are "smarting" as they always do in moments of pressure. Later, in a longer and more threatening confrontation with Heron, he fails completely by refusing to admit that Una spent the night at his apartment.

That night at the apartment is crucial in Devine's failure to forge a new self and find love. On a number of occasions before the night in question, he had planned to tell Una of his love but could not bring the matter into the open light. Finally he speaks out at the dance club, but is immediately taken aback when Una suggests they go to his place. Fearful of what his landlady would say—she is "careful of the proprieties" (11), and no girl other than his sister has entered his digs—but also fearful of insulting Una, he acquiesces. But Dev is uneasy from the start. Afraid that his rooms will undermine the new image he has been forging, he believes that as soon as he "put the lights on in his den, he would lose her respect" (141). Then, when Una begins speaking of her Dublin affair, he cannot bear to look at his father's photo above the fireplace. To make matters worse, when Una asks that he kiss her, he misses her mouth completely.

Moore, through religious diction, suggests that Devine is a faithless supplicant at the altar of love. He makes a "pilgrimage" (145) toward Una, and kneels "as though in genuflection before the altar of her body." She asks that he express his love in words, "as though, like prayer, repetition would buy grace for the thought" (146). But Devine, because of his puritanical Irish Catholicism, cannot equate love and sex: "And that was the difference between love and lust, he remembered a missioner once saying. Love was pure. Love was respect" (53). So that when Una expresses love for him, "Gratefulness filled him" (145); but when she French kisses him, "The reverence was profaned." Unable to handle the reality of love when his youthful fantasies are "made flesh" (145), Devine is afraid to sin but also afraid of offending Una by not sinning.

During the scene of sexual failure, Moore, in addition to employing religious diction, brings in two motifs that weave in and out of the novel—punishment and mirror reflection—and once more utilizes light and dark imagery. As Devine reluctantly undresses and waits for Una in his room, he knows he will fail the test: ". . . he was sick as a boy who had not prepared: the role had been reversed, he was victim, he would be punished for his failure" (149). Ashamed of his flesh, "his naked body," he sees his face in the dresser mirror "weak with fright" (146). As he has done frequently in his life when confronted with reality, Devine hides in the darkness, first backing into the "shadows" (147), then "squatting down behind the far side of the bed . . . " (148). But there is no avoiding reality this time, and he fails to make his love flesh.

A greater failure is his betrayal of Una. In several confrontations with Tim Heron, he cannot bring himself to admit that the girl was at his lodgings all night. Ironically, although Dev and Una did not sleep with each other, ". . . who'd believe us?" (184). Devine's fears conquer him. Going to consult with Una, he runs from the Herons's front door like a guilty child when he hears an unidentifiable voice in the hallway. Moore suggestively sets the subsequent discussion with Una in a playground. Devine, the man-child, despite shame at his cowardice and despite the shame of Una's literally going down on her knees to him, will not agree to help by admitting they spent the night together. He has lost his chance to live. When marriage comes up in the discussion, Una speaks words almost identical to those of James Madden in *The Lonely Passion,* "Marry? Who's talking about marriage?" (189). She accurately sums up the incompatible difference between them: "I want to fight against what life's doing to me, and you're afraid to" (192).

As gossip about Devine, Heron, and Una begins threatening the reputation of St. Michan's, Dev admits to his older colleague that Una was at his digs all night, and then, to prove the girl's innocence of wrongdoing, admits his own virginity and impotence. Then, in a scene foreshadowed during the unsuccessful sexual encounter by Dev's certainty that he would be punished and thematically related to the novel's title and Dev's schoolroom lesson that morning, Heron canes the abject master. However, unlike the women who suffer the Lupercalian lash in hopes of fertility, Devine will remain barren. "How can I try again with another girl, how can I try without remembering Una and worrying that I will fail a second time?" (218).

Devine attains self-knowledge. He accuses himself of sinning in losing Una (206). He thinks, "To fail to sin, perhaps that is my sin" (218), and also admits that the "real sin" was "keeping quiet" for so long. But he will not use this knowledge to change his life. Furthermore, even when he asserts himself with Father MacSwiney and Dr. Keogh, President of St. Michan's, this miniature rebellion is overlooked and brushed aside. Although Devine is relieved that he has not lost his position as a result of his strong words and the whole Una-Heron affair, he is also disappointed. To protect St. Michan's by presenting "an appearance of perfect amity" (238), Devine "had not even been allowed to disgrace himself . . ." (241). Like a shroud, the system enfolds him.

Diarmuid Devine, "whose body was unpublic, skin never sunned" (14), returns to the darkness of his basement rooms—Mrs. Dempsey is going to keep him after all—after some blinding glimpses of the light. "For the rest of his life he'd go on telling people what they wanted to hear" (246). He is like the horse that on the last page watches with him as Una disappears down the street, blinkered and harnessed.

The protagonist of *The Luck of Ginger Coffey* (1960) is more outgoing and less introverted than both Judith Hearne and Diarmuid Devine. Furthermore, unlike these two, he has a mate and child, and has flown past Stephen Dedalus's nets to settle in Montreal, Canada, and start a new life. But Ginger Coffey has as much trouble as Judy and Dev separating illusion and reality, and throughout most of the novel is on the verge of losing his wife and child and his chance for a happier existence. Ultimately, after some romantic fantasizing and painful truth-facing, this thirty-nine-year-old boy jettisons his youth and becomes a man. In the process of realizing his true self, he comes to understand his relationship with Ireland and Canada, and with his wife and daughter.

Moore's title—in particular, the word "luck"—is suggestive and central, pertinent to both Ginger's fall and, later, his rise. Out of work and money, as the book opens, Coffey believes his luck is due for a change,[2] and the clerk at the unemployment office wishes him luck and alludes to the luck of the Irish (13). But Ginger's flaw is an overreliance on luck. His goals and aspirations as well as his assessment of himself always have been inflated and unrealistic, and as a result so have the promises made to his wife during fifteen years of marriage. As promise after promise fails to reach fulfillment, Ginger never seeks the true reason but merely manufactures another promise, continually believing that "his ship would come in" (7).

This motif of luck ties in with a theme prominent in Moore's novels: the openness, freedom, and opportunity of North America vis-a-vis the restrictive nature of life in Ireland. Coffey contrasts the "rags to riches" rise possible in the New World to the Chinese box arrangement in his native land, "one inside the other, and whatever you started off as, you would probably end up as" (15). However, when Fox and others of his fellow galley slaves at the Montreal *Tribune* speak disparagingly of Canada, he begins to wonder if he should have stayed in his "box" at home (67). He is troubled when another of his *Tribune* cohorts, Old Billy Davis, turns out to be a Donegal man who never found any gold streets, and wonders whether he will also "end his days in some room, old and used, his voice nasal and reedy, all accent gone?"(189).

Coffey clearly remembers a sermon preached by a Redemptorist Missioner at his school which warned those young boys who were not satisfied with their lot in Ireland that both material and spiritual ruin awaited them. The boy unable to accept his "God-given limitations" (20) and remain in Ireland, according to the preacher, was not really seeking "adventures" but an excuse "to get away and commit mortal sins. . . ." Ginger considers this "missionary malarkey," but he thinks of the sermon frequently. In fact, on his way to a job interview, he goes to church, his first such visit since coming to Canada some six months before. Sitting in church and wondering if there really is a God and an afterlife, he considers the idea that God might be trying to get him back in line by withholding worldly success. In the face of such a thought, he refuses to buckle under and asserts himself:

> I came in here to maybe say a prayer and I'll be the first to admit I had a hell of a nerve on me, seeing the way I've ignored you these long years. But now I cannot pray, because to pray to you, if you're punishing me, would be downright cowardly. If it's cowards you want in heaven, then good luck to you. (24)

Although these thoughts indicate that Ginger possesses some courage, he does not know who he is and what he wants from life. In fact, during his church visit he asks himself what he believes and what are his aims. The best he can contemplate are some vague thoughts about providing for his wife and child, being his own master, and making something of himself. This is a start, but he has much to learn.

In many ways, Coffey is still a young boy uncertain of his identity. Throughout the novel, Moore uses a number of devices to underline this lack. Aside from his reliance on luck, Ginger enjoys playing with Michel, a neighbor's small boy, and longs to be a boy himself again. "Oh, to be a boy . . . tears one moment, all wiped away the next. A world of toys" (84). On several occasions, he childishly avoids or puts off painful confrontations instead of facing them like a mature adult. For example, when he has to admit to his wife there is no money for return fare to Ireland, he acts "like a child" (31), "hiding" in his daughter's room and fondling a doll. Later, when he spots Vera, his wife, having lunch with Gerry Grosvenor, he flees the restaurant like a "boy escaping a pair of bullies" (81). Reminiscent of Diarmuid Devine, he always avoids "scenes."

His belief that "clothes made the man" (10) is also suggestive of his lack of identity. Sporting a Tyrolean hat, a hacking jacket like Devine's in *Lupercal,* gray tweed trousers, and brown suede boots, Coffey believes he has made himself a "Dublin squire." However, his costume and military mustache (also reminiscent of Devine) have the opposite effect from that intended. The first job interviewer to see him thinks a man of thirty-nine should not dress like a "college boy" (25), and later A. K. Brott takes him for a "burleycue comedian" (126). As to the mustache, ironically, Vera wrenches him back into the reality of their separation by yanking it when he attempts to assault her sexually; and toward the end of the book when his fortunes are approaching their nadir, Rose Alma discerns behind the "facade" of middle age and mustache "a boy . . . Lost" (197).

As is his custom, Moore makes frequent use of a mirror motif to chart his protagonist's sense of himself. Ginger's gradual movement toward a more mature and realistic assessment of self and life is reflected in the following:

He looked at him [self]. A stupid man dressed up like a Dublin squire. Looked at the frightened childish face frozen now in a military man's disguise. He hated that man in the mirror, hated him. Oh, God, there was a useless bloody man, coming up to forty and still full of a boy's dreams of ships coming in. . . . (88)

Later in this scene and in some of the other mirror scenes Moore emphasizes the identity theme by having Coffey refer to his reflected self as "impostor" (88, 147, 203).

For years Ginger has been so filled with boyish dreams and himself that he has failed to consider his wife and child as people. This is reflected in his habit of calling his wife "Kitten," and his daughter "Pet" and "Apple." He can't believe that his wife has had enough of his unrealistic and unfulfilled promises and wants to leave him and then divorce him: ". . . his wife sat alone, sick with some madness he could not understand" (119). And he is shocked when the fourteen-year-old Paulie rebels against his parental authority: "Now, she was not his little Apple any more" (163). Ginger's reassessment of self must involve a reassessment of human relations within the family circle.

Coffey is launched reluctantly on his voyage of self-discovery when the only job he can get is that of proofreader for the Montreal *Tribune,* paying only half the money he needs, and when Vera angrily tells him he has an inflated view of his capabilities, always blaming others for his failures, and then states she is going to get a job herself and leave him. He considers this "malarkey," but is "troubled as he had rarely been" (60). Vera does leave and when Ginger moves from their apartment he begins the process of change by bequeathing the two Alpine buttons and brush from his Tyrolean hat to Michel. Of course, he is still filled with illusions: in no time at all he will be raised to the position of reporter or editor.

Even as he moves into his cell-like room at the Y.M.C.A., Coffey manufactures romantic visions of self pity: "No ties, no responsibilities, no ambitions. By the holy, that would be a grand gesture. To retire from the struggle, live like a hermit, unknown and unloved in this faraway land" (98). But meeting and observing a fellow tenant, Warren K. Wilson, provides him with some insight about himself. Wilson, an older man with no ties or roots, still dreams "youth's dreams" (104). He is an inveterate participant in correspondence courses—for becoming a TV repairman, a private detective, a magazine photographer—and his room is jammed with evidence of "boyish schemes, boyish pursuits—yes it was familiar. A world of toys. . . . Was manhood that Wilson had missed?" After half a day's freedom, Ginger concludes that it is too late for him to start life alone.

In addition to this insight, Wilson provides Ginger with a lead for a second job, delivering and picking up for a diaper service. He takes the position, now working night and day at two rather menial tasks, to prove to his wife that he wants her back and can support the family. Shedding his Dublin squire outfit for the Tiny Ones uniform, "anonymous and humiliating" (107), he becomes a member of the "shit brigade." This job brings about another break with the past, and Ireland, when one of the customers on his route recognizes him as a former Dublin acquaintance: ". . . he knew that, sink or swim, Canada was home now, for better or for worse, for richer or for poorer, until death" (123).

Although Coffey is beginning to understand that love is selfless and involves acceptance and giving, he still is not sure that it is possible to keep another's love "without a promise or two" (148). He also continues to be susceptible to romantic illusions. For example, he refuses to face the reality that MacGregor will not promote him to reporter on the *Tribune,* and after enduring many sleepless nights during which he envisions his wife participating in sexual acts with other men, he begins to believe he does not love or need her anymore. Acting on this last illusion, he agrees to be caught in adultery to facilitate divorce proceedings, and tells himself that the arrangement is not "sordid" but an "adventure" (154).

At the last minute, however, Ginger does not go through with the plan. Trying to kill time before the arranged adultery at a downtown hotel, he decides to take in a movie, and as he stands outside the theater, watching the "pairing," "the world going two by two" (154), the reality of his situation closes in on him: "He had no one." The movies, which Moore frequently uses as embodiments of illusion, offer Coffey no solace, or escape, so he walks out. He perceives the difference between illusion and reality. "What had these Hollywood revels to do with the facts of life in a cold New World?'' (157). Thus when the prostitute meets him, as planned, in the hotel cocktail lounge, he goes home rather than upstairs, and determines that he must get his wife back. Even when Vera returns to Ginger temporarily in order to control their daughter's social life more effectively, she refuses to accept as real his protestations of love and his promise of a promotion to reporter by the end of the week. In an effort to prove the selflessness of his love, he makes one final promise—to give her freedom and Paulie if the promotion fails to come through. He is sincere this time, but his rise at the *Tribune* is an illusion, his last. Foolishly, he quits Tiny Ones, despite the offer of a position as personal assistant to the head of the firm, in anticipation of his new job at the *Tribune.* Thus when MacGregor refuses to make him a reporter, Ginger, intending to stand by the words to his wife, can no longer dream. ''Ah Dear God, what did you do when you could no longer dream? How did you reconcile yourself to those humble circs?'' (194).

In his despair, Ginger gets drunk, and is arrested for indecent exposure when the police spot him relieving himself in a doorway. Thrown into jail, he identifies himself as Gerald MacGregor to spare his wife and daughter an embarrassment. This thoughtful and selfless act gives evidence that the adult Ginger Coffey has emerged, as does his pre-trial discovery that a ''man's life was nobody's fault but his own. Not God's, not Vera's, not even Canada's. His own fault. *Mea culpa*'' (203).

In court, Coffey sees his case, his life, and himself as the source of some witty courtroom humor, but the judge compassionately lets him off with a suspended sentence. A detective-sergeant comments on the ''luck of the Irish,'' but Ginger, believing that Vera has fled the courtroom to join Gerry Grosvenor, does not feel lucky: ''Nobody cared'' (213). At this moment of emptiness and apparent abandonment on the courthouse steps, he experiences a moment of ''unpredictable joy'' (214), a Wordsworthian spot of time, and asks himself whether all he can hope for is a ''few mystical moments spaced out over a lifetime'' (215). Unlike the old Ginger Coffey, he refuses to wish for more.

True to his word, Ginger goes home to pack and leave. Once there, he finds that his daughter has been worried about him, and that Vera wants him back. His attempt to use a false name to protect his family has convinced her that he has truly changed. He accepts her offer and, illusions abandoned, is willing to try to get back the previously rejected position at Tiny Ones. ''Didn't damn nearly everyone have to face up someday to the fact that their ship would never come in?'' (220).

Ginger Coffey is truly a lucky man. Unlike Diarmuid Devine, he has not merely gained insight into himself and the meaning of life, but has the opportunity and courage to build a new and better life. It is perhaps no accident that Brian Moore's first novel to end on an affirmative and hopeful note is also the first to be set in the New World rather than Ireland. Of course, Coffey's rise at the end is not patterned on the "rags to riches" aspect of the American Dream that the author has scrutinized in a number of his novels, but is based upon a realization of true freedom and its concomitant sense of responsibility. Ginger Coffey has come to realize that financial and social success is not what matters: ". . . on the courthouse steps he had learned the truth. Life was the victory, wasn't it? Going on was the victory" (222).

Notes

1. *The Feast of Lupercal* (Boston: Little, Brown and Co., 1957), p. 6. Further citations will appear in parentheses.
2. *The Luck of Ginger Coffey* (New York: Dell Publishing Co., 1962), p. 22. Further citations will appear in parentheses.

William Trevor's
Stories of the Troubles

Robert E. Rhodes

William Trevor was born Trevor Cox in Mitchelstown, County Cork, in 1928, spent his boyhood in provincial Ireland, and was educated at St. Columba's and Trinity College, Dublin. Since 1958—and mostly since 1964—he has been the author of nine novels, five collections of short stories, and a number of radio and television dramas as well as plays for the stage.[1] A member of the Irish Academy of Letters and the recipient of an honorary C.B.E., an unusual distinction for a non-British writer—although he has lived in Devon for a number of years—he has garnered several literary awards, including the Hawthornden Prize, the Royal Society of Literature Award, the Allied Irish Banks Prize for Literature, and the Whitbread Prize for Fiction. Brian Cleeve's 1967 *Dictionary of Irish Writers* observes that his works "have won Trevor a great critical reputation as well as popular success in America, Britain, and Europe";[2] and an August 1981 interview by Elgy Gillespie in *The Irish Times* notes that "These days he is a very famous writer indeed. . . ."[3]

In addition to the formal honors that have come his way, it is true that Trevor's novels and short story collections have consistently enjoyed favorable reviews, that a number of his books have been reprinted, and that he now appears with regularity in such periodicals as the *New Yorker*. But it is also apparently and surprisingly true, despite declarations by Cleeve and Gillespie and a growing reputation, that thus far Trevor has been the subject of only two moderate-length critical studies: Mark Mortimer's 1975 "William Trevor in Dublin" and Julian Gitzen's 1979 "The Truth-Tellers of William Trevor."[4]

Given the size of his canon and his putative reputation, it seems only a matter of time before Trevor receives the kind of critical examination that will test the works against the reputation. For the time being, at least, most such attention is likely to focus on Trevor's "non-Irish" fiction—most of which has its scene in England—since only one of his nine novels and nineteen of the fifty-five or so of the readily available short stories are "Irish," which may explain why he is not even listed in such relatively recent compilations as *A Bibliography of Modern Irish and Anglo-Irish Literature* and *Anglo-Irish Literature; A Review of Research.*[5] Such omissions are perhaps reason to call attention to some aspects of Trevor's work that fall under the rubric "Irish."

Although Irish characters figure fairly prominently in *Elizabeth Alone* (1973) and *Other People's Lives* (1981), only *Mrs. Eckdorf in O'Neill's Hotel* (1969) among the novels takes Ireland—specifically Dublin—as its scene, and except in some fairly conventional ways it is difficult to think of this as an "Irish" novel. Of the short stories, four do not really qualify as "Irish." Of "Miss Smith," Trevor himself has said that it "might perhaps have come out of anywhere, but in fact is set in a town in Munster. . . ."[6] "The Forty-Seventh Saturday" is a rather comical story of the affair of two lovers with Irish names, but the scene is London and there is nothing to distinguish these lovers as "Irish" or, indeed, as different in nationality from many other pairs of lovers in Trevor's stories. The action of "The Grass Widows" takes place in Galway, but the story is about two English couples; and "Memories of Youghal" features a seedy private detective who recalls his Youghal boyhood, but the scene is a Mediterranean resort and the protagonist is really an elderly English schoolteacher.

The remaining fifteen Irish short stories form a moderate-sized but solid accomplishment, a body of work meriting the attention of ordinary discriminating readers and critics alike. Almost all of them deal with rural and small-town Irish life and reveal both knowledge of and sympathy with that life. It is not necessary, of course, to reduce the stories to categories, but it does seem that in them Trevor has played variations on a handful of themes that have unusual significance for those who would use the artist's insights to understand contemporary Irish life: repression, coming of age or failing to come of age, parent-child relationships, and love—usually thwarted.[7]

Five of the readily available Irish stories that have appeared since 1975 show that Trevor has addressed himself to a subject that very few Irish writers have been able to avoid: the renewal of Ireland's ancient Troubles in Northern Ireland since the late 1960s and the impact of that violence on people in the North, in the Republic of Ireland, and in England. That Trevor's attention has been increasingly riveted by the Troubles is suggested by the fact that his first full-length stage play, *Scenes from an Album,* which opened in Dublin's Abbey Theatre in August 1981, clearly takes its motive from the history of the Troubles. Writing in *The Irish Times,* Elgy Gillespie notes of the play, "Once again . . . it will allow him to examine the interfaces between cultures, between Protestant and Catholic and English and Irish and Planter and Gael, toying [with] the ambiguities of their mingled lives," and she quotes Trevor as saying, "Because I *do* feel the countries are inextricably dependent on each other, and it's what I still want to write about."[8] Add to these views Trevor's own Protestant background and his many years of writing about the English in England and he seems particularly suited to have written the five stories we will examine here: "The Distant Past," "Saints," "Attracta," "Autumn Sunshine," and "Another Christmas."[9]

On the whole, the protagonists in these stories differ markedly from those in Trevor's other Irish stories, and differ in ways that are significant both for their own lives and for the insights Trevor offers through their dramas.

First, there is a significant age difference. In the other stories, protagonists range from age seven to age thirty-seven at the time of significant action, with most of them being under twenty, two in their early twenties, and two in their early thirties. On the other hand, all of the protagonists in the Troubles stories are clearly older and generally well set on their life courses. Only the couple in "Another Christmas"—who also differ in other ways from most of these protagonists—are identified only as "middle-aged," the rest ranging from sixty-one to sixty-nine and in one case perhaps to the early seventies.

Essentially well set on their life courses by their ages, they are further defined by their religious backgrounds. Almost all the protagonists of Trevor's other Irish stories come from often repressive Catholic backgrounds. To the contrary, only the protagonists of "Another Christmas" and important characters, though not protagonists, in "Attracta" and "Saints" are Catholic. The rest are clearly identified as Anglican or Anglo-Irish; indeed, one is a Church of Ireland rector, and protagonists in two other stories define much of their position in Irish society by their Protestantism. In words that to some degree apply to most of these protagonists, Trevor writes of the titular character in "Attracta": "Within the world of the town there was for Attracta a smaller, Protestant world. Behind green railings there was Mr. Ayrie's Protestant schoolroom. There was the Church of Ireland, with its dusty flags of another age, and Archdeacon Flower's prayers for the English royal family" (198).

Furthermore, most of the protagonists of Trevor's other Irish stories belong to a socio-economic stratum somewhat lower than that of protagonists in stories about the Troubles, a condition that may be related to their Catholicism. With few exceptions—and even these cannot be called unusually prosperous—the Catholic protagonists and their families are working class people: a farmer, a shop assistant, a butcher, a mechanic, for instance. Conversely, again with the exception of the protagonists of "Another Christmas," the protagonists come from at least moderately affluent backgrounds that confer certain social distinctions. If the elderly brother and sister of "The Distant Past" are only shabby genteel relics of the Ascendancy Big House tradition, the protagonist of "Saints" is a wealthy and cultivated inheritor of the same tradition; and the other protagonists are a respectable teacher in a Protestant school and a Church of Ireland rector.

In short, by age, religious persuasion or probable inclination, and socio-economic status, the protagonists of these stories are insulated from the imperatives that often drive their younger, poorer, Catholic neighbors: sexual desire, the search for identity, establishing places for themselves in their communities. Furthermore, though these are indeed stories of the Troubles and therefore of lingering animosities, latent danger, and explosive violence, these protagonists when we first meet them are neither obvious perpetrators nor immediately personal victims of violence. While there may sometimes be some mild disharmony, on the whole their relationships with their Catholic countrymen have been amiable and sometimes affectionate. Despite their distinct minority position, they are people who seem to have achieved some kind of equilibrium in the business of living. Essentially impregnable in ways the young are not, even as members of minority in a troubled place and time, they seem capable of emerging unscathed from their contact with the renewed British-Irish conflict of the present. Still, they are victims of the past as much as Irish Catholics.

While the youthful protagonists of Trevor's other Irish stories characteristically inhabit two worlds, the everyday world and the world of fantasy or imagination, and sometimes seek harmony between them, Trevor's older protagonists, at the outset, typically seem to have left a conflict between two worlds behind or at least to have resolved such a conflict satisfactorily. Very often, however, this is because they have put the past to rest. What shatters the illusion of safety and impregnability and forever alters their worlds is the renewal of outright violence in the late 1960s *and* the recollection of past violence and its relationship to present violence. Sometimes it is a personal past, too, but, if so, it is bound inextricably to the violent English-Irish past that eventually and inevitably merges with today's violence. In short, the past not only repeats itself but is a continuation of what for the Irish has been "the cause that never dies" and for the protagonists results in almost every case in increased loneliness and isolation.

The title of "The Distant Past," perhaps the earliest of Trevor's Troubles stories, signals what has become his continuing exploration of the ways in which apparently dead events of past conflicts obtrude on the present and shape the future. "The Distant Past" and "Saints," one of Trevor's most recent stories, have as protagonists survivors into the 1970s of the Anglo-Irish Ascendancy and, in particular, survivors of the burning of the Big Houses and the killing of their occupants during the 1920–1922 period.

The protagonists of "The Distant Past" are a brother and sister now, in the early 1970s, in their mid-sixties, the sole survivors of the Middletons of Carraveagh. Sixty miles south of the border separating the Republic of Ireland from Northern Ireland, the once splendid Carraveagh, built during the reign of George II, now barely shelters the Middletons as its roof suffers continued neglect and rust eats at its gutters, apt reminders of the straitened circumstances of brother and sister and of the dwindled importance of the tradition they represent and doggedly uphold. Reduced to a few acres, four cows, and some chickens, the Middletons believe the local story that their father had mortgaged the estate in order to maintain a Catholic Dublin woman, so that on his death in 1924 the two children inherited a vastly diminished estate. Consistent with their attitudes toward the new order in Ireland, "they blamed . . . the Catholic Dublin woman whom they'd never met and they blamed as well the new national regime, contriving in their eccentric way to relate the two. In the days of the Union Jack," they believe, "such women would have known their place: wasn't it all part and parcel?" (28).

Following the middle course suggested by their name, brother and sister have achieved—on their own terms—a *modus vivendi* for holding onto their version of the British presence in Ireland and for living with their neighbors, who know they are anachronisms. They achieve a delicate balance by the rituals of their Fridays and Sundays. On Fridays, they visit the town to sell eggs and to deliberately cultivate social intercourse with tradespeople in their shops and with other townsfolk over drinks in the bar of Healy's hotel. On Sundays, they attend St. Patrick's Protestant Church and say prayers for the king. What is symbolized by their Sunday ritual is borne out by their quietly voiced loyalty to pre-Treaty Ireland; their rising when B.B.C. plays "God Save the King"; their display of the Union Jack in the rear window of their car when Elizabeth II is crowned; their declaration that the revolutionary regime won't last—green postal boxes and a language no one can understand, indeed!

So successful are the Middletons in establishing an equilibrium that the townsfolk cherish them and their eccentricities. Visitors to the town are impressed that the Middletons can keep the old loyalties and still win the town's respect and affection, so much so that they and town are pointed to as an example that old wounds can heal and that here at least people can disagree without resorting to guns. The one nagging reminder that the revolutionary past has brought irrevocable change to Ireland and has done so with blood is the joking reminder by Fat Driscoll, butcher, that he and two others had stood in the hall of Carraveagh in the days when they might have burned it and slaughtered its occupants and instead waited with shotguns ready to kill British soldiers.

This delicately balanced situation continues during the post-World War II prosperity in the town created by an influx of tourists, and starts to end only in 1967, when news comes that sub-post offices in Belfast have been blown up, news that leads Fat Driscoll to say, "A bad business. We don't want that old stuff all over again," and Miss Middleton lightly to remind him, "We didn't want it in the first place" (33). As British soldiers arrive in the North and incidents in Fermanagh and Armagh and in Border towns and villages multiply and create fear in the hearts of tourists, despite assurances that the trouble in the North has nothing to do with the Republic, the town's prosperity begins to wane and with it tolerance of the Middletons. Now Fat Driscoll wishes that people would remember that he had stood in the Middletons' house fifty years earlier ready to kill British soldiers instead of knowing that he has given them meat for their dog, and brother and sister are pointedly cut by former friends, even the local Catholic priest.

The resurgence of violence in the present brings to the surface not only an awareness by all that the present violence is a renewal of past violence but a sharp reminder that the specific event at Carraveagh fifty years earlier took place in the home of those who, in Irish Catholic eyes, were responsible for violence in the first place. In mourning for the end of their *modus vivendi* rather than in fear of their lives, the Middletons remove from the walls of Carraveagh the icons of their distant past: a portrait of their father in the uniform of the Irish Guards, the family crest, and the Cross of St. George, and prepare "to face the silence that would sourly thicken as their own two deaths came closer and death increased in another part of their island. . . . Because of the distant past they would die friendless. It was worse than being murdered in their beds" (36).

If there is something quixotic about the Middletons' version of the proper relationship between England and Ireland and their choice to remain in a town that thinks otherwise, inhabit the crumbling Carraveagh, and patch together a relationship with their neighbors, there is also something gallant about their efforts to stave off isolation and loneliness, and it is not difficult to think that their efforts to create and sustain friendship—even on an illusory basis—are more admirable than their neighbors' denial of friendship because of the cash nexus, loss of income from the tourist trade, and that they deserve better than exile at home.

Contrary to this, it is difficult at first to rouse much compassion for the nameless sixty-nine-year-old narrator of "Saints," inheritor of the Big House of Kilneagh, near Cork, and of enough revenues in Ireland to have been able to spend forty years in luxurious self-imposed exile in Italy in the Umbrian town of Sansepolcro. However muddled the Middletons may be about their national identity, they at least win our understanding and perhaps our compassion for seeking friendship, for dealing with the past as best they can in the home place, and for enduring a cheerless exile they neither choose nor deserve; whereas, this protagonist confesses without apparent regret that "In national terms, I've become a nothing person" (30). Reluctant to visit Ireland, he has not returned to Cork for forty years, and when he does visit Ireland it is strictly on business and he is always glad to leave. Nor has Italy been a place of friendships or commitments to the living. Here, he confesses, he has indulged himself in drink, music, women, and the wonders of the Italian Renaissance, and we easily conjure up a cross between an old-time absentee landlord and a Roman sybarite, more a figure for contempt than compassion. But this is a story of how the Troubles reach from Ireland to Italy and from past to present to touch a life seemingly on a steady course.

And so the first impression is undercut at the very time it is being made because Trevor piques our curiosity about the reason for his protagonist's fierce rejection of Ireland, and he early on whets our curiosity further with at least three clues about the past. First and most obvious is his receipt from Cork of a telegram saying only "*Josephine is dying. Hospital of St. Bernadette,*" and his reactions: pleasure that he has been sent for, determination to go to Ireland on a personal affair, and immediate departure. Second is his observation that he has been lost in the world of Ghirlandaio and Bellini, "preferring its calmness to the pain of life," and third is his reflection that at sixty-nine he still indulges himself as best he can, "continuing to redress a balance" (29).

The truth as we come to discover it is that he and the devoutly Catholic Josephine—his family's domestic-of-all-work sixty and more years ago—are the sole survivors of the burning of Kilneagh and the murder of the protagonist's father, sisters, and three domestics by die-hard republicans in 1922, and of his mother's subsequent suicide by slashing her wrists with a razor ten years to the day after the events at Kilneagh, the despairing act which finally drove him to make financial provisions for Josephine and to leave Ireland for Italy.

With Trevor's characteristic method of revelation, we do not learn all of this at once; and neither we nor the protagonist learn until later that Josephine had endured her own forty-year exile as a result of the burning and deaths. Trevor so designs his story that the journey from Italy to Josephine's bedside in Cork, which takes fully half the story, must be made by bus, train, taxi, plane, train, and taxi, with temporal cross-cuttings between the present journey to places associated with the painful past and the story of why those places and that past are painful. It is as if the narrator were delicately peeling back layer after painful layer of still tender scar tissue to fully expose to himself—as well as to us—for the first time in many years the horror that drove him from Ireland. As he sits by Josephine's deathbed, he realizes that she, too, is remembering the experience:

Tears oozed from her eyes and I could tell from the contortion in her face that she was remembering not just my mother's suicide but my sisters and my father burnt alive and Mrs. Flynn [the cook] burnt also. The fire had started in the middle of the night and we were all trapped except O'Neill and John Paddy [the gardener and his son], who lived in the yard, though they always ate in the kitchen. They hauled us out the best they could, but only my mother and Josephine and myself survived. We had not been murdered when the men returned because we were not conscious, but O'Neill and John Paddy, faced by the men, were instantly shot. After my mother's burial, ten years later, Josephine said to me: "You and I are what's left of it now." (33)

So completely has the narrator effaced his human Irish past that it is only now, after his forced recollection of that past, that he learns that he and Josephine have shared more than he knew—that in 1932, the year of his mother's suicide and the beginning of his exile from Ireland, Josephine began her own very different forty-year exile as an inmate of St. Fina's insane asylum, driven there by her memories of the burning and deaths. As Sister Power tells him what she knows of Josephine's years there, the starkest of contrasts with the narrator's exile emerges. Whereas he was driven to self-indulgence in a foreign land to redress, as he has put it earlier, a balance—the losses he had suffered in Ireland—Josephine has devoted her life to prayer for others and has come to be regarded as a saint by her fellow inmates, who attribute miracles to her. Unlike the protagonist, Josephine has neither forgotten nor tried to forget the massacre and suicide; indeed, in words that reveal Trevor's intention to underscore the continuity of the Irish Troubles into the present, Sister Power says, "She hardly ever ceased to pray. She was confused, of course. She confused the tragedy you spoke of and your mother's death with what is happening now: the other tragedies in the North. She prays that the survivors may be comforted in their mourning. She prays for God's word in Ireland" (34).

After a brief visit to Kilneagh, "windowless and gaunt, a hideous place now" (35), and Josephine's death and funeral, the narrator, glad as always to leave Ireland but in isolation and loneliness and trailing bitter introspection about his failures in human relations, rejects the claim of Josephine's sainthood and miracles on rational grounds. But irrationally and under the influence of considerable wine, he meditates on a long procession of saints and sees with certainty the story of Josephine taking its place with them in scene after scene in the work of Fra Angelico, Giotto, Lorenzo di Credi, and Ghirlandaio, a pageant culminating in

the miracle that crowned them all: how she had moved that embittered man to find pleasure in the wisp that remained of a human relationship. On her deathbed she prayed that Ireland's murders might be forgiven, that all survivors be granted consolation, and rescued from the damage wrought by horror. Josephine of the Survivors they called her, Ghirlandaio and all the others.

Before I fell asleep, I wept on the terrace, the first time since my mother's death. It was ridiculous to weep, so old and wrinkled like a crab, half drunk and even senile. And yet it wasn't in the least ridiculous: it was as right and fitting as the sainthood imparted by the inmates of St. Fina's. For a moment she stood in glory on my terrace and then she disappeared. (36)

What are we to make of this conclusion, so close to sentimentality, skirting bathos with a narrator whose vision may be only alcohol-inspired? To put the worst construction on it, it is both sentimental and bathetic, an alcohol-induced and therefore unreal acceptance of the past. On the other hand, without this or a similar conclusion, the protagonist would remain essentially unchanged by his return to the past and the past's intrusion on his present and future, and Josephine's life of prayer and forgiveness would mean no more than the narrator's life of self-indulgence and denial of others—one survivor driven to nearly total isolation, the other to madness by the Irish Troubles. This grim possibility may be Trevor's intention. But to put the most hopeful construction on the ending, the conclusion, appropriately in a section of the story devoted to a litany of the saints, can also be read as an exemplum of the power of prayer and forgiveness, which may depart from the reality of the situation, but which softens the narrator's bitter self-reproaches, lessens his isolation, holds out some mild hope for regeneration, and in the larger context of the Troubles points beyond political and military solutions. That the story ends as it begins, in Sansepolcro—Holy Sepulcher—only adds to the ambiguity of Trevor's conclusion.

''Attracta'' and ''Autumn Sunshine'' are recent stories dramatizing the themes of betrayal, violence, revenge, guilt, forgiveness, redemption, and reconciliation in past and present. They are also stories in which the Anglican Protestantism of the protagonists figures more prominently than in any other of Trevor's Troubles stories, Attracta being the only teacher in the one-room Protestant school in a small town near Cork; Moran being the rector of St. Michael's Church of Ireland. Because of the authority derived from both their positions and long tenure in them, Attracta and Moran might have been but have chosen not to be aggressively Protestant in their work with their charges. Both are peaceable people who as adults have remained apart from religious and secular disputes and have no serious differences with their Catholic neighbors. But in the face of past violence renewing itself in the present, both depart from prepared teaching-preaching texts and counsel their small flocks to reconciliation in place of the revenge that has again become part of their human environment—a message their listeners find odd.

"Attracta" is Trevor's most complex examination of religious and sectarian allegiances. In present action that occurs in about 1975, Attracta, in her sixty-first year—after forty-some years of untroubled teaching and happiness—is haunted by a newspaper account of the death of a British army officer and the subsequent suicide in Belfast of his English wife of twenty-three, Penelope Vade. Attracta is strangely moved by these deaths, particularly Penelope's, for two reasons. First, this is a notably grisly tale of murder, vengeance, and suicide in contemporary Ulster:

> It was Penelope Vade's desire to make some kind of gesture, a gesture of courage and perhaps anger, that caused her to leave her parents' home in Haslemere and go to Belfast. Her husband . . . had been murdered in Belfast; he'd been decapitated as well. His head, wrapped in cotton-wool to absorb the ooze of blood, secured within a plastic bag and packed in a biscuit-tin, had been posted to Penelope Vade. Layer by layer the parcel had been opened by her in Haslemere. She hadn't known he was dead before his dead eyes stared into hers.

> Her gesture was her mourning of him. She went to Belfast to join the Women's Peace Movement, to make the point that somehow neither he nor she had been defeated. But her gesture, publicly reported, had incensed the men who'd gone to the trouble of killing him. One after another, seven of them had committed acts of rape on her. It was after that that she had killed herself

by swallowing a bottle of aspirin (195). Second, Attracta is haunted by this story because it both parallels and differs from her own story, one with its beginnings in the Black-and-Tan phase of the English-Irish conflict nearly sixty years earlier.

When Attracta was three, her parents, nonmilitant Irish Protestants, had been killed in an ambush meant for the Black-and-Tans, British military terrorists. That the architects of these deaths were an Irish Protestant guerrilla and his adulterous Catholic mistress, Devereux and Geraldine Carey, suggests the complexity of loyalties Trevor brings to this story.

Thus, for example, Devereux and Geraldine, who had not stopped at any violence in the Irish cause against the British, are guilt-stricken at these innocent deaths. They stop their guerrilla activity and devote much of their lives to seeking redemption. For Devereux, this means unusual devotion to the child Attracta—elaborate birthday presents, spending long hours with her, visiting her at her Aunt Emmeline's house, for example—until, ironically, when Attracta kisses him good night she imagines it is what having a father is like. For her part, Geraldine remains in Devereux's home as housekeeper and undergoes a sea change from violent revolutionary and adultress to the quietest and most devout person Attracta has ever known:

Geraldine Carey was like a nun because of the dark clothes she wore, and she had a nun's piety. In the town it was said she couldn't go to mass often enough. ''Why weren't you a nun, Geraldine?'' Attracta asked her once. . . . But Geraldine Carey replied that she'd never heard God calling her. ''Only the good are called,'' she said. (199)

The story of her parents' death is not revealed to Attracta until she is eleven and the relationship with Devereux and Geraldine well established. Then the story is told to her by Purce, whose aggressive Protestantism and bigotry embarrass the town's few other Protestants. By telling Attracta and trying to sever her relationship with Devereux and Geraldine, Purce seeks revenge against Devereux, a Protestant who never goes to church and is thus a betrayer of his faith; a renegade for having fought against the British Black-and-Tans, for having been responsible for the deaths of two Protestants, and for endangering Attracta's Protestantism by allowing her contact with the formerly adulterous but now piously Catholic Geraldine Carey.

Because they have won redemption, Purce does not gain revenge against Devereux and Geraldine, which would have destroyed Attracta, too. Instead, she survives because of those she might have hated, develops an affection for the town and is happy there: ''There'd been tragedy in her life but she considered that she had not suffered. People had been good to her.'' (194)

Now, in 1975, Attracta, realizing that she has survived and been happy because of the goodness of those who had harmed her nearly sixty years earlier, realizes that Penelope Vade did not survive because of the continued violence of those who had killed her husband when she, instead of seeking revenge, sought reconciliation by joining the Women's Peace Movement. Realizing these things, she meditates on her life as a teacher, wondering if she has not taught the wrong things:

She was thinking that nothing she might ever have said in her schoolroom could have prevented the death of a girl in a city two hundred miles away. Yet in a way it seemed ridiculous that for so long she had been relating the details of Cromwell's desecration and the laws of Pythagoras, when she should have been talking about Devereux and Geraldine Carey. And it was Mr. Purce she should have recalled instead of the Battle of the Boyne. (196)

In a mood of black guilt, she reflects that in a lifetime she has neither learned nor taught anything and, in atonement for not having taught her pupils the lesson from the past that had led to her own happiness, she reads to them the account of Penelope Vade and her husband and asks what they think of it. Faced with their puzzlement, she tells her own story, identifying in the telling with Penelope in detail after painful detail, and explaining further that Penelope was also like Devereux and Geraldine in offering peace and friendship. But because they have grown calloused by the horrors of the new Irish Troubles, the children only stare and wonder what on earth Penelope Vade has to do with anything, and think that Attracta does not "appear to understand that almost every day there was the kind of vengeance she spoke of reported on the television. Bloodshed was wholesale, girls were tarred and feathered and left for dead, children no older than themselves were armed with guns" (213).

At the last, then, Attracta, named for an Irish saint of the fifth or sixth century, succeeds only for herself but fails with others and so begs ironic contrast with Josephine of "Saints," who in bringing an otherwise bitter and lonely old man some consolation might be said to have some sort of success. They have both suffered grievous personal losses at about the same time in the past; but because she has never forgotten the past, Josephine brings it into the present and is able to console an old man; whereas, ironically, Attracta, who was able to forget the past because of the goodness of others, cannot bring the lessons of the past into the present for anyone but herself. Not only does she fail to teach the lesson to her pupils, but because they report her peculiar behavior to their parents she is eased into retirement—and thus loneliness and isolation—at the end of the term. Instead of defending her eccentric lesson, Attracta offers words that underscore the necessity of bringing the lessons of the past into the present: "Every day in my schoolroom I should have honoured the small, remarkable thing that happened in this town [i.e., that people *can* change for the better]. It matters that [Penelope Vade] died in despair, with no faith left in human life" (214).

In "Autumn Sunshine," Canon Moran of St. Michael's Church of Ireland is probably the oldest and most parochial protagonist of this set of stories. At the time of present action—September 1978—he lives alone in an eighteenth-century rectory, standing alone and looking lonely, two miles from the village of Boharbawn and eight miles from the town of Enniscorthy, County Wexford. Ministering to a small flock, a man abstemious and unambitious, he has for the most part been content, though the ordinary mild melancholy of the season is now deepened for him by the recent death of his wife of fifty years, Frances, and because his youngest and favorite daughter, Deirdre, has been in England for three years and did not return home or even write at her mother's death.

Not only is Moran rather isolated in his home, he has also always been insulated from even the mild conflicts of an Anglican pastor in a predominantly Catholic area. A man who has always disliked disorder, he had relied on Frances to resolve skirmishes with neighboring Catholics; for example, the ticklish situation of a girl in his parish made pregnant by a Catholic lad was settled when Frances had a chat with Father Hayes and the girl's mother.

Furthermore, Moran is largely at peace with his personal past. True, Frances's death is still difficult for him because it is not truly past and she has yet to become a ghost for him. True, too, he is troubled that Deirdre, always somewhat rebellious, had gone off to England without telling her parents, but she is too much the favorite to have alienated them by this. So on the whole Moran is not a man much troubled by his own past.

Nor does Trevor allow him to be very aware of the historical past of County Wexford, a past that perhaps should have engaged his attention more than it has; for, during the unsuccessful Irish rebellion of 1798 against the British, the Wexford rising was largely religious and animated by Catholic sentiments; Wexford held out against the British forces longer than any other section of Ireland; and Vinegar Hill, headquarters of the Wexford insurgents and scene of a famous Irish defeat, is only eight miles away in Enniscorthy. But the historical past is to be forced on Moran in a personal way and is to be the source of conflict, pain, and loss that are ultimately resolved only at the cost of denying to himself the truth of his own perceptions.

In this September, Deirdre returns, needing, she writes to her delighted father, to get back to Ireland for a while. She is soon followed by her English young man, Harold, too thin, wearing a black leather jacket; an electrician with dirty fingernails, bad manners, and a cockney accent. His face bears a birthmark, an affliction almost belligerent and that comes to symbolize his birth into England's lower orders and his rebellion against any establishment. It is Harold who forces the violent Irish past and an awareness of a violent Irish present into Moran's consciousness and compels him to connect the two.

For Harold is a radical who supports the Irish cause against England or any established social order. His pronouncements—he seldom converses, and in this and other ways Trevor has made him nearly a caricature—are largely cant: England has been "destroyed by class consciousness and the unjust distribution of wealth," "the struggle is worldwide," and "I'm not answerable to the bosses," for example, and his favorite catchcry, "the struggle of the Irish people." That Deirdre—named for the heroine of Irish legend's greatest love story, of whom it was prophesied at her birth that she would bring Ireland bloodshed and death—appears to be in love with him distresses Moran, and all the more when it seems possible that she is Harold's "Irish connection," that is, that he may have formed his liaison with her because she is Irish and possibly even because she is from Wexford.

If Moran is innocent of Irish history, Harold knows a great deal, including the story of Kinsella's Barn. There, in 1798, a Sergeant James, as an example to the countryside, burned in the barn twelve men and women accused of harboring insurgents; and Kinsella, innocent of either sheltering rebels or the executions, was murdered by his own farm workers. Returning from a visit to the site with Deirdre, Harold vents his hatred against James, a man who boasted that he had killed a thousand Irishmen and who had amassed great wealth at Irish expense, and further declares that Kinsella got what he deserved. When Moran protests gently that it was all two hundred years ago—implying that the past is past and best forgotten, certainly not to be dragged into the present—and that in any case Kinsella was innocent of any complicity, Harold automatically interjects that in two hundred years nothing has changed, that "The Irish people still share their bondage with the twelve in Kinsella's Barn," and that as for Kinsella, "if he was keeping a low profile in a ditch, it would have been by arrangement with the imperial forces" (50).

So virulent is Harold's hatred and so determined is he to cast his lot with Ireland's new revolutionaries that Moran is forced to connect past and present in two ways. First, when he addresses his small flock the following morning he departs from his prepared text and, in a spirit not unlike Attracta's when speaking to her uncomprehending pupils, "tried to make the point that one horror should not fuel another, that passing time contained its own forgiveness" (50) and that Kinsella was innocent of everything. He thinks:

> Harold would have delighted in the vengeance exacted of an innocent man. Harold wanted to inflict pain, to cause suffering and destruction. The end justified the means for Harold, even if the end was an artificial one, a pettiness grandly dressed up. . . . He spoke of how evil drained people of their humor and compassion, how people pretended to themselves. It was worse than Frances's death, he thought, as his voice continued in the church: it was worse that Deirdre should be part of wickedness.
>
> He could tell that his parishioners found his sermon odd, and he didn't blame them. He was confused, and considerably distressed. In the rectory Deirdre and Harold would be waiting for him. They would all sit down to Sunday lunch while plans for atrocities filled Harold's mind, while Deirdre loved him. (51)

The kinship between past and present is yet more specific that evening when Deirdre and Harold announce their departure for Dublin the next day, but Harold, reading a book about Che Guevara, is evasive about their exact movements. Certain that Harold intends to meet others like himself in Dublin and that Deirdre has turned her back on the rectory to join a man who plans to commit atrocities, Moran thinks:

Harold was the same kind of man Sergeant James had been; it didn't matter that they were on different sides. Sergeant James had maybe borne an affliction also—a humped back or a withered arm. He had ravaged a country for its spoils, and his most celebrated crime was neatly at hand, so that another Englishman could make matters worse by attempting to make amends. In Harold's view the trouble had always been that these acts of war and murder died beneath the weight of print in history books, and were forgotten. But history could be rewritten, and for that Kinsella's Barn was an inspiration: Harold had journeyed to it as people make journeys to holy places. (52)

Returning to the rectory the following morning from delivering Deirdre and Harold to the Dublin bus and deep in gloom because he believes Deirdre to be a befuddled girl under Harold's influence, Moran connects all that has happened with Frances, who had always resolved conflicts for him. Conjuring her up in the autumn sunshine, he hears her say, "Harold's just a talker. Not at all like Sergeant James," words that Moran clings to as truth because they take the curse off what he had clearly perceived to be so. In this mood of new hope, he hears Frances laugh,

and for the first time since her death seemed far away, as her life did too. In the rectory the visitors had blurred her fingerprints to nothing and had made her a ghost that could come back. The sunlight warmed him as he sat there; the garden was less melancholy than it had been. (52)

On the one hand, the conclusion of "Autumn Sunshine" is similar to that of "Saints," with the spirit of a dead woman bringing comfort to a lonely old man who has been dispirited by an excursion into the past. On the other, while the protagonist of "Saints" appears, in one interpretation, to undergo a change that allows him to deal, perhaps ineptly and at a distance, with the reality of a violent Irish past, Moran's change is only to put the past firmly into the past once again and to determine not to accept and to deal with the reality he had earlier perceived: that Harold is really a contemporary Sergeant James. When he calls up Frances, it is for her to do what she has always done—resolve his problem for him, here by denying that Harold *is* like James. As Frances is now properly dead, so is his probably accurate discernment of Harold and Deirdre.

Although ''Another Christmas'' dramatizes similar themes and arrives at not dissimilar resolutions, it differs in several ways from other Trevor stories about the Troubles. The protagonists, Dermot and Norah, are a middle-aged Irish Catholic couple. They are working-class people, Dermot having been a gas company meter-reader for twenty-one years, during which time they have rented the same small terrace house from the same landlord, Mr. Joyce. What is most important for Trevor's purpose is that this middle-aged, working-class Irish Catholic couple have lived in London since the early days of their marriage in Waterford. Thus, Trevor here reverses a familiar pattern. Instead of giving us Anglo-Irish Protestants in a distinct minority position in predominantly Catholic Ireland, he gives us Irish Catholics in a distinct minority position in predominantly Protestant England, and wonders, perhaps, if they'll behave any differently from their counterparts when faced with the same violent past renewed in the present, in this instance, about 1976. On the whole, this is another story in which apparently firm human relations unravel under pressures from the renewed past.

Initially, at least, it appears that Dermot and Norah have achieved about the same *modus vivendi* in their community as that reached by the Middletons in ''The Distant Past.'' Although there are several reminders in the opening pages that their background is Irish Catholic—two pictures of Waterford scenes and a picture of the Virgin and Child on the living-room walls, for instance—most of the opening pages are devoted to establishing that Dermot and Norah are at home here and doing what most English couples are doing at the same time: decorating the house for Christmas and drinking tea and talking about past Christmases, their five children, and the joy and peace of the present Christmas. On the other hand, as if showing that Dermot and Norah are simultaneously content and yet rather isolated, Trevor confines present action almost entirely to their living room. Later in the story, this suggestion of isolation becomes more sinister as Norah thinks of their entire situation in England as a trap,

the trap they'd made for themselves. Their children spoke with London accents. Patrick and Brendan worked for English firms and would make their homes in England. Patrick had married an English girl. They were Catholics and they had Irish names, yet home for them was not Waterford. (34)

At the opening of the story, too, it appears that Dermot and Norah have achieved a personal *modus vivendi* that is not simply a reflection of the warmth of the Christmas season. They have not had a serious quarrel in all their married life. She recognizes that he is ''considerate and thoughtful in what he did do, teetotal, clever, full of kindness for herself and the family they'd reared, full of respect for her also'' (28), and he knows how to compliment her for managing things so well. But there are also intimations in these early pages that their equanimity has cost Norah something. She is a plump, cheerful, easygoing woman whose Catholicism is relaxed and practical, and she has always deferred to Dermot, who is her opposite in mien and manner: "thin and seeming ascetic, with more than a hint of the priest in him . . ." (27), a man who gives much time to pondering religious matters while on his meter-reading route; a slow and deliberate man who, having arrived at a position, will not change his mind. As Norah well knows, "it was his opinion that mattered" (28).

The catalyst for a serious rift between them and their English neighbors is an issue that has developed between Dermot and their landlord, Mr. Joyce. Ironically, despite his name, Mr. Joyce is not Irish but thoroughly English. This fact has not mattered for over twenty years because Mr. Joyce, now a frail and bent old bachelor, has established his own warm and human relationship with the couple and their children, spending every Friday evening with them, kissing the children good night, joining them every year for Christmas, bringing presents for the children and small gifts for themselves. More than his tenants, Norah and Dermot are his friends; and to judge from the evidence of the story, he seems to be the sole valued long-time friend they have in England.

When the I.R.A. first started bombings that took civilian lives in England, Mr. Joyce did not stop his Friday evenings with Norah and Dermot, believing, perhaps, that their friendship was not based on religious or political considerations. However, perhaps assuming that for Dermot and Norah the friendship also transcended such lines, Mr. Joyce had not hesitated quietly to condemn the I.R.A. bombers, and they had not contradicted him until one Friday night in August when Dermot had shaken his head in agreement with Mr. Joyce over the latest outrage and

had added that they mustn't of course forget what the Catholics in the North had suffered. The bombs were a crime but it didn't do to forget that the crime would not be there if generations in the North had not been treated like animals. There'd been a silence then, a difficult kind of silence which she'd broken herself. All that was in the past, she'd said hastily, in a rush, nothing in the past or the present or anywhere could justify the killing of innocent people. Even so, Dermot had added, it didn't do to avoid the truth. Mr. Joyce had not said anything (35),

and he had stopped coming Friday evenings.

Now, in the midst of Christmas preparations, the issue of Mr. Joyce hangs unspoken between Norah and Dermot, and she delays until halfway through the story to say to Dermot that she is not counting on Mr. Joyce being with them for Christmas. Certain that he has been right in his condemnation of the treatment of the Catholics in the North and that Mr. Joyce would understand the justice of the I.R.A. bombings in England, Dermot insists that Mr. Joyce will come, that he has missed his Friday evenings because of illness, and that he wouldn't let the children down by not coming. Dermot refuses Norah's plea that he try to make it up with Mr. Joyce and instead says that he will pray that Mr. Joyce will come.

What emerges strongly in the second half of the story is what has been latent in the first. There is Dermot's deadly calm—he never displays emotion—and certitude that he is right; his conviction that they must keep faith with other Catholics; his belief that his position is God's position and that he has done his Catholic duty. Invoking the need for good will at the Christmas season, he repeats that one wrong leads to another wrong and that perhaps Mr. Joyce has seen this by now, failing on the one hand to see the bitter irony of his statements and on the other that Norah is tormented by the fact that seeming to condone what Mr. Joyce has condemned—the killing of innocent people—is to appear to condone the bombings.

For her part, Norah's conviction that Dermot is dead wrong and must be challenged is betrayed by manner and feelings never before associated with him: the increased impatience in her voice, her unusual edginess of manner, her raised voice, her feeling of wildness—as if she should rush into the streets to harangue passersby with her belief that the bombers are despicable and have earned hatred and death for themselves—and her impotent will to strength to pour out her rage at him:

> She looked at him, pale and thin, with his priestly face. For the first time since he had asked her to marry him in the Tara Ballroom she did not love him. He was cleverer than she was, yet he seemed half blind. He was good, yet he seemed hard in his goodness, as though he'd be better without it. Up to the very last minute on Christmas Day there would be the pretence that their landlord might arrive, that God would answer a prayer because his truth had been honoured. She considered it hypocrisy, unable to help herself in that opinion. (37)

At the end of the story we know that the relationship between Dermot and Norah has changed irrevocably. Seeing him guilty of a cruelty no one would have believed of him, she knows that he will be as kind as always to the children on Christmas Day but that Mr. Joyce's absence—the seal on the end of a cherished friendship—will be another victory for the bombers. And she thinks that "whenever she looked at him she would remember the Christmases of the past. She would feel ashamed of him, and of herself'' (38).

Despite differences in characters and setting, "Another Christmas" does not differ significantly from the other stories in its conflicts and resolutions, except, of course, to parcel out approval and condemnation to Irish Catholics, too. Except for their nominal tags, Norah shares much with the Middletons, Attracta, and Canon Moran; and Dermot is brother under the skin with Fat Driscoll, Purce, and Harold. In simpler terms, both Dermot and Norah understand how the past renews itself in the present; but where Dermot blindly perpetuates that past, Norah is willing to break the circle of violence begetting violence by forgiveness. In even simpler terms, he wants justice; she wants mercy.

As reported in *The Irish Times,* William Trevor's first full-length stage play, *Scenes from an Album,* takes photographs, so to speak, of a Tyrone Anglo-Irish family from Jacobean times to the present, and takes their home from castle to the present "decaying heap in which the occupants find themselves caught between the Orange Order and the IRA." If this is not precisely the situation of the protagonists in most of Trevor's Troubles stories, it is near to the spirit of those stories, an approximation whose meaning deepens when Trevor says that this Tyrone family is "the kind of Anglo-Irish family that I would have great respect for, not being that kind of Anglo-Irish myself . . . ," that is, more Irish than the Irish themselves rather than his "own kind of small-town Protestant bank manager's background. . . ."[10]

The Anglo-Irish protagonists of Trevor's stories, rather than being caricatures that might serve some propaganda, have his understanding and compassion, sentiments not withheld from the Irish Catholics of "Another Christmas," either, though, on the whole, their problems seem less provocative. This is because the situation of the Anglo-Irish, deep-rooted in Ireland but retaining at least traces of a different heritage and withal often more Irish than the Irish themselves, is so anomalous that their dilemmas generate greater and more complex and more subtle conflicts and thus more opportunities for insights than the situation of either Irish Catholic nationalist or British imperialist. The arena for conflict in Trevor's stories thus opens up more than most Troubles fiction has human issues that time has not solved and that cannot be solved by merely partisan positions. Upon reflection, Trevor's Troubles stories sometimes seem so open-ended that one must hesitate before pronouncing judgment on their collective "meaning"; but if there is one consistent view, it seems to be that the past cannot be forgotten but that with resolution and forgiveness it need not be perpetuated.[11]

Notes

1. With the exception of his first novel, *A Standard of Behavior* (London: Hutchinson and Co., 1958), Trevor's novels and short story collections have been published in England by Bodley Head and in the United States by The Viking Press. The novels are *The Old Boys* (1964), *The Boarding House* (1965), *The Love Department* (1966), *Mrs. Eckdorf in O'Neill's Hotel* (1969), *Miss Gomez and the Brethren* (1971), *Elizabeth Alone* (1973), *The Children of Dynmouth* (1976), and *Other People's Lives* (1981). The short story collections are *The Day We Got Drunk on Cake and Other Stories* (1967), *The Ballroom of Romance and Other Stories* (1972), *Angels at the Ritz and Other Stories* (1975), and *Lovers of Their Time and Other Stories* (1978). In addition, a selection of Trevor's Irish short stories has appeared as *The Distant Past and Other Stories* (Swords, County Dublin: Poolbeg Press, 1979).

2. (Cork: The Mercier Press, 1966), p. 134.

3. "Mr. Trevor Writes a Play," August 8, 1981, p. 12, col. 7.

4. Mortimer, *Etudes Irlandaises,* 4 (1975):77–85; Gitzen, *Critique* 21, no. 1 (1979):59–72.

5. Frank L. Kersnowski, C. W. Spinks, and Laird Loomis, *A Bibliography of Modern Irish and Anglo-Irish Literature* (San Antonio: Trinity University Press, 1976); *Anglo-Irish Literature: A Review of Research,* ed. Richard J. Finneran (New York: Modern Language Association, 1976).

6. "Author's Note," *The Distant Past,* p. 5.

7. These stories are "The Ballroom of Romance," *The Ballroom of Romance* and *The Distant Past*; "An Evening with John Joe Dempsey," *The Ballroom of Romance*; "A Choice of Butchers," *The Ballroom of Romance* and *The Distant Past*; "Teresa's Wedding," *Angels at the Ritz* and *The Distant Past*; "Mr. McNamara," *Angels at the Ritz* and *The Distant Past*; "Death in Jerusalem," *Lovers of Their Time* and *The Distant Past;* "The Raising of Elvira Tremlett," *Lovers of Their Time;* "The Time of Year," *The Distant Past*; "The Death of Peggy Morrissey," *The Distant Past*; "Downstairs at Fitzgerald's," *New Yorker,* July 13, 1981, pp. 28–37.

8. "Mr. Trevor Writes a Play," p. 12, col. 6.

9. "The Distant Past," *Angels at the Ritz* (Harmondsworth, England: Penguin Books, 1979), pp. 28–36; "Saints," *Atlantic Monthly,* January 1981, pp. 29–36; "Attracta," *Lovers of Their Time* (London: The Bodley Head, 1978), pp. 193–215; "Autumn Sunshine," *New Yorker,* March 10, 1980, pp. 44–52; "Another Christmas," *Lovers of Their Time* (London: The Bodley Head, 1978), pp. 27–38. Further references are to these sources and will appear in parentheses in the text.

10. "Mr. Trevor Writes a Play," p. 12, col. 6.

11. As this essay neared completion, my attention was called to a new Troubles story by Trevor, "Beyond the Pale," *New Yorker,* August 10, 1981, pp. 32–50. In it, Trevor plays yet another variation on themes examined in this essay, this time by bringing two Englishmen and two Englishwomen to an almost exclusively English resort in County Antrim, where they encounter an outsider from the streets of Belfast.

The Novels of John McGahern:
The Road Away Becomes the Road Back

Eileen Kennedy

Well known and highly praised in Ireland and England, John McGahern—whom Julian Jebb in the *Times Literary Supplement* ranked as "among the half dozen practicing writers of English prose most worthy of attention"[1]—was relatively unnoticed in this country until the publication of his novel, *The Pornographer,* in 1979, and a collection of short stories, *Getting Through,* in 1980. Both books received wide critical attention; but so far as I can determine, no one has pointed out how *The Pornographer,* despite its lurid title, is essentially conservative, a circling back to ideas and values explored in McGahern's first novel *The Barracks* (1963).

The circling back is unexpected because McGahern, once he had portrayed provincial life in his first novel, shows his protagonists, in later novels, finding some hope of fulfillment, by moving from their small farms and restrictive villages to the city. In *The Barracks,* McGahern portrays the monotonous rural village from which Elizabeth, the heroine, is alienated; and then, in *The Dark* (1965), the author has young Mahoney, a studious farmboy, deciding to confront his destiny in the city—Dublin. In the third novel, *The Leavetaking* (1974), McGahern's schoolteacher, Patrick Moran, has moved from the country to Dublin and then, ultimately, chooses London over Dublin. But in *The Pornographer,* McGahern's urban protagonist, who spends his time drifting into bars, dance halls, and affairs, decides—after several painful events—to leave the city for the farm he had inherited. This essay will explore the themes running through McGahern's novels and assess the significance of the circling back in *The Pornographer.*

Born in a nursing home in Dublin, in 1934, John McGahern spent his early years in various small towns in County Monaghan and County Leitrim with his mother, a schoolteacher. Because of their work, his parents lived apart. When McGahern was about ten, his mother died of cancer, and he went to live with his father in the barracks at Cootehall, County Leitrim, where his father was a police sergeant. He was educated at Presentation College in Carrick-on-Shannon and from there he studied at St. Patrick's, Dublin, graduating from University College Dublin. For several years he was a primary teacher in an Irish Catholic school; and then, in 1963, Faber and Faber published his first novel, *The Barracks,* which won Ireland's important literary prize, the AE Memorial Award.

McGahern's achievement in that first novel—the only one in which his protagonist is a woman—is so extraordinary, its tone so distinctive, and its poise so remarkable that some feel it is his best. Life as a passage from darkness to darkness is the theme of this finely crafted novel, which opens with the children querying their stepmother Elizabeth "Is it time to light the lamp yet?" and closes with the boy asking his widowed father the same question.[2]

The story is set in a rural Irish village, west of the Shannon. Sergeant Reegan, a fifty-year-old policeman, lives there in the barracks with his second wife Elizabeth (his first had died) and his three children, who never call her mother. Reegan and Elizabeth, in her early forties at the novel's opening, have been married four years—they had met when she was home in Ireland worn-out after nursing through the London Blitz—and the unrelenting demands of their hard life cause Elizabeth to think that perhaps Reegan had married her to have a housekeeper.

Elizabeth is gracious but keeps to herself, sensing that no one in this forgotten outpost can understand the daring voyages of the soul that she ventures on. Reegan is hot-headed and sardonic, a man born to authority—he had fed on the wild ideals of the Irish Free State—but hounded now by a self-important Superintendent whom he hates. Stern with his children, inexpressive with his wife, Reegan is driven by an overwhelming desire to throw off his hated job and take up small farming. In spring, when he plants the potato crop "the frustrations and poisons of his life [were] flowing into the clay he worked" (p. 90).

The plot of this somber novel is simple. Elizabeth discovers that she has cysts on her breasts, and the almost-certain knowledge that she only has a brief time to live causes her to examine and reexamine the meaning—if there is any—of her life. As she looks back, she realizes that she had tasted life feverishly only once, and for a few months: in London, she had fallen in love with a doctor, Halliday, who had made love to her and who off-handedly had offered to marry her, even as he told her he could love no one, he found life so meaningless. Shaken by his nihilism, realizing that marriage with him would be bitter, she had refused him. When she learned of his death in a car crash, she buried him in her mind. But Halliday had awakened her to a sense of herself, to her uniqueness, and his insistent question, "What is all this living and dying about anyway?" torments Elizabeth confronting her own death.

Reegan unthinkingly accepts the Church's teachings, praying the rosary with his family, implicitly believing in life after death; Elizabeth is a solitary seeker whose quest for meaning is knitted to the turning of the seasons, to the ritual of the church year. McGahern masterfully re-creates the rhythms of these two cycles signalling the passage of time so that the tension in the novel arises from Elizabeth's participation in the events of these cycles and her knowledge that time is bringing death closer. She takes joy in seeing the rushes and wildflowers, sign of Lady's Eve, sprinkled on the doorsteps by the children, as they kick off their boots to walk barefoot in May; in making her pilgrimage in August to Mary's Well, next to the church she loves, where she finds quietude but no answers to her questions; and in placing candles in her windows on Christmas Eve to light the way for the Christ Child, even though she cannot believe with the fullness of faith.

Concealing her physical pain and mental torment from the family, Elizabeth struggles to keep house. Tempted to go away and have other loves, she realizes

. . . that her life with these others, their need and her own need, all their fear, drew her back into the activity of the day where they huddled in their frail and human love, together. (p. 126)

Her illness causes Reegan to unearth in himself a capacity for tenderness, to put into words his passionate concern. If before his conversation had centered on his hate for the Superintendent, now he goes out of his self-pitying moods to meet her needs, and to take courage to change the direction of their life. Driven by a brutal intensity, he forces the children to drag turf that will be sold in town; and, with the profits, he plans to leave the police force, to take up small farming.

In McGahern's wedding of the church year to Elizabeth's life, he makes the Christmas celebration, five months before her death, a climactic scene. Exhausted from her holiday preparations, Elizabeth goes to bed late on Christmas Eve; and Reegan, returning from his night patrol much later, joins her. After making love, they "lie in the animal warmth and loving kindness of each other against the silence of the room. . . . And they were together here. It didn't have to mean anything more than that, it'd be sufficient for this night" (p. 150). Their physical and emotional union is paralleled in the Christmas dinner scene where the family are united in a human communion, the ritual of the meal taking on a spiritual dimension, transcending the here-and-now. It

began and ended in the highest form of all human celebration, prayer. It was a mere meal no longer with table and tablecloth and delf and food, it was that perfectly, but it was above and beyond and besides the wondrous act of their reality. (p. 151)

There are hints, more suggestive than conclusive, that Elizabeth's search for meaning has been touched by flashes of grace. Early one November morning, when as she looks out on the river and up to the woods across the lake, she utters softly ''Jesus Christ'' as she gazes at the winter beauty which culminates in the ''radio aerial, that went across from the window to the high branches of the sycamore, a pure white line through the air'' (p. 141). Reflecting on the Stations of the Cross, ''She saw her own life declared in them and made known, the unendurable pettiness and degradations of her own fallings raised to dignity and meaning in Christ's passion.'' If she cannot take hope in Christ's Resurrection, she does sense that ''on the cross of her life she had to achieve her goal'' (p. 161).

And if her passion for Halliday had awakened in Elizabeth a desire for a total love, she ultimately glimpses a vision of love that is transcendent:

She had come to life out of mystery and would return, it surrounded her life, it safely held it as by hands; she'd return into that which she could not know; she'd be consumed at last in whatever meaning her life had. Here she had none, none but to be, which in acceptance must be surely to love. (p. 174)

She moves to further statement:

All real seeing grew into smiling and if it moved to speech it must be praise, all else was death, a refusal, a turning back. . . . (p. 174)

Elizabeth's triumph over pain and nothingness is seen by F. C. Molloy merely as ''A moment of relief: no searching after explanations, being satisfied with the need to love, and letting life and death take their course.'' He believes ''The vision of despair continues to the end. . . .''[3] My view of her death is not so bleak: Elizabeth's life has been a day-to-day enactment of her love for her family. Her unfailing kindness to the stepchildren, her holding back sharp words when the pain overwhelms her, her persistence at the household tasks, give her life a radiance, some shining splendor of the spirit; and, during her illness, her emotional relationship with her husband intensifies and deepens. She had always kept back, hidden in her trunk, some money saved from her days in London; and when she reveals this small treasure to him, her disclosure underlines her coming to trust him completely, just as his concern for her causes her to realize "how lucky she was to have found Reegan, to be married to him and not to Halliday, where she and he would drive each other crazy with the weight and desperation of their consciousness" (p. 127).

Elizabeth may not have found a completely fulfilling answer to Halliday's question about the meaning of life; but the reader is aware—much more than she— that she has taken her existential situation and, within the limits of her freedom, has shaped her life into one of significance and meaning. *The Barracks* is a somber novel, but it is neither grim nor depressing. Elizabeth's struggle and limited achievement leave the reader feeling some exaltation: she has not succumbed to defeat or despair. In her own way, Elizabeth has given her life meaning, one lit up with the luminosity of love.

McGahern's second novel, *The Dark,* has a cast of characters who may seem like a continuation of the story of Reegan and his children. *The Dark* opens with a widowed father, named Mahoney, threatening his son, who is nameless throughout the novel, with a brutal whipping for saying "Fuck." Mahoney is a small farmer, whining and hard-working, who by turns beats and cajoles his children; and in this isolated family group, the children are at war with their father. Set in the rural west of Ireland, this *Bildungsroman* tells how young Mahoney, influenced by his dead mother's wish that he become a priest, weighs a vocation to Holy Orders. His cousin, Father Gerald, a country pastor, also urges him to consider the possibility. But the boy is torn by strong feelings of adolescent sexuality, and the sexual acts with himself described in graphic detail underline even more his isolation and loneliness. He feels drawn by the "security" of the priesthood, the serenity and sureness of heaven; but he knows, from his masturbatory fantasies, he cannot live a celibate life. In a visit to Father Gerald, he is compelled to tell the priest his reason for not becoming a priest; and, surprisingly enough, the man seems to understand the boy's troubled sexuality. His final advice is something he would never admit in public—people would think him a madman:

Remember your life is a great mystery in Christ and that nothing but your state of mind can change. And pray. It's not merely a repetition of words. It's a simple silent act of turning the mind on God, the contemplation of the mystery, the Son of God going by way of Palm Sunday to Calvary and on to Easter.[4]

Returning to the farm, young Mahoney informs his father of his decision; but he cannot answer his father's question of what he would do with his life. Instead, the adolescent begins the working out of his life through a tentative exploration of the possibilities of freedom, a liberation from his father's bullying and the drudgery of the farm. Highly intelligent and sensitive, he is determined to go to the university. He spends his high school years in incessant study, helping on the farm, and cunningly overcoming his father's domination; and with no human outlet for his sexual energies, he continues his masturbatory fantasies. His hour of triumph arrives when he wins a scholarship to the University of Galway. The summer before entering the University, he sees that he excels his father in physical strength. Young Mahoney feels he is a man, "able to take a man's place," and, as he notices that his father is growing old, he finds it "hard to imagine that this was the same man who'd made the winters a nightmare over the squalid boots, the beatings and the continual complaining" (p. 111).

But at Galway, young Mahoney is unhappy. Unable to decide on a career, he watches the other grim, security-driven students choose courses that will give them a living. Drifting through classes, the boy senses that "there'd be little dream, mostly the toil of lectures, and at night the same swotting and cramming in a room for the exams same as last year" (p. 129). He fears that he will fail or fall sick or lose his scholarship; he longs to dance, but cannot bring himself to enter the dance hall. A pompous lecturer, falsely accusing him of "hooliganism," dismisses him from class. The professor's bullying, the boy realizes, is the mirror of his father's; and he sees tyranny as the way of university life. Riddled by self-doubt, he uncertainly makes a bid for freedom, one which brings his father to Galway. Young Mahoney is considering leaving the University to work as a clerk for the Electrical Supply Board (E.S.B.) in Dublin. "Chained to a desk all day would be the worst part" (p. 133), but he would have money and be freed from his dependence on his father and the dread of sickness and failure. The father and son talk with the Dean of Students, who seems to the boy another contemptuous tyrant. He decides to enter the E.S.B. "If it was no use you could leave again, and it didn't matter, you could begin again and again all your life, nobody's life was more than a direction" (p. 139). For the first time, he can

laugh purely, without bitterness . . . and it was a kind of happiness, at its heart the terror of an unclear recognition of the reality that set you free, touching you with as much foreboding as the sodden leaves falling in the day, or any cliché. (p. 140)

The book closes with a quiet scene of reconciliation in which the father asks the son for mutual forgiveness. Young Mahoney tells him: "I wouldn't have been brought up any other way or by any other father" (p. 142).

Although *The Dark* has some apparent similarities with Joyce's *Portrait of the Artist as a Young Man,* the comparison should not be pressed. Like Stephen Dedalus, the boy in *The Dark* has overpowering sexual drives and considers a vocation to the priesthood. Young Mahoney is highly intelligent and excels in his studies, but he has none of the intellectual arrogance and psychic certainty with which Stephen Dedalus leaves Ireland to "encounter for the millionth time the reality of experience." Unlike Stephen, the boy does not desire to be a creator of mortal beauty nor does he reject his faith. Instead, young Mahoney fumblingly works out his life, walking hesitantly toward freedom. It is significant that in scenes at Father Gerald's house where he weighs the decision to become a priest, he picks up the one volume that seemed livelier than the rest, Tolstoy's *Resurrection*. By choosing not to become a priest, the boy is beginning the resurrection of his own life; but it will move by fits and starts—no one choice is clear-cut before him. McGahern, through his protagonist, seems to be indicating that human decisions are fraught with uncertainty but that to achieve some happiness, freedom must be won daily. Stephen Dedalus is an urban hero who can leave Ireland boldly; but young Mahoney is a farmboy whose sights are set no higher than the city.

The Dark, with its sexually explicit scenes, caused a *succès de scandale* for McGahern, a teacher in a Dublin Catholic boys' school. Following the banning of the book for indecency or obscenity by the Irish Censorship Board and McGahern's marriage outside the Church, the author was forced out of his teaching position.[5] Perhaps, for these reasons, McGahern makes the flight to freedom even more explicit in his third novel, *The Leavetaking,* where he draws heavily upon his personal experiences. That book portrays a single day in the life of the protagonist, Patrick Moran; and the decisive event of that day is linked to his whole biography through stylistic devices like reverie, association, and recurring imagery. These techniques emphasize one of the thematic concerns of the novel, the long shadow time past casts on time present.

Part One focuses on Patrick's parents and their strange marriage. His mother, a deeply religious schoolteacher who had thought of becoming a nun, unwittingly encourages her son's attachment, strongly oedipal, to her. Patrick's father, a police sergeant, unfeeling to the point of emotional brutality, lives away at the barracks, so that the boy, raised almost wholly by his mother, is pliant to her wishes, especially her hope that someday he will say Mass for her. McGahern probes in detail the histories of the parents as though to discover what emotional alliance could produce a Patrick Moran. The author describes Patrick's mother's work as a teacher, her sensitivity to beauty, and her odd courtship by Sergeant Moran. The searing poverty out of which Sergeant Moran comes, raised by a mother deserted by her husband, is also portrayed. This marriage of gentleness to harshness, of passivity to authoritarianism forms the background of Patrick's early years until his mother develops cancer, and the young boy watches her fading away. Part One culminates in the break-up of the family. In a heavily charged scene, which symbolically re-creates the long erosion of the marriage, Sergeant Moran, remaining at the barracks, orders his men to remove the furniture from the house and bring the children to him. The men arrive and as they hammer apart the beds—which have rusted too much in the damp to come apart—their blows resound through the house and into the room where the mother lies dying. In the first leavetaking of the novel, the boy goes to his father, and that night they receive word the mother has died. Guilt-ridden, Patrick feels he has not loved her enough, has not told her enough that he loved her; and these feelings color his attitude toward himself and life.

In Part Two of the novel, Patrick, knowing that he cannot give up his longing "to enter the mystery of the lovely and living flesh of women,"[6] chooses his mother's path of teaching; and wanting the anonymity of the city, he moves from his position as country schoolmaster to a teacher in a Catholic boys' school in Dublin. In many ways, Patrick, up to this point, could be young Mahoney of *The Dark.* Both are intelligent men, inclined toward dream and reverie; both have lost their mothers who have wanted them to be priests; both have authoritarian fathers with whom they are in conflict. But if, in *The Dark,* the protagonist only can grope his way toward some freedom, Patrick Moran, in *The Leavetaking,* strikes a decisive blow for it. If young Mahoney cannot bring himself to enter the dance hall, Patrick pursues pleasure, which McGahern captures in a brilliant contrast that underlines the difference between Patrick's mother's great wish for him and his own desires. Patrick describes the queue for the dance hall where there was

. . . Matt Talbot's altar against the wall, the little wooden kneeler and the statue of the Virgin dustcoated and shabby, dustcoated too the glass jars in which fresh daffodils and narcissi stood: old mad Dublin labourer who fell with chains festering in his flesh where we queued to dance. (p. 86)

At the dance he meets and falls in love with a country girl studying to be a teacher—she is very much like his mother—but she ultimately rejects him. Succeeding women find him attractive, and he has several affairs, hoping to find love and, therefore, a meaning to life.

Taking a year's leave of absence from his position, he travels to England where he falls in love with Isobel, a young American divorcée. The scenes in London are lively but unconvincing: McGahern's strength lies in his treatment of Irish figures and especially the rural landscape. Patrick marries Isobel in a registry office, and they return to Ireland where he does not reveal his marriage because it will mean the loss of his job. Learning of the marriage outside the Church, the school manager asks him to resign. Patrick refuses, thus forcing his dismissal: he will not make it easy for the oppressive authority of the Church to be rid of him. At the end of the novel, Patrick has cast away all hopes for security in Ireland—he will go to England with his wife—but he finds meaning and strength in his love. He has taken a definitive stand for freedom, even though this final leavetaking demands exile. With Isobel, he will find an inner freedom as well because he will be able to throw off his guilt-ridden memories of his mother, "the life would have made its last break with the shadow, and would be free to grow without warp in its own light" (p. 82).

If *The Dark* explores the father-son relationship, in which the mother was virtually nonexistent, *The Leavetaking* explores the mother-son relationship, in which references to the father, after Part One, are scarce. In *The Dark,* the father is the major influence against whom the son must do battle; in *The Leavetaking*—though her influence is more subtle, and hence, more invidious, the mother is. In both novels, McGahern seems to be suggesting that the freedom to grow into personhood comes from throwing off the powerful parental forces that have shaped one; that one comes into some fullness of being by choosing, whatever insecurities follow, freedom. And both young Mahoney and Patrick Moran must leave their country villages, their rural landscape and its restrictions, for the city where they can test the possibilities of that freedom.

The cold, nameless narrator—he is the protagonist—of McGahern's fourth novel, *The Pornographer,* lives in the city, in a room where daylight rarely filters in. The anonymous city—Dublin's bars, dancehalls, bus stations, train platforms—is the gray landscape where this rejected lover and pornographer broods over the dualism between body and soul. His brooding does not prevent him from making a comfortable living from his hack work, a metaphor, in the book, for his deadness of heart; and the city, where no one questions his habits or his occupation, gives him the freedom to follow his sexual desires, to drift from one woman to the next, to assuage, temporarily, his sense of anomie. At thirty, almost rootless, he has one strong tie: his love for his aunt, dying of cancer, and her brother, his uncle, relatives who had raised him in the country after his mother died.

The narrator picks up at a dancehall Josephine, a sturdy near-virgin (in an unfulfilling one-night stand earlier, her membrane had been only partially penetrated), and they go to bed together that night. Casually he begins an affair with her, she more the aggressor than he; and when they make love, she refuses to use contraceptives, saying they are unnatural. Predictably, she becomes pregnant. More comic than tragic, Josephine is drawn in bold strokes. Conventionally Catholic, she works in a bank and at thirty-eight is eager for marriage and motherhood; but in some ways she seems unrelentingly contemporary, like a caricature of Ireland coming into the twentieth century, studding her conversation with American slang gleaned from the movies and writing tourist articles for *Waterways,* a magazine that promotes travel on the Shannon by houseboats equipped with ". . . hi-fi, central heating, fridges, push-button starters."[7] And she bursts with energy as she connives to trap the narrator into marriage. She refuses to have an abortion, and he will marry her only to legitimatize the child; then he will divorce her. In an unconvincing turn of plot, she moves to London where her protector is an elderly magazine publisher who wants to marry her and adopt the child after it is born. She cannot bring herself to marry him, flees his house, and some time later she is taken in by an Irish construction worker and his wife, the Kavanaghs. After the baby is born, the protagonist goes to see her in London but refuses to see the child, knowing that it is part of her scheme to have his heart so moved by the baby he will marry her. He arranges to meet her in a Fleet Street bar where she arrives accompanied by Michael Kavanagh, who beats him so mercilessly that his face is disfigured for weeks. The beating is the moment of grace for the narrator who hides from his assailant in the sheltered doorway of a church.

Intertwined with this plot, which McGahern often treats with a touch of humor which has not been present in his writing before, is another story. Visiting his aunt in a Dublin hospital, the narrator meets Nurse Brady, a dark-haired country girl, "man-mad," his caustic aunt calls her. Raised on a farm with her brothers, she is frank and unaffected; and subsequent meetings with him culminate in his making love to her, which he associates with "the sweet fragrance of the new hay" (p. 175). His numb heart is beginning to come alive, he feels the twinges of love for the nurse. But he feels he should not see her until he is free of his responsibility to Josephine; and when he finally confesses that affair to the nurse, his painful admission, a realization of his fault in the matter, signals a step in his growth as a human being.

The narrator is learning that his uncaring ways and irresponsible behavior have continuing repercussions. The beating he gets from Michael Kavanagh parallels his recognition that he has used Josephine coldly, that he has been "shamefully shallow" in his initial encounters with the nurse. And his coming to terms with his aunt's painful illness causes him to think about the meaning of life. If at the opening of the novel, he had felt of his aunt's approaching death, "Now that it was taking place it amounted to the nothing that was the rest of our life when it too was taking place" (p. 13), he can assert, near the close of the book, that the struggle to find meaning is the important thing:

We can no more learn from another than we can do their death for them or have them do ours. We have to go inland, in the solitude that is both pain and joy, and there make our own truth, and even if that proves nothing too, we have still that hard joy of having gone the hard and only way there is to go, we have not backed away or staggered to one side, but gone on and on and on even when there was nothing, knowing there was nothing on any other way. (p. 203)

Using echoes of Biblical images, he continues his reflections—their import will not be clear until the book's final pages:

All the doctrines that we had learned by heart and could not understand and fretted over became laughingly clear. To find we had to lose: the road away became the road back. . . . All the time we had to change our ways. We listened to others singing of their failures and their luck, for we now had our road. All, all were travelling. Nobody would arrive. The adventure would never be over even when we were over. (p. 203)

When his aunt dies, the narrator goes to the country for her funeral. There his uncle shows him his newly bought farmhouse, completely furnished down to the blue and white mugs in the kitchen and the wedding and baptism photographs, as well as an ordination one, amid the religious pictures on the wall. The narrator finds these emblems of stability and permanence, of tradition and commitment "very lovely." And he observes that the house has a "solid hall door looking confidently down the road" (p. 233), a telling detail because of his earlier reference that he now has his road. And it is the "road back" for the narrator because after his aunt's burial, he reaches a decision. He is "going to try to make a go of" his life, to change his ways. He sums up his past:

By not attending, by thinking any one thing was as worth doing as any other, by sleeping with anybody who'd agree, I had been the cause of as much pain and confusion and evil as if I had actively set out to do it. I had not attended properly. I had found the energy to choose too painful. (p. 251)

His road back will be to propose marriage to his dark-haired nurse and to return here, to his roots, to his inherited farm. Moving out of his narcissism, he feels a "fierce need to pray" (p. 252), for himself and his friends, even though prayers could not be answered. The novel ends on an exultant note, in which the rain is a kind of baptism for the narrator. He remembers, with respect, his uncle standing on the platform of the railroad station, a scene that had opened the book. Like *The Barracks, The Pornographer* circles back, opening and closing with the same scene, but the later novel is less fearful, more affirming of life. The urban protagonist, who as pornographer had counterfeited the act of love, who had allowed his personal pain to make him an outcast from life's feast, has slowly and painfully realized that he must follow his "instinct for the true, to follow it with all the force we have, in all the seeing and the final blindness" (p. 252).

If Elizabeth in *The Barracks* had found some meaning to her life in the living out of her love, the protagonist of *The Pornographer* also seems drawn to the need for some roots, for commitment to a person. Like the protagonists of *The Dark* and *The Leavetaking,* he, raised in the country, chooses the city. But the city, where he has exterior freedom, also helps to keep him "dead of heart," as he follows its ways, trading the permanence and stability of the land for the city's commercialism. Nurse Brady, spontaneous and direct, raised on a farm, is the protagonist's choice over Josephine: the smell of freshly cut meadows turning to hay is preferred to the fridges and hi-fis of the Shannon houseboats. McGahern's fourth novel, then, is a circling back to the conservative ideas and traditional values explored in *The Barracks:* the road away becomes the road back.

Notes

1. 10 January 1975, p. 29.
2. *The Barracks* (1963; rpt. London: Quartet Books, 1977), p. 7. All further references to this work appear in the text.
3. "The Ireland of John McGahern," *Critique: Studies in Modern Fiction* 19 (1977):12.
4. *The Dark* (1965; rpt. London: Quartet Books, 1977), pp. 74–75. All further references to this work will appear in the text.
5. See Bruce Cook, "Irish Censorship: The Case of John McGahern," *Catholic World,* 206 (1967):176–79. Although some critics, like Bruce Cook and F. C. Molloy, have pointed out apparent structural flaws in *The Dark,* Paul Devine, in "Style and Structure in John McGahern's *The Dark,* " *Critique: Studies in Modern Fiction* 21 (1979):49–58, provides a close and illuminating study of McGahern's technique in the novel.
6. *The Leavetaking* (1974; rpt. London: Quartet Books, 1977), p. 85. All further references to this work will appear in the text.
7. *The Pornographer* (New York: Harper & Row, 1979), p. 55. All further references to this work will appear in the text.

The Romanticism of Brian Friel

Daniel Leary

> Some day when I'm awf'ly low,
> When the world is cold,
> I will feel a glow just thinking of you
> And the way you look tonight.

The Kern-Fields song runs throughout Brian Friel's *Faith Healer* (1979) and resonates in all his earlier stories and plays.[1] Friel is part of the romantic tradition, a sour variety that foresees little for man, but one that treasures early memories as visions to be drawn upon in later, bleaker years and views authority in its various forms—familial, religious, civil—as the destroyer of that vision.

Citing that Fields verse may be misleading. The vision in Friel is seldom of an amorous nature. The memories are prepuberty and often—again a romantic tendency—involve a magical place in Northern Ireland, often in County Donegal, frequently in Derry City, the town where Friel was born in 1928 and has lived most of his life.[2]

Our concern is the plays but occasionally I will refer to stories from Friel's first collection of fiction to illustrate recurring themes. In the story that furnishes the title of his first volume, *The Saucer of Larks* (1962), Friel's description of a blessed place in Donegal where a World War II aviator is buried—a German aviator, an alien and an enemy—captures the mood of the narrator, contrasts it with the "obdurate, peaty, rocky earth," and conveys a complicated feeling about life and death, exile and home, being and loss that is quintessentially Frielian, typically romantic:

The path dipped sharply into . . . a saucer of green grass bordered by yellow dunes. . . . For a few seconds after they entered the valley, their ears still heard the rush of the breeze and they were still inclined to call to one another. Then they became aware of the silence and then, no sooner were they hushed by it, than they heard the larks, not a couple or a dozen or a score, but hundreds of them, all invisible against the blue heat of the sky, an umbrella of music over this tiny world below.

All the romantic themes are caught in this depiction of a womb-tomb place revealing a sensibility half in love with easeful death.

In the plays the romanticism is seldom as pure. It is self-conscious, wry, often humorous. Kern's song on a battered Astaire record serves as a pathetic introduction to the faith healer's meetings with the blind, the lame, the diseased of whatever woebegotten town he has stumbled upon, seated anxiously, despairingly before him. This blending of reality and show, pain and dream, sensitivity and routine, is the basis for most of Friel's humor, but though we laugh, we do so conscious of the frustrations at the heart of the humor. The minor key of the song and the graceful colloquial line of the verse nicely mirror the controlled rhythms Friel uses as he has characters almost touch the lost vision. Controlled, I say, because Friel uses the Irish cadences while avoiding the Irish blather.

Friel's career as a playwright began with radio scripts for the Northern Ireland B.B.C. in the late 1950s. The two I have read, "A Sort of Freedom" and "To This Hard House," focus on fathers: in the first a man loses contact with family and friends because of his need to maintain authority, in the other a father loses a sense of purpose as his children demand and win their freedom. Taken together the two scripts suggest there is happiness neither in having authority nor in losing it, that it is impossible to strike a balance between autonomy and loyalty to family.

In 1959 Friel wrote his first stage play, *A Doubtful Paradise,* which is clearly a reworking of materials in "To This Hard House." Friel confessed that it was a very bad play and we can safely move on to his next, *The Blind Mice* (1960). This one too Friel dismissed but I find the dialogue very much alive. Some of it may have been drawn from conversations leading to Friel's decision not to enter the priesthood upon leaving the Catholic seminary at Maynooth College. In the play Father Cris Carroll returns to Derry City, a hero, after five years in a Communist Chinese prison. Triumph turns to disgrace, however, when it is revealed that Father Carroll was released because he signed a confession renouncing his faith. As in Ibsen's *An Enemy of the People,* the conflict is between the individual and society with an ending both ambiguous and unresolved. Two people stand by him: a "whiskey priest" who warns him not to indulge in a sense of guilt; and his mother who sees him experiencing the humiliation of Christ's lowliest. Their loyalty may be ill-placed since Father Carroll gives signs of becoming the worldly compromiser he was before his ordeal. The lost vision of a triumphant martyr and the reality of a calculating priest are juxtaposed and linger bitterly in the mind long after the final curtain.

One play in the Friel canon presents a priest positively, *The Enemy Within* (1962), his first truly successful play. The hero is the sixth-century Irish founder of monasteries, Saint Columba. His vision, as in "The Saucer of Larks," is of an Ireland worth dying for. Columba explains why he was late in returning from the fields with Father Cormac and confesses his growing weakness:

And I was back in Tirconaill; and Cormac was Eoghan, my brother, humming to himself; . . . and the blue sky was quick with larks as long as I did not lift my head; and the white point of Errigal mountain was behind my shoulder as long as I kept my eyes on the ground.

Columba has much in common with Father Carroll of *The Blind Mice:* he too is a practical man, a man of action in the world. The enemy within is the Columba who prizes Ireland more than service to God. His temptation is to return to "the wrack of Gineebarra, the woodpigeons in the oaks of Derry" and fight for the honor of his family, using his calling as a weapon.

Like Father Carroll, Columba is warned that he must prevent guilt from destroying his mission. The guilt stems from Columba's angry slapping of a postulant who idealizes him. The boy's vision disturbed Columba because it was another form of the enemy within. In confronting that guilt with humility, Columba avoids the mistake of using his priestly role for secular purposes, though now cursed by his own people. All the major characters are Columba's inner enemy, his Irish family obviously so but also his monastic family from the youngest postulant to the oldest of the fathers. When Columba's beloved old associate Father Caornan dies we are told that Caornan's final wish was to "go to the Isles of Orkney and . . . do penance for all the joy he found in the life here." The wish ironically reflects on the lifetime mission of Columba, who sought exile by founding homes away from home, away from the Ireland he loved so much.

The Enemy Within was a commercial and critical success but Friel was not satisfied. The historical distancing of the play had certainly given him more artistic freedom than he had had in *The Blind Mice,* but the narrative line was still that of the short stories. He may have released himself enough to shift from place and focus on person but the first three plays were not truly dramatic events. Of Friel's preoccupations, the sense of home might be realized but the sense of loss, of exile, of yearning, the dynamic presentation of those living experiences eluded him. He took a kind of sabbatical for five months in 1963 to observe Tyrone Guthrie in Minneapolis at work directing *Hamlet* and *The Three Sisters.*

We have seen the repetitive romanticism in Friel, how the plays return to the stories, more specifically how *A Doubtful Paradise* was a reworking of *To This Hard House,* how *The Enemy Within* was a reworking of *The Blind Mice.* It is a pattern that continues in the plays to follow. In those few months with Guthrie, Friel must have seen what that return implies. The content remains much the same as in the stories and earlier plays but the innovations in form—breaking of time frame, opening of subconscious drives, fragmenting of central characters—reveal the awakening of the true dramatist to the truth of Eliot's "We had the experience but missed the meaning / And approach to the meaning restores the experience / In a different form. . . ."[3] Friel's real interest, he discovered, was in the inner movement, the inner action. Drama was a search but, unlike the writing of a short story, this search needed an audience which ritualistically had to share in the search and the discovery. The dislocations in the rhythms of Friel's subsequent dramas reflect his search, but are also attempts to produce a dislocation in audience consciousness, attempts to break through its confused dream of life in order to place it before the reality of a human action to be purely contemplated and judged by author, players, and audience. The discovery is twofold with both insights involving death: death in life and death in masks. Friel is in the tradition of Ibsen, who knew that when we dead awaken we will find that we were dead; and he is in the tradition of Jean Genet, who knew we are prevented from living our lives by the constant and inevitable conflict between the part we find ourselves playing and the image we have of ourselves as free agents. In a play such as *Philadelphia Here I Come!* (1964) Friel gives us both the living dead and the acting non-actors.

"Philadelphia here I come / Right back where I started from." The melody lingers on. In two hours and three episodes *Philadelphia* presents eight hours in the life of young Gar O'Donnell as he prepares to become an exile from Donegal by emigrating to America, by leaving an antiquated general store and his inarticulate father for a second-rate hotel in Philadelphia and his crudely demonstrative aunt. Gar leaves to find the City of Brotherly Love that he never found in Donegal, leaves to find—and he knows the truth even before he goes—to find that he is "right back where I started from."

Gar's vision of Philadelphia is not of America at all. It has to do with a remembered moment of what he believes was a shared vision:

The music says . . . that once upon a time a boy and his father sat in a blue boat on a lake on an afternoon in May, and on that afternoon a great beauty happened, a beauty that has haunted the boy ever since, because he wonders now did it really take place or did he imagine it? There are only the two of us, he says; each of us is all the other has; and why can we not even look at each other?

The vision is as elusive as the gold the California-here-I-come 49'ers sought. It is the same vision that crops up in his short stories "Among the Ruins," "My True Kinsman," and "Mr. Sing My Heart's Delight"; it is a moment of understanding and fellowship between authority and self, a remembrance from childhood of a fleeting harmony between a boy and a parent in a place that suggests organic harmony between man and nature. In the play we find that all authority figures fail: the local priest makes no effort to initiate real conversation; the old teacher is caught in his own memories; his girl's father breaks up the relationship between his daughter and Gar.

But *Philadelphia* goes beyond the stories. Friel actually communicates the longing, the frustration of a young man discovering how close to impossible it is to communicate that longing. The principal dramatic device is the dividing of Gar into two actors—Public Gar and Private Gar, with Public maintaining the usual mask demanded by society while Private gives voice to all the unsaid remarks, enacts all the gestures that we live our days suppressing. The effect is hilarious as Private, anticipating every exchange in the conversation of Public and his father, the Canon, and the housekeeper, seems to be pulling their dummy strings, speaking lines just before they are spoken, anticipating actions a moment before they are repeated by those capable of nothing but rehearsed responses. The resulting laughter is a dislocation that leads to audience recognition. The place may be Donegal but on stage it is represented by a stylized interior. Gar may be a Donegal boy debating the wisdom of leaving home but his is also the universal experience of finding that though you have outgrown the nest, it is painful to face the fledgling flight.

In terms of the play Gar never leaves home. The hours on stage are spent with Public/Private Gar confronting his "enemies within," the other selves he might become if he stayed in Donegal: his dour father, the fossilized Canon, the broken schoolmaster, the aimless "boys" bragging of their imaginary sexual adventures. The closing lines of the play, Gar's to himself, underscore the play's inner action: "Why do you have to leave? Why? Why?" The answer rests not so much in what he does not want to become as in his vision—his father now displaced—of his young vital mother who died in his infancy. It is a vision adumbrated in the short story "Mr. Sing My Heart's Delight" in which an impulsive girl is forced to marry an old farmer who is as rocky and forbidding as the spot in Donegal where they live. She remains, nonetheless, so vital, curious, and playful that she becomes a perennial vision for the now adult narrator. Why does Gar leave Donegal? Perhaps to find the mother he never knew, to find the free impulsive life, the dream of the romantic.

Friel's next play, *The Loves of Cass McGuire* (1966), dramatizes the return of the exile and the displacement of vision with illusion. Cass's return to Ireland from America after fifty-two years to live with her brother's family might be one version of the other half of Gar's story. Cass is a variation of the strong, life-loving woman caught in the deadly drabness of a morally smug society that we have already heard of in the reports of Gar's mother. Cass's vitality surfaces soon after her return in a bar-room brawl which so offends her brother's genteel wife that she has Cass sent off to a rest home called Eden House.

The vision this time is of total independence with an understanding father who worked on the railroad in the background. As Cass drifts into illusion she tries to reassure herself: "I live in the present . . . if things get too rough I can go and hide in the signal box. . . . The signal box . . . it's the safest . . . no one ever looks there." In the home, the overwhelming temptation is to succumb to a re-created, comfortable past. The play, however, is not a dramatized lecture on geriatrics. The passage above ends with Cass's cry to the audience, "Where are You?" She frequently addresses the audience from the opening scene when she insists that the play begin with her arrival at Eden House until the close when she can no longer see the audience.

As in *Philadelphia,* time shifts between then and now and Cass's dialogue, like Gar's twin self, catches the audience off guard, makes them laugh, and then, when the mood shifts abruptly, uneasily consider what they have been laughing at. The audience sees that all the characters inside and outside Eden House are sustained not by visions but by illusions: the elderly in the institutional home obviously but also in the domestic home of Cass's brother where the grandmother lives in another generation, where the brother and his wife speak affectionately of their children who never visit them, where their youngest son has day-dreams fed by pulp magazines. Cass's last line is her capitulation to Eden House, the giving up of the autonomy Adam and Eve had sinned for, the return to unthinking dependence. Her line refers to all the characters and perhaps most of the audience: "Here at last. Gee, but it's a good thing to be home."

I find something of a falling off in *The Lovers* (1967). The play is actually two one-acters which deal with the theme of love from the vantage points of youth in "Winners," and middle age in "Losers." Experimentation with form continues but the content does not come alive. The fault may be in the brevity of the plays that affords only short-story-like glimpses of the charac-ters. Moreover, "Losers" is a reworked version of Friel's short story "The

Highwayman and the Saint'' and its appearance with ''Winners'' seems forced, since the forms of the two works are quite different.

In the first segment, two teenagers are ''winners'' in the game of love because they die before being tested by time. At first it seems to offer only the wryly romantic lyrical cry of Housman's ''To An Athlete Dying Young,'' but there is more. Joe and Mag's last afternoon together is in microcosm a lifetime of work, fun, arguing, planning, sensing defeat and sensing also the vision. Mag confides to Joe that ''I think this is the most important moment in my life. . . . I think sometimes that happiness, real happiness, was never discovered until we discovered it. . . . And I want to share it with everyone, everywhere.'' The vision is undercut by two dispassionate commentators who fill in family and social background, make clear that no adult in either family is happily in love, that the youngsters, if they had lived, were doomed to repeat the pattern. Those commentators also bother me. I recall *Our Town,* but the irony of their distanced omniscience is too easy; they should have had more of the balanced concern of Wilder's Stage Manager.

The middle-aged love affair of ''Losers'' is recounted by Andy, who good-naturedly tells of his frustrated mating with Hanna when they were both in their fifties. He wins his bride despite the efforts of Hanna's mother, but in the end he and Hanna are losers. The old lady, who is described as looking ''angelic . . . with a sweet, patient invalid's smile,'' uses her illness and her religion to beat them both into submission. Paired with ''Winners,'' the second play throws Friel's love message off balance: one is too distant; the other too light. Still, in fairness to Friel, these plot accounts miss the sound, verve, humor of the dialogue. Andy and Hanna do have their initial victory and Andy at least preserves a kind of balance as he grudgingly admits, ''By God, you've got to admire the aul bitch. She could handle a regiment.''

Crystal and Fox (1968) is next in a string of plays investigating love. From *Philadelphia* on they had their center in drab middle-class homes. This time the characters have no home and are in constant exile. They are a group of itinerant players offering a romantically sentimental play—sections of which we see—that heavy-handedly treats of Friel's central theme, the conflict between a calling and individual love. The central love in the play proper is that of Fox Melarkey and his wife Crystal, owners of the raggle-taggle traveling show, who as middle-aged lovers recalling the vision of their young love merge the two plays of *Lovers.*

The search this time is a total stripping. By the close Fox has separated himself from everything and everyone including all the members of his group, the show itself, and his only son. He proves to himself that even

Crystal's love can break when she leaves on being told by Fox—falsely—
that he betrayed their son to the police for a reward. Even the audience that is
experiencing this exercise in nihilism seems to be rejected: in the show
within a show, Fox loses patience with the absurdly romantic play he puts on
and the audience that supports it—"All the hoors want is a happy ending."
At the close of the play, alone on the stage, Fox twirls a wheel of fortune—
the last remnant of his show—and mumbles, "That's what I remember, just
you and me as we were, but we were young then, and . . . there were
hopes—there were warm hopes; and love alone isn't enough now, my
Crystal."

Recall "The Saucer of Larks," the title story of Friel's first short-story
collection and its depiction of an idealized harmony between a Donegal
scape and man both living and dead. In *The Mundy Scheme* harmony is
impossible in a world where the authorities replace scape with scheme.
Self-serving politicians propose to solve Ireland's fiscal problems by turning
the western counties into an international cemetery. The satire is in the
Jonsonian vein, but in lacking a moderating sensibility to measure its
madness against, it becomes a caricature. The play could use the voice of the
Sergeant in the early short story who bewailed what the land developers were
doing: "They would destroy it! . . . Dig it up and flatten it out and build
houses on it and ring it round with cement!" It is the laying waste of the spirit
as much as of the land that he cries out against. In spite of its outrageously
funny dialogue the play fails because it is filled with fools. We miss the other
voices, internal and external, that flesh out Friel's more naturalistic plays.

The Gentle Island (1971) is thematically related to *The Mundy Scheme* for
it also deals with the dying of Ireland and the waning of a romantic, pastoral
life. The vision and the voices articulating the vision form a complex
dramatic pattern which suggests that the roots of evil are found not simplisti-
cally at the politician's doorstep but in the heart of man. The island in
question, if not gentle, is passive, allowing each character to see it in terms
of his own needs. Literally, it is Inishkeen, off the Donegal coast, recently
abandoned by all but one family, but it is by extension Ireland with love of
the land coupled to high emigration figures, and symbolically it becomes the
home some in the audience cling to, others escape from, most are formed by.

The Sweeneys are the family that remains on the island: Manus, the father,
with his two sons, Joe and Philly, and Philly's wife, Sarah. The two other
characters are a pair of summer tourists, the middle-aged Peter Quinn and his
young lover Shane Harrison. Each character is revealed through his attitude
toward the island. Manus presides over a family that has begun to question
his authority. For him the island is a tribal territory in which he is chief. For

Joe it is a place to leave as soon as possible. For Philly, it is justification through unending labor; for his wife, Sarah, there is the dream of having a child. To Quinn's tourist eyes, the island is an idyll, with man "a part of a permanence" with the sea and the land. Shane Harrison, however, sees beneath the gentle dream of harmony. He notices the war booty taken from the sea by Manus, has to refuse Sarah's advances, probably has a sexual encounter with Philly, is shot almost fatally by Sarah. Shane introduces and mocks a series of romantic myths he associates with the island: cowboys and Indians, the Pied Piper; plantation life in the old south—all of them tales in which the innocent suffer. Shane, shipped back to Dublin with a shattered spine, is another damaged innocent. But then it was Shane who questioned whether "there is an ultimate reality." Neither his cynicism nor their dreams have anything to do with the reality of the island.

In the confrontation of rural family and urban tourist that is the action of *The Gentle Island,* Friel was experimenting with an insight that obviously continued to trouble him. On Saint Patrick's day, 1972, he observed in an article in the *Times Literary Supplement* that "What may well be worthy of the dramatist's probe is the deep schizophrenia of the city, because it is there, and only there, that the urban man and the rural man meet and attempt to mingle."[4] In *The Freedom of the City* (1973)—Friel's first dramatic attempt to engage the problem of increasing violence in Northern Ireland—he has three characters meet in Derry City: Lily, Michael, and Skinner, representing respectively the peasant mind, middle-class values, and urban cynicism. When the play begins they are already dead, having been killed by English soldiers, justly according to the play's Judge who conducts an inquiry into their deaths, unjustly in the light of the play which itself is an inquiry. A number of impersonal authorities report to the Judge including a sociologist who also acts as a commentator as in "Winners," dispassionately noting that the real conflict is not so much between the three "outlaws" and the authorities as among the three while they illegally but accidentally occupy the Guildhall for a day. In the short time and tight area they share, we see that the old culture is breaking up: for Lily the securities of place and family, however dismal, are being eroded; for Michael, middle-class values no longer work; for Skinner, his urban Dandyism, his calculated dismissal of place, family, and values, threaten to evolve into a commitment to international terrorism.

Escalating civil tensions are faced by characters who refuse to be reduced to the political banalities of T.V. commentary or the sentimentalizing of a balladeer's verses. Friel avoids what I find to be the dangerous tendency toward icy distance of his earlier plays and permits—controlled and

warranted—sympathy for his characters. In a brilliant stroke he has the dead
provide their own epilogue. Lily, speaking now with words she could never
have mustered while alive, sums up the blind acceptance of Michael and the
blind rejection of Skinner in a confession of her own blindness that reminds
me—and this not for the first time in Friel—of Thornton Wilder:

And in the silence before my body disintegrated in a purple convulsion, I thought I
glimpsed a tiny truth: that life had eluded me because never once in my forty-three
years had an experience, an event, even a small unimportant happening been
isolated, and assessed, and articulated. And the fact that this, my last experience,
was defined by this perception, this was the culmination of sorrow. In a way I died of
grief.

Again we have a human action purely contemplated and judged by an author,
by an audience, after wrenching dislocation of consciousness.

Volunteers (1975) continues Friel's inquiry into the breakup of our culture. The place is an excavation of a Viking site that is soon to be buried
under a multi-story hotel. The volunteers are five political prisoners on
parole helping with the work. Now that the dig is drawing to a close, they
learn that their fellow-prisoners intend to kill them when they return to the
cells because they cooperated with the authorities. Two of the prisoners, Butt
and Smiler, are from the country, two others, Keeney and Pyne, in their city
brashness and flow of routines and impromptu jokes, recall Skinner in *The
Freedom of the City*. The fifth prisoner, Knox, comes from an upper-level
family but has abandoned all the values held by his class. The five represent
the three social levels of *Freedom* and share with the three characters of the
earlier play an intimate awareness of death.

The site is described as an "encapsulated history, a tangible précis of the
story of Irish man." But like *Freedom* it expands beyond Ireland. The site
"looks more like a bomb crater—or maybe a huge womb—or . . . like a
prison-yard." The play becomes an "encapsulated history" of the culture
that is passing, including references to God, Adonis, Thor, Jesus, the Queen
of the May, Leif Erikson, the Pope, Calvinism, Knox, Sir Thomas More, Sir
Francis Drake, Shakespeare, the Christian Brothers, Keats's "To a Grecian
Urn" and "To Autumn," Wellington, Karl Marx, the Titanic, Woodrow
Wilson, Parnell and O'Shea, De Valera, Hitler, and King Kong. I am
tempted to include King in the list, the often repeated name of the off-stage
chief archeologist who profits from everyone's digging while aborting the
whole effort.

The major findings are the remnants of a Viking home, the skeleton of a
tenth-century exiled Viking, and the patched-together shards of an ancient

vase. The home and Viking dominate the stage, though all that is left of the home is an outline; of the Viking, a skeleton. The home, particularly cared for by the countryman Butt, is described as "the size of a prison cell." Again home is lost security, prison, need for escape. As with the home, so with the digs which are described as looking like a womb and a bomb crater: security, prison, need for escape. As with the digs, so with the world. The prison officer says of the prisoners: "Outside it's the same thing—they're a dirty word with their mates outside, too." There is no security out there and there is no place to escape.

Keeney, describing the aims of archeology, provides us with the inner action of the play: "What we are all engaged in here is really a thrilling voyage in self-discovery." The prisoners' speculations about the life and death of the skeleton—familiarly known as Lief—become a Rorschach test. Characteristically, Keeney does not tell a direct story; he plays around the skeleton, calls to it, unveils it, provides it with a mock Christian burial—a clown being his own grave digger. No wonder Keeney asks at the beginning of the play and reports that Lief asks the same question at the close: "Was Hamlet really mad?"

Smiler, a simple, inarticulate countryman, does not tell his story. His intellect—like the urn he is associated with—has been shattered, in his case, by police brutality. Smiler was the one who found the urn shards. When patched together, the urn is identified by Keeney as "Smiler restored; Smiler full, free and integrated." But for all our science and art, culture fails. Near the close we hear that during her music exams the prison officer's daughter played the cello with "grace and discretion" but presumably without understanding, duplicating her father's performance with the men. At the close, Butt, the other countryman and protector of Smiler, picks up the urn and smashes it in front of the archeologist. The remnants of the Viking home are already washing away, the urn is smashed, the Viking is described at his reburial as "one of nature's gentlemen" and "hungry and vicious." Science and art fail man, and man fails himself.

In his recent work Friel has been continuing his experiments searching for new methods to express recurring patterns while avoiding allegorical rigidity by remaining true to the cadences and characters of the people he knew and knows. In *Living Quarters* (1977), the self destruction of an Irish family is informed by a Celtic variation of the House of Atreus. In his last play to date, *Faith Healer* (1979), the informing vision is the scapegoat, who saves by dying, the fate of Christ.

The Clytemnestra of *Living Quarters* is related to women in such stories as "Aunt Maggie" and "Stories on the Verandah," as well as the "aul bitch'' in ''Losers''—women who control through sickness, religious commitment, and willfulness. The deadly mother, Louise Butler, died six years before the events of the play and we only see her in the disturbed family she leaves behind: her husband Frank Butler, her twenty-four-year-old son Ben who is described as a ''mother's boy,'' and her three daughters, Helen, a divorcee of twenty-seven, Miriam, a married woman of twenty-five, and Tina, eighteen, ''the pet of the family.'' When the play opens the Commandant is the returning hero of a U.N. campaign in the Mid-East. This Agamemnon attributes his victory to the memory of his young bride of a few months, Anna. He meets death at his own hand but it is as though the house rose against him. Butler fulfilled his duty toward his family but was never able to communicate with them. His wife held him responsible for her ill health and alienated him from both Ben and Helen. During the father's absence, Ben has an affair with his father's young wife and permits the news to spread to the barracks. Helen gives the father no support since she feels he failed her at the time of her divorce by not standing up to her willful mother's intimidating ways. In the dead Mrs. Butler and the living Mrs. Butler, Friel contrasts the two types of women that recur in his work: the death bringer, usually associated with religion, and the life bringer, ''passionate,'' as Anna is described, and ''direct in speech and manner.''

Friel's formal approach in *Living Quarters* is reminiscent of Pirandello's *Six Characters in Search of an Author*. The events leading up to Butler's suicide are reenacted by the family years afterward. Again Friel uses a commentator, who also is the director of the action. ''Sir,'' as he is called, prompts thoughts of Auden's ''Petition'' and a distant, formal God. But Friel succeeds in both distancing and giving warmth to ''Sir'' because he is made in the characters' own images. He reads from a ledger which he explains the family conceived ''out of some deep psychic necessity'' to ''record . . . everything that was said and done that day.'' He himself was conceived of the same psychic need as ''the ultimate arbiter'' to whom they give a total authority they constantly try to circumvent. Under ''Sir's'' direction the reenactment is a realization of Lily's longing in *The Freedom of the City* to have had even one experience in life ''isolated, and assessed, and articulated.'' From another perspective ''Sir'' is the ideal psychologist opening the play's Oedipus/Atreus implications, leading characters into a better understanding of themselves, especially Ben who recalls his uncontrollable laughter at his mother's funeral and his childhood confession to his father that ''I always loved him and always hated her.'' At the close ''Sir'' apologizes to Anna for not introducing her. She claims there is no need and intimates that her story is not over. The curse of the House of Butler is upon her and will continue to be worked out in her life, Helen's and Tina's.

In the four monologues that are *Faith Healer,* the play's three characters attribute the choice of "The Way You Look Tonight" as a theme song to one of the others: Frank, the faith healer, in his opening and closing monologues, attributes it to his manager Teddy, who, in his monologue, attributes it to Frank's mistress, Grace, who, in her monologue, attributes it to Frank. Facts are evasive even when the action, as here, is stripped to essentials.

The monologues go beyond the facts in their search for meaning. Teddy and Grace try to understand their years with Frank and he tries to understand the life he spent with them. Faith, art, people, prove as illusive as facts. Frank's final insight is the ultimate romantic one:

I became possessed by a strange and trembling intimation: that the whole corporeal world—the cobbles, the trees, the sky . . . somehow they had shed their physical reality and had become mere imagings . . . that even we had ceased to be physical and existed only in spirit, only in the need we had for each other.

Frank speculates about whether he has awesome powers or is only a con man, wonders whether when his powers work upon a maimed man, the cure is due to faith in the healer, the healed, or faith itself. In this multi-leveled narration all speculations are right and wrong. The one certainty is Frank's scapegoat role, his taking on others' pain, his emptying himself of vision, until finally upon his homecoming to Ireland, he is savagely murdered by disappointed peasants. Before his death, he celebrates with the wedding guests who will kill him, "toasts to the departed groom and his prowess, to the bride and fertility . . . to all things ripe and eager for the reaper. A dionysian night."

Exile, homecoming, loyalty, but autonomy at any cost, they are all in the play but the romantic theme that dominates is the search for harmony. Frank intones the names of the little towns his wagon wheels through in an incantation to the spirit of the land and a preparation for the broken-spirited audience he is to meet. Grace says of him that "Before a performance he'd be . . . in such complete mastery that everything harmonized for him." Teddy says of a successful performance that the wonder was not only in the cures but that "he had given them some great content in themselves." Before the bloody sacrifice of Frank's death, the thought crosses his mind of "a fulfillment, an integration, a full blossoming."

And in no play since *Crystal and Fox* does Friel better grapple with the question of drama itself and the ritual it is. The play opens with Frank addressing three rows of on-stage chairs so placed that the actual audience is a continuation of that other audience. The magic Frank's "other audience" half fears, half expects is the same magic Friel's "actual audience" has its ambivalences about. How many want the miracle of being raised from the dead? To draw the parallels more exactly between scapegoat and dramatist is outside the range of this paper. Grace touches on the matter when she recalls that the sick people who came to Frank were "to him . . . real enough, but not real as persons, real as fictions, his fictions, extensions of himself that came into being only because of him."

Friel seems quite conscious of his bitter romanticism. In the *T.L.S.* article already cited, he writes that to understand anything about the history or present health of Irish drama, one must first ". . . recognize two dominant elements in the Irish mind: One is a passion for the land; the other a paranoiac individualism." Whether it be a monastery, a tent, a peasant hut, an archeological dig, a nursing home, a traveling show, we find the central character preoccupied with home, knowing that even if you could go home again, you would not. Both Frank and Grace tell of earlier attempts to go home only to return to the road. Frank's final homecoming is the ultimate autonomy, the harmony of death.

In the *T.L.S.* article, Friel writes of form as well as content. He concludes that "there must be a far greater distinction between the Irishman who suffers and the artist's mind which creates." His plays taken in sequence are a demonstration of his effort to make that distinction, achieve that distance: the split character, the disinterested commentator, the voices of the dead, juxtaposed time, the play within a play, the prison within a prison, the myth within a plot. At his best the matter and the form are one, as in *Faith Healer* where he merges all his techniques and has the dead act out their own commentaries while maintaining a loyalty to his romantic contents, a vision of home that is so complex it demands being retold in new forms, though always in the cadences and confines of Northern Ireland.

Notes

1. The short stories were published in England by Gollancz and in the United States by Doubleday: *The Saucer of Larks* (1962); *The Gold in the Sea* (1966). The following plays were published in England by Faber and Faber: *Philadelphia, Here I Come!* (1965), *The Loves of Cass McGuire* (1967), *Lovers* (1969), *Crystal and Fox* (1970), *The Gentle Island* (1971), *The Freedom of the City* (1974), *Living Quarters* (1978), *Volunteers* (1980), and *The Faith Healer* (1980). Plays published in the United States were *The Enemy Within* (Newark, Del.: Proscenium Press, 1975) and *Two Plays: Crystal and Fox* and *The Mundy Scheme* (New York: Farrar, Straus & Giroux, 1970).

2. My source for this information as well as other facts about Friel's life is D. E. S. Maxwell, *Brian Friel* (Lewisburg, Pa.: Bucknell University Press, 1973).

3. ''The Dry Salvages,'' *The Complete Poems and Plays* (New York: Harcourt, Brace and Company, 1952), p. 133.

4. ''Plays, Peasant and Unpeasant,'' *Times Literary Supplement,* March 17, 1972, pp. 305–6.

Elegy for Aran:
The Poetry of Máirtín O'Direáin

Maureen Murphy

In his Introduction to *Nuafhilí 3,* Séamas O'Céileacháir credits Máirtín O'Direáin with a pioneering role in the development of modern poetry in Irish. "Sa bliain naoi-deag, ceirthe's dó d'fhoilsigh Máirtín O'Direáin cnuasach de dhánta *Coinnle Geala* agus ceaptar gurbh é sin an tús."[1] (In 1942 Máirtín O'Direáin published *Coinnle Geala,* a collection of poems that is considered the beginning [of poetry in Modern Irish].) The title *Coinnle Geala* (Bright Candles) comes from a line in the poem "Coinnle ar Lasadh" (Lighted Candles) that describes the rural custom of putting candles in the windows on Christmas Eve as a welcome to Mary and the Child. The poems in *Coinnle Geala* were themselves welcoming lights to poets writing in Irish and to their readers.

There was virtually no contemporary literature in Irish when Eoin Mac-Neill founded the Gaelic League in 1893. While the League's aim was not to create a literature in Modern Irish but to preserve and extend the use of Irish as a spoken language, literature was clearly essential to the language revival. As editor of *Irisleabhar na Gaedhilge* (The Gaelic Journal), MacNeill realized the need to demonstrate that a contemporary national literature could be created in the Irish language and that such a literature should be based on living speech.[2] When he became the first editor of the League paper *An Claidheamh Soluis* (The Sword of Light), he continued to encourage the use of the *caint na ndaoine* (ordinary speech) and to argue for a modern literary language based on actual use.

It was a decision that among other things encouraged writers in the Connacht Gaeltacht, a region that did not claim a classical poetic tradition like that of seventeenth- and eighteenth-century Munster, but a region whose folk tradition, the intense feeling and natural imagery one observes in Douglas Hyde's collections *The Love Songs of Connacht* (1893) and *The*

Religious Songs of Connacht (1906), provided writers of the first generation—Padraic O'Conaire, Padraic Pearse and Douglas Hyde—as well as of the later generation—Máirtín O'Cadháin, Liam O'Flaherty and Máirtín O'Direáin with both subject and language based on everyday life and speech.

Critics frequently quote Thomas MacDonagh's remark introducing his discussion of Padraic Pearse's modest volume of lyrics *Suantraidhe agus Goltraidhe* (Lullabies and Laments) in *Literature in Ireland,* "Irish has produced very little original personal work since the beginning of the revival"; however, in his survey of literature in Irish he neglected to mention Padraic O'Conaire's seven short stories published in *An Claidheamh Soluis* between 1906 and 1913, stories included among the ten in the standard O'Conaire collection *Scothscéalta* (Best Stories).[3] While an authentic prose developed within the first decade of the language revival, Irish would have to wait till the 1940s for a poetic voice with equal authority. That voice emerged partly as a result of history—isolation as a consequence of Ireland's neutrality during World War II, certainly as a result of literacy: a generation of writers, many with university educations, combined a fluency in the Irish language with a knowledge of literature.

In 1935 Irish students at the colleges of the National University formed an organization called An Comhchaidreamh (Association) to coordinate the activities of their respective college Irish societies. In 1942 An Comhchaidreamh launched a monthly magazine called *Comhar* (Partnership); the Gaelic League followed with *Feasta* (Henceforth) in 1948. Both provided outlets for poets writing in Irish.

The Gúm (Plan) was established by the Irish government in 1926 to publish books in Irish, but it was Seán Sáirséal O'hEigeartaigh's firm of Sáirséal agus Dill, founded in 1945, whose titles and whose high standard of book production demonstrated that there was a market for literature in Irish. The creation of An Club Leabhar (The Book Club) in 1948 and another for junior readers, Club Leabhar ne Sóisear in 1956, further provided a reading public for poets writing in the Irish language. In more recent years two substantial prizes created by the Irish American Cultural Institute recognize achievement in Irish letters.

The best measure of the success of these efforts is the appearance of a second generation of poets writing in Irish: Mícheál O'Siadhail, Tomas MacSiomóin, Nuala ni Dhomhnaill and Michael Hartnett to follow the three major poets in Modern Irish: Máirtín O'Direáin, Seán O'Ríordáin and Máire mhac an tSaoi. O'Direáin, O'Ríordáin and mhac an tSaoi, the poets of the

Renaissance of Modern Irish Literature, brought a whole new direction to poetry in Irish. Unlike some Irish poets writing in English who have experimented with traditional Irish prosody, notably Austin Clarke, O'Direáin, O'Ríordáin and mhac an tSaoi chose *vers libre* and the more natural rhythms of speech.[4] O'Direáin reaches further back than seventeenth-century classical poetry or thirteenth-century medieval poetry to the compact, concrete imagery of early Irish nature poetry. The only native speaker, O'Direáin's real ease with the Aran idiom provides the basis for a poetic diction that is broad enough to include all dialects, borrowings from past poets and particularly words from a favorite source, Father Dineen's *Irish-English Dictionary*.

He was born November 10, 1910, on Aran (Inishmore), the island that in the twentieth century has produced two sets of writing brothers: Máirtín and Tom O'Direáin and Liam and Tom O'Flaherty as well as Breandán O hEithir and Pat Mullen. Apart from what he learned at the local national school, O'Direáin says his education came from life, from other people and from reading. The death of his father when O'Direáin was a child further limited the opportunities for a poor boy on Aran; however, at seventeen he had a chance to sit for the Post Office examination. Tutored by his schoolmaster, O'Direáin passed the examination in 1927 and went to the Galway Post Office in January, 1928. He was transferred to Dublin in August, 1937. He continued to work as a civil servant but in later years moved to the Secondary Branch of the Department of Education and finally to the position of Registrar in the National College of Art.

O'Direáin was introduced to the literary movement in Modern Irish during his Galway years. He served as secretary to the local branch of the Gaelic League; he acted in the Taibhdhearc na Gaillimhe (Galway Theatre) and in December, 1938, at a lecture given by Torna (Prof. Tadhg O'Donoghue), he discovered poetry. Like Moliere's M. Jourdain, he was astonished to realize his people had been speaking poetry to him all his life. O'Direáin says he does not recall a single sentence of the talk but that he remembers that Torna contrasted the way a thing is expressed in prose with the way a thing is expressed in poetry and that convinced him to stop experimenting with prose and to turn to poetry (''Mise agus a Fhilíocht,'' p. 12). He was twenty-nine.

In the next forty years O'Direáin wrote nearly three hundred poems, mainly lyrics. The most prolific of the Modern Irish poets, he is the author of nine books of poetry: *Coinnle Geala* (Bright Candles, 1942), *Dánta Aniar* (Poems from the West, 1943), *Rogha Dánta* (Selected Poems, 1949), *Ó*

Mórna agus Dánta Eile ("From Mórna" and Other Poems, 1957), *Ár Ré Dhearóil* (Our Wretched Era, 1962), *Cloch Choirnéil* (Cornerstone, 1966), *Crainn is Cairde* (Trees and Friends, 1970), *Ceacht an Éin* (The Bird's Lesson, 1979) and *Dánta 1939–1979* (Poems 1939–1979, 1980). A collection of essays *Feamainn Bhealtaine* (May Seaweed) appeared in 1961.

His work has won recognition at home and abroad. In 1965 he won the Arts Council Prize; in 1967 he won one of the prizes given by the Irish American Cultural Institute and in 1977 he was awarded a D. Litt. by the National University of Ireland and the Ossian Prize by the Foundation F. V.S. in Hamburg.

Aran is a major theme in O'Direáin's work. His poem "Ionraiceas" (Honesty), which may be an allusion to the proverb "Tá ionraiceas os cionn margaidh" (honesty is above bargaining or honesty is the best policy), explains the choice:

> Dúirt file mór tráth
> go mba oileán is grá mná
> Ábhar is fáth mo dháin;
> Is fíor a chan mo bhráthair.
>
> Coinneod féin an t-oileán
> Seal eile i mo dhán,
> Toisc a ionraice atá
> Cloch, carraig is trá.
>
> A great poet once said
> an island and a woman's love
> are the matter and reason for my poems.
> It is truth you speak, my brother.
>
> I'll keep the island
> another while in my poem
> because of the integrity
> that is in stone, rock and strand.[5]

Aran offers O'Direáin not just integrity but the intensity of feeling that is essential to the lyric, the emotional ties to place—particularly to one's own place or ancestral place—that informs Irish poetry. His own recollection of his leave-taking of Aran as place, written some thirty years later, still reflects that depth of feeling.

Chuaigh mé suas ar na creaga tráthnóna De hAoine agus bhuail sprocht de chineál eile mé. Chonaic mé an raithneach mar bheadh féasóg rua ar éadan lom na gcreaga. Chonaic mé Dún Eoghanachta agus teach na scoile siar uaim. Bhí Dún Aongusa ansiúd thoir go maorga aonraic ar bharr na haille. D'fhág mé slán ag raithneach is ag dúnta, ag creaga is ag buailte. Ní fheicfinn go deo arís iad, ach ar feadh cúpla seachtain den bhliain.[6]

I went up to the crags Friday evening and sadness of another kind struck me. I saw the bracken like a red beard on the bare face of the cliffs. I saw Dun Eoghanacht and the schoolhouse to the west. Dun Aengus was over to the east in solitary dignity on top of the cliff. I said good-by to the bracken, to the forts, to the crags and to the booleys. I would never see them again except for a couple of weeks each year.

O'Direáin wasn't going to America. He was going to Galway, a city in his own county some thirty miles away.

It is precisely O'Direáin's position as an Aran emigrant that provides the distance to watch the traditional culture being eroded by forces outside and inside the island. Even the simple lyrics observant of Aran life like "Cuimhní Cinn" (Mind's Memories), "Cuireadh do Mhuire" (Invitation to Mary), and "Rún na mBan" (Women's Secret) have a special poignancy.

> Cuimhní Cinn
> Maireann a gcuimhne fós i m'aigne:
> Báiníní bána is léinte geala,
> Léinte gorma is veistí glasa,
> Treabhsair is dráir de bhréidín baile
> Bhíodh ar fheara cásacha aosta
> Ag triall ar an Aifreann maidin Domhnaigh
> De shiúl cos ar aistear fhada,
> A mhusclaíodh i m'óige smaointe ionamsa
> Ar ghlaine, ar úire, is fós ar bheanníocht.
>
> Maireann a gcuimhne fós i m'aigne:
> Cótaí cóirithe fada dearga,
> Cótaí gorma le plúirín daite,
> Seálta troma aníos as Gaillimh,
> Bhíodh ar mhná pioctha néata
> Ag triall ar an Aifreann mar a gcéanna;
> Is cé go bhfuilid ag imeacht as faisean,
> Maireann a gcuimhne fós i m'aigne
> Is mairfidh cinnte go dté mé i dtalamh. (*Dánta 1939–1979*, p. 23.)

> Their memory lives in my mind
> White flannel and bright shirts
> Blue shirts and grey vests
> Trousers' tweed of homespun frieze
> Worn by men of venerable age
> On Sunday morning going to mass
> Travelling the long way by foot

That in my youth inspired thoughts
Of purity, freshness—
Always of blessedness.

Their memory lives in my mind
Long, patched petticoats of red
Blue coats dyed with indigo
Heavy handsome Galway shawls
On comely women, tidy, trim
Going to mass as they've always done
And though they're going out of fashion
Their memory lives in my mind
It will live there surely—
Till I'm in the ground.

There is more than nostalgia here. O'Direáin's association of traditional clothes with traditional virtues recalls Brian Mac Giolla Phádraig's poem "Faisean Chláir Eibhir" (These Fashions on the Plains of Eibhear) where the poet's scorn for English clothes on Irish upstarts is a way to criticize the English social order that replaced Gaelic society. In "Cuireadh do Mhuire" when the poet asks Mary where she will seek shelter this year (1942), his invitation to his island brings with it the suggestion that in a darkened Europe there is still light in Aran.

An important early poem "Aran 1947" uses the disappearance of local customs to symbolize the decline or death of the island. The ominous refrain "Níor chualas" (I did not hear) marks the end of communal activities: visiting in houses at night and storytelling, but it is the end of the "stone of strength" competition after mass that is particularly portentous, for it is a sign that the young male strength on the island has gone and that "Ní don óige feasta / An sceirdoileán cúng úd" (Dánta 1939–1979, p. 34). (The young shall not again / possess that bleak narrow island.)

O'Direáin has catalogued the kinds of threats to Aran: historical, natural and human. "Sic Transit," the title of a 1955 poem that alludes to Thomas á Kempis's quote from the Imitation of Christ "Sic transit gloria mundi" (O how quickly doth the glory of the world pass away), is based on Aran history that O'Direáin knew from local folklore and from Father Martin O'Donnell's Oileain Arann (1930). The poem refers to the Mac Teige O'Briens of Thomond, "Lords of the Islands" from the thirteenth century until they were defeated by Morogh na Doe O'Flaherty, one of the Iar-Chonnacht O'Flaherties who defeated the O'Briens in 1584. The O'Briens petitioned Elizabeth I for return of the Islands, but advised of their strategic position, she awarded them to John Rawson of Athlone in 1587 who promised to garrison English soldiers there.[7] Sir Morogh O'Flaherty of Bunowen is buried in Teglach Enda (Enda's Household), the graveyard southeast of Kilronan believed to be the burial place of 120 saints (*RSAI*, p. 83). The last local landlord, O'Flaherty Johnson, lived in the big house near Kilmurvey and was reputed to have driven the local people to the crags at the back of the island.[8] A poem of dispossession, "Sic Transit" owes something to O'Direáin's poetic predecessors of the seventeenth century Dáibhí Ó Bruadair and Aogán Ó Rathaille.

> Sic Transit . . .
> Clann Mhic Thaidhg, na flatha
> Faoi raibh na hoileaín thiar
> Cúig céad bliain go léir,
> Síol Bhriain na n-éacht,
> An pór teann tréan,
> Cá bhfuil a nead cré?
>
> Na flatha a bhris a réim,
> A choinnigh a gcion féin
> Den talamh garbh gann
> Ceithre céad bliain dá n-éis,
> Gheobhair i reilig thuas ar aill
> Leaba a bhfualais is a nead.
>
> Cois cuain atá a bhfeart
> Láimh le trá ne gceann,
> Ar an tuama tá armas greanta
> Is mana ar leacht in airde,
> Mana a bheireann dúshlán Flaitheartach:
> *Fortuna favit fortibus-*
> Ach tá meirg ag creimeadh an ráille.
>
> Tá meirg ag comhrá le seanchóiste
> I gclós an tí mhóir le seal anall,
> Níl lua ar na flatha ná tuairisc,
> I dteach a sean ná i gCill Cholmáin,
> Ó chuaigh an Flaitheartach deiridh síos,
> Le líon a fhualais san uaigh láimh le trá. (*Dánta, 1939–1979,* p. 70.)
>
> The O'Briens of Thomond
> Were lords of the islands
> Five hundred years
> The sword their sceptre
> Their blood as strong as their name—
> Where is their resting place?

Lords of Connaught replaced them
Conquered and kept
A parcel of gaunt ground
For thirteen generations—
The graveyard on the cliff
Is their resting place.

The O'Flaherties lie on the cliff
Above the blood-soaked strand
On their tomb a coat of arms
A slogan carved on the headstone
Their proud defiance perpetuated
But rust eats at the rail.

Rust talks to an ancient coach
In the close of the big house
But no one talks of the lords themselves
In their ancestral house in Kil Colman
Since the last O'Flaherty went to join
His kin in the graveyard above the sea.   trans. Douglas Sealy.[9]

Like Donagh MacDonagh's poem on the Anglo-Normans "A Warning to Conquerers," "Sic Transit" pauses over the monuments of former conquerers reclaimed by the Irish countryside; however, the Aran invaders were not Anglo-Normans but the Irish themselves: the O'Briens and the O'Flaherties. The poem also reflects the extraordinary psychological distance between the islanders and the rest of Ireland. The truth of Benedict Kiely's remark "so far as Ireland was concerned, Liam O'Flaherty always remained a tourist from his native rock" can be demonstrated by an Aranman's conversation with his parish priest, "Thall annsin thoir atá Eire" (Over there in the east is Ireland).[10]

Some Aran tradition suggests it is neither the people nor the land that will prevail; it will be the sea. Engulfing waves are part of Aran history and are a vivid memory in the folk mind. The extraordinary wave that swept across Aran from east to northwest about 1640 could still be recalled in 1878 (RSAI, p. 73). More menacing still was the spectacular mountain of water that rose up the cliff on a calm day, August 15, 1852, and washed fifteen fishermen off to their death (RSAI, pp. 84–85). In his recent study of Liam O'Flaherty, P. A. Sheeran refers to a recurrent image of an apocalyptic flooding of Gort na gCapall and the middle of Aran by a giant wave from the Atlantic (Sheeran, p. 15).

O'Direáin's poem "Bua na Mara" (The Victory of the Sea) is less evocative of an apocalyptic wave than of the isolating forces of the sea which will gradually erode the islanders' will to remain "imprisoned on bleak cliffs and black skerry."

> Ní mhairfidh na fir fada
> Feasta san oileán rúin,
> Ní bheidh neach ar an gcladach
> Chun dúshlán na mara a thabhairt;
> Cuirfidh an fharraige
> An sceirdcharraig úd
> Faoina glas-smacht dubhach
> Canfaidh sí a buachaintic
> Sin creill an oileáin rúin. (*Dánta, 1939–1979,* p, 51.)

>   Defeat
> My people, the gallant, the tall
> Will leave Aran forever—
> No one will stand on the beach
> To defy the rising waves—
> The sea will imprison
> Bleak cliffs and black skerry
> With its curtain of cold chains,
> The ocean's triumphant chant
> Sounds the knell of Aran.   trans. Douglas Sealy, p. 65.

Seamus Heaney's "Lovers on Aran" shares neither the destructive vision nor the desolation of O'Dircáin's poem, but its relationship of mutuality between sea and land excludes the islander.

> Did sea define the land or land the sea?
> Each drew new meaning from the wave's collision
> Sea broke on land to full identity[11]

It is emigration, of course, that is the real threat to Aran. While the population in the Irish countryside has declined, the consequences are not as dramatic for any part of the Irish mainland as they are for Ireland's islands, some of which have been cleared when their populations have fallen too low to provide basic services. The population of Aran, for example, dropped from 2,312 (1852) to 933 (1961).

Emigration as a theme has been a shaping force in O'Direáin's world and work. Among his earliest recollections are those of stories told around the fire by people who had lived in America.

Ní raibh máthair clainne ar an dá bhaile nár chaith seal éigin i Meiriceá. Chloisinn féin cuid mhaith cainte uatha ar Boston, ar Dorchester, ar Woburn agus áiteanna eile tráth a mbídís cruinnithe cois tine.

Bhí an oiread eolais acu ar na cathracha céanna is bhí acu ar Ghaillimh. Déarfainn go raibh agus níos mó. Ní bheadh eolas ar bith ag a leithéidí ar Bhaile Átha Cliath ná ar aon chathair i Sasana an tráth úd. (*Feamainn Bhealtaine,* pp. 27–28)

There wasn't a mother of a family in the two villages who hadn't spent some time in America. I myself used to hear a good bit of talk from them about Boston, Dorchester, Woburn and other places when they would be gathered around the fire.

They knew as much about those cities as they knew about Galway. I would say as much and more. They had no idea at all about the likes of Dublin or any English city of that time.

To read O'Direáin is to realize the extent to which emigration is a controlling force in the Irish countryside. While emigration is a more modest proposal than Swift's, the phenomenon of children raised for export has shaped rural Irish culture for the past century. Social scientists have paid surprisingly little attention to this phenomenon, but the works of Aran writers reflect the significance of emigration in the culture and, like the islanders for whom emigration is a preoccupation, they equate emigration with a kind of death. Tom O'Flaherty has written ". . . this going to America was the nearest thing to death. It was a life sentence of exile, except in rare cases."[12]

O'Direáin also links emigration and death. His poem "Dínit an Bhróin" (The Dignity of Sorrow) juxtaposes women in black and the Kilronan pier, the Aran embarkation point, to suggest that their mourning clothes could be related either to death or to emigration.

> Nochtaíodh domsa tráth
> Dínit mhór an bhróin,
> Ar fheiceáil dom beirt bhan
> Ag siúl amach ó shlua
> I bhfeisteas caointe dubh
> Gan focal astu beirt:
> D'imigh an dínit leo
> Ón slua callánach mór.
>
> Bhí freastalán istigh
> ó línéar ar an ród,
> Fuadar faoi gach n-aon,
> Gleo ann is caint ard;
> Ach an bheirt a bhí ina dtost,
> A shiúil amach leo féin
> I bhfeisteas caointe dubh,
> D'migh an dínit leo. (*Dánta 1939*–1979, p. 21.)
>
> Once I was shown
> The great dignity of sorrow

> On seeing two women
> Walk out from the crowd.
> In their clothes of sadness
> Not speaking a word,
> Dignity went with them
> In the murmur of the crowd.
>
> There was a tender at quayside
> From the liner in the bay,
> And everyone was busy
> With noise and loud talk,
> But two there were quiet,
> Who walked out by themselves;
> In their clothes of sadness,
> Dignity went with them.

The poem speaks to the community values of restraint and acceptance of personal tragedy, values reflected in Aran literature in the stoicism of John Millington Synge's Maurya in "Riders to the Sea" and in the resignation at the end of Liam O'Flaherty's short story "Going into Exile" when the two old neighbors lead Mrs. Feeney back to her kitchen after seeing her children leave to go to America. " 'There is nothing that time will not cure,' said one. 'Yes. Time and patience,' said the other.' "[13]

It may be that part of the acceptance is tied up with ambivalence, for it is not only the young emigrants who have mixed feelings about staying or going; parents share the same ambivalence. Children leave so the family can survive.

O'Direáin's poems of the passing of traditional life on Aran do not simply express the romantic theme of primitive life doomed, but they name the forces on the island that encourage it. "Deireadh Oileáin" (Death of an Island), a fine later poem from *Ó Mórna* (1957), sympathetically considers the reason why young women leave the island taking with them the promise of future generations. The quality of their lives—the drudgery, the world bound by field and fireside, the menace of local gossip send the women away leaving the islandmen cheerless bachelors.

The urbanized peasant, the gombeen man whose greed corrupts rural society, the figure of whom both O'Direáin and O'Flaherty are contemptuous, is associated with sterility. In "De Dheasca an Úis" (Because of Usury), O'Direáin indicts usury, or the habit of mind it produces, with the responsibility for sterility on the island.

> De dheasca an úis:
> Tá an ghin sa mbroinn

> I ngeall don léan dubh,
> Is tuilleadh a ghinfí
> Gan ghineadh in aonchor (*Dánta 1939–1979,* p. 72.)

> Because of the interest on the loan:
> The embryo in the womb
> Is mortgaged to grief
> And women mourn the children
> They never conceived.   Sealy, p. 64

Frank O'Brien has identified Ezra Pound's Canto 45 "With *Usura*" as a major source for the poem.[14] Both contrast natural increase and sterility and suggest that procreation proceeds from goodness; both charge that usury cripples and corrupts.

> Usura slayeth the child in the womb
> It stayeth the young man's courting
> It hath brought palsy to bed, lyeth
> between the young bride and her bridegroom
>
>   CONTRA NATURAM
> They have brought whores for Eleusis
> Corpses are set to banquet
> At the behest of usura[15]

For O'Direáin emigration is a personal as well as communal tragedy. Eoghan O hAnluain traces O'Direáin's concern with the countryman transplanted to the city in his poem "Stoite" (Uprooted), which appeared in *Rogha Dánta* (*Selected Poems,* 1949) and which compares the kind of work done by Aranmen as they tamed their rocky island with the work done in dusty offices by their sons, ". . . a theme which O'Direáin has pursued relentlessly ever since: uprooted rural man astray in the complexities of the city and cut loose from the moral sanctions of traditional life. The theme received its most exhaustive treatment in *Ár Ré Dhearóil* where he explores the moral crisis inherent in 'an chathair fhallsa,' the city of deceit."[16] Not only is O'Direáin's islander alienated in the modern city, but he also experiences the particular sense of loss in being not only away from his community but divorced from it as well.

However much O'Direáin criticizes rootless life in the *cathair fhallsa,* he admits that life there will continue. While the civil servant's monument of paper is no match for the monument of stone in walls and cottages Aranmen have wrested from nature, civil servants have sons. Aran may survive, but if it does not, the stone walls and cottages, like the stone monuments to the dead along the road from Kilronan to Kilmurvey, will bear mute witness to the deeds of Aranmen, and O'Direáin's Aran poems, his *beochaoineadh* (elegy for a living person) for his native island, will bear witness to their passing.

Notes

1. Seamas Ó Céilacháir, *Nuafhilí 3* (Baile Átha Cliath: An Gúm, 1980), p. v. Also see Flann Mac an t Saoir, "Smaointe Faoi Nua-Fhilíocht na Gaeilge," *Comhar* 25 (Bealtaine, 1967):87–94. O'Direáin believes the growth of modern poetry in Irish was a far more gradual process. See "Mise agus a Fhilíocht," his introduction to *Ó Mórna agus Dánta Eile* (Baile Átha Cliath: Cló Morainn, 1957), p. 13.
2. See discussion in Brian O'Cuív, "MacNeill and the Irish Language," in F.X. Martin and F.J. Byrne, eds., *The Scholar Revolutionary, Eoin MacNeill 1867–1945* (Shannon: Irish University Press, 1973), pp. 9–10. MacNeill's decision to publish An t-Athair Peadar Ua Laoghaire's *Séadna* in *Irisleabhar na Gaedhilge* between 1894–1897 was based on that commitment to literature in the living language.
3. Thomas MacDonagh, *Literature in Ireland* (Dublin: Talbot Press, 1916), p. 143.
4. O'Direáin discusses his use of the natural rhythms of language as he heard it in his "Mise agus a Fhilíocht," p. 14. For Austin Clarke's notes on his use of traditional Irish versecraft see his notes to *Pilgrimage and Other Poems* (1929), in *Selected Poems*, ed. Thomas Kinsella (Dublin: Dolmen Press, 1976), p. 190. For a judgment on Clarke as a poet in the Irish mode see John Montague, "In one aspect of his work Austin Clarke is the fulfillment of MacDonagh's dream of a separate Irish mode" in *Tribute to Austin Clarke* (Dublin: Dolmen Press, 1966), p. 9.
5. Máirtín O'Direáin, "Ionraiceas," *Dánta 1939–1979* (Baile Átha Cliath: An Clóchomhar, 1980), p. 69. Unless otherwise indicated, the translations are my own.
6. Máirtín O'Direáin, *Feamainn Bhealtaine* (Baile Átha Cliath: An Clóchomhar, 1961), p. 34.
7. *Illustrated Guide to the Northern, Western and Southern Islands and Coast of Ireland.* Royal Society of Antiquaries of Ireland Handbook, 4 (Dublin: Hodges, Figgis, 1905), p. 61.
8. Patrick F. Sheeran, *The Novels of Liam O'Flaherty* (Atlantic Highlands: Humanities Press, 1976), p. 15.
9. Douglas Sealy, "Five Poems by Máirtín O'Direáin," *Dublin Magazine* 8 (1969):63.
10. An t-Athair Martin O'Donnell, *Oileáin Árann* (Baile Átha Cliath: hOifig an tSoláthair, 1930), p. 255.
11. Seamus Heaney, "Lovers on Aran," *Poems 1965–1975* (New York: Farrar, Straus and Giroux, 1980), p. 35.
12. Tom O'Flaherty, *Aranmen All* (Dublin: At the Sign of the Three Candles, 1934), p. 136.
13. Liam O'Flaherty, "Going into Exile," *The Short Stories of Liam O'Flaherty* (London: Jonathan Cape, 1948), p. 150.

14. Frank O'Brien, *Filíocht Ghaeilge na Linne Seo* (Baile Átha Cliath: An Clóchomhar, 1968), p. 238.

15. Ezra Pound, Canto 45 "With *Usura*," in "The Fifth Decade of Cantos," *The Cantos of Ezra Pound* (New York: New Directions, 1948), p. 24.

16. Eoghan OhAnluain, "The Twentieth Century: Prose and Verse," in Aodh DeBlácam, *Gaelic Literature Surveyed* (New York: Barnes & Noble, 1974), p. 391.

Some Aspects of
Contemporary Prose in Irish

Charles B. Quinn, C.F.C.

With the collapse of the Gaelic polity in the seventeenth century there began the decay of a centuries-old literary tradition. In the late nineteenth century, when the language revivalists initiated their crusade to restore the Irish language, the lack of a continuous literary development posed serious problems for those who began to use Irish as a literary medium. The literary output since the turn of the century has been an interesting and significant one and for convenience' sake may be considered under two periods: the time before World War II and the years since. This essay will review some aspects of the prose of the latter period with particular attention to the short story.

It was in the Gaelic League's ideal of saving and restoring the language that the writers of the first period found their main inspiration. Fortunately, early on the decision was made to reject the archaic literary diction in favor of *caint na ndaoine,* the living language of the people of the Gaeltacht, the Irish-speaking areas. The richness and liveliness of the language was readily apparent; much of its attraction lay in its freedom from tired literary clichés. Its adaptability and suitability as a literary medium was soon established. It is not surprising that the literature would focus on the country people of the Gaeltacht where Irish was the medium of communication.

By 1940 the first generation to learn Irish in school was coming to adulthood, a generation which found little to relish in the predominantly rural-oriented writing then in vogue. It is significant that one of the first efforts of the newer school of writers was a satire on the fíor-Ghael, the stock Gaelic League figure, and on the Irish writers. In *An Béal Bocht* (1941) by "Myles na gCopaleen" we find the city worm turning on the depressing repetition of the narrowness, poverty, and misery of the Gaeltacht found in earlier writings. At this time, also, the Comhchaidreamh, the union of university Gaelic societies, founded the monthly, *Comhar* (1946), which together with the Gaelic League's monthly *Feasta* (1948), became the vehicles for the essays, short stories, poetry, and criticism of the new generation. Signs of the new vigor were apparent in the founding of the weekly paper *Inniu* (1943) and the publishing house of Sáirséal agus Dill (1945). This latter venture had remarkable success in producing a steady stream of worthwhile books and, in particular, in creating a market for literature in Irish.

If the writing of the second period is less parochial in content, more open-minded, and more in touch with modern life than that of the earlier decades, it is because the writers of the earlier period were more concerned with the problems of restoring the language and making it a vehicle of expression rather than using it as a philosophical means of seeing personal identity as a mirror of the national identity they were trying to preserve. The newer writing focuses on the individual, his inclinations and expectations, his place in society, his need to understand and explain himself.

The oral tradition of story-telling still very much alive in Ireland at the turn of the century was, no doubt, a strong influence on the popularity of the short story form. The *seanchaí* or story-teller recited his tales around the fire to winter-night gatherings. These tales differed little in plot and story outline from generation to generation and from teller to teller and so, of necessity, the prowess of the *seanchaí* depended (apart from the extent of his repertoire) on the way he spun his tale, that is, on the vividness and drama of his imagery, the sharpness of his detail, and the charm of his turn of phrase. That attitude to story-telling, to the impact of the teller's voice actually speaking, was part of the heritage of the Irish short-story writer.

The development of the short story in Irish we owe to Pádraig Mac Piarais (1879–1916) and Pádraig Ó Conaire (1883–1928), both of whom were familiar with the genre from their acquaintance with English and other European languages. In all, about thirty-nine collections of short stories were published before 1940. The popularity of this genre may be explained by the fact that Irish literature was in the main a periodical literature. Short story writing was a part-time occupation and the individual with literary talent had a better chance of success with it than with the novel form which requires time and leisure for reading and research.

Máirtín Ó Cadhain is the most significant prose writer of the later period. Evident in all his work is a concern with language, the language of his native Connemara Gaeltacht, but used with a richness and vitality and sometimes obscurity hitherto unknown. From the pages of *As an nGéibheann* and from his own *Páipéir Bhána agus Páipéir Bhreaca* (1969) we learn much about his literary education, his wide reading in Irish and a half-dozen European

languages, and his interest in the short story form. The listing of his
collection of short stories is impressive: *Idir Shughradh agus Dáiríre*
(1934), *An Braon Broghach* (1948), *Cois Caoláire* (1953), *An tSraith ar
Lár* (1967), *An tSraith dá Tógáil* (1970).[1]

People caught up in the problems of living in a period of changing values
and life styles, of being isolated in a world they do not comprehend, of
deciding questions that admit of no easy solutions—these are his topics. It is
not surprising that the people of the Gaeltacht figure largely in his stories,
particularly the early ones. Other writers had written of these folk as types
rather than characters, as repositories of all that was best in the ancestral
culture. Ó Cadhain is more realistic in his treatment: he shows them as they
are, very human Irish men and Irish women. This integrity of presentation,
although deplored by some, has been generally praised by the critics. Later
on, as his experience widened, he wrote of urban life with confidence and
conviction.

His growth as a writer is apparent as he freed himself from dependence
upon earlier short story writers such as Pádraig Ó Conaire, Séamas Ó
Grianna, Tomás Báiréad, and others. The very titles of his stories in the first
collections are traditional: "Idir Shughradh agus Dáiríre," "Gan an
Craiceann ná a Luach." The story about three birds in snowy weather is
reminiscent of Tomás Báiréad as is "Mac Rí na nDeachmann," the narrative
about a young boy who climbs the walls of an old castle to rob a bird's nest
but is killed in the attempt. The writer's imagery has a distinct rural and
agricultural base. The style is verbose and plot development depends upon
what one reviewer terms "modh an charntha,"[2] a method of accretion by
which incident is piled upon incident, reflection upon reflection. However,
the reader is aware of the hard realistic tone of the author, the eye for detail,
the tendency to examine events minutely, and to probe the minds and actions
of the characters in order to understand their motivation.

The Gaeltacht and its people, particularly the women folk, are major
themes of the two succeeding collections: *An Braon Broghach* and *Cois
Caoláire*. As *de facto* head of the household, the woman directs all her
energies and devotes all resources to the continuity of the family, of religion
and tradition. The author's understanding of these women, long-suffering
and leading very circumscribed lives, is remarkable and his treatment is
sympathetic. His ability to inhabit their minds, as it were, perhaps explains
his fondness for the kind of interior monologue he employs so successfully.

A woman's long meditation on her poverty-stricken situation is the
substance of "An Bóthar go dtí an Ghealchathair." Bríd, a strong
independent-minded woman, is forced to walk the nine long miles each

Saturday to the city market with her basket of produce. The pathos of her plight and her secret longings are revealed through the accumulation of details that chase through her mind: memories, hopes unrealized, the rumors, gossip, and backbiting of the neighbors, even the physical features of the road and names of the townlands. As the ruminations go on and on, the concentration one expects in a short story is weakened.

"An Strainséara" is the story of a woman, Nora, whose five children were stillborn and whose husband has invited a nephew to manage and inherit the farm. Nora's antipathy to the stranger is based on the fact that he, the nephew, will eventually succeed to what should have been her children's inheritance. She broods over her dead children, who her distorted mind tells her are in Limbo. Under the weight of sorrow and delusion she dies. The melodramatic ending, a departure from the probable or likely event, is unusual in Ó Cadhain. The focus of the narrative is divided between Nora's irrational resistance to the stranger whose every act and utterance intensifies her dislike, and her brooding over her dead children. The story has power to move the reader deeply as it reveals the tortured mind of Nora through the agony and gloom of her thoughts.

The interior monologue with its tones of anxiety, irony, and frustration is used very effectively in "Ciumhas an Chriathraigh," the story of a middle-aged unmarried woman, Muiréad, whose mind and sensibilities are hardening under the daily drudgery of farming, unaided, a poor piece of land. The soil is unproductive. She, too, is infertile. She regrets that she rejected the young man who had proposed to her years before. She envies the married women with their homes and children and security. A recent experience at a wedding when a young man embraced her troubles her conscience and sets her mind dreaming of what might have been. Through the illumination of a small incident Ó Cadhain gives a passionate reading of the deeply troubled mind of a woman hemmed in and restricted by the circumstances of life and thus leads the reader to a sympathetic understanding of the pathos of her plight.

The most mature of the writings of Ó Cadhain are found in *An tSraith ar Lár* (1967) and *An tSraith dá Tógáil* (1970). The verboseness is not so pronounced, diffuseness of plot is less noticeable, and dialogue is used effectively to advance the story. Much variety is found in these collections: urban life as well as country life, men as principals in the stories with women in the roles of companions and helpmates, the bizarre and the fanciful side by side with the realistic.

The theme of conflict runs through the stories of the first collection. There is the struggle between the old and the young, between new ways and old ways, between life and death. "An Sean agus an Nua" and "Úr agus Críon" might well be pieces from the literature of despair. In the latter tale the shell of an old decaying currach symbolizes the de-Gaelicification of the Gaeltacht. The terrible final moments in the struggle with death through famine are acutely portrayed in the story "Gorta." But Ó Cadhain is not all gloom: the celebration and affirmation of life is the theme of the stories "An Bheo agus an Marbh" and "An Bheo agus an Críon."

"Sraith Eile ar Lár" posits a fanciful world where horses speak and seek to break the chains of slavery to their master, man. This search for freedom from tyranny is a satire on man's vaunted pride in his achievements and, at the same time, an allegory of man's own unending search for a Utopia here below. There is a strain of fantasy running through the theme of the story "Cé Acu? . . .," a mixture of the exaggeration and broad humor so characteristic of the old comic tradition of Irish prose. Fundamentally, it is a bitter attack on the philistinism of modern city life.

The study of the grotesque, of the malicious and brutish in man seems to fascinate Ó Cadhain as evident in the stories "Fios" and "Fuíoll." In "Fuíoll" a former footballer recounts the glory of his prowess on the playing field, a strange kind of fame in that for him "getting the man" was more important than getting the ball. The author invests this "tough" man with the trappings of the hero of folklore and succeeds in producing a hilariously biting satire on the brutality of the playing arena, thereby deflating the vulgar hero-worship attending some athletic greats. The piece "A Simple Lesson" written in the style of *Finnegans Wake* still remains unexplicated. One wonders how much further this obscure incomprehensible language can go.

There are two long stories, "An Eochair" and "Fuíoll Fuine," that reveal the author's interest in the dark, gloomy aspects of modern life. Ó Cadhain understands and treats sympathetically those melancholic, alienated ones who feel themselves hedged in by the uncertainties of life and seem unable to understand or direct their own lives. It is significant that two such nameless alienated ones are introduced as J. in "An Eochair" and N. in "Fuíoll Fuine." J., a civil servant, a "handler of paper," manages to lock himself in his office overnight. Bureaucratic red tape and the petty regulations of the service are unable to provide the key for his release. In all, the story is an indictment of the impersonality of modern-day government. Despite the long wearying interior monologue the character of J. is inadequately developed; the apparent irony and the satire on bureaucracy is less than subtle.

"Fuíoll Fuine" is a more successful composition. N., another civil servant, receives a call in his office on Saturday morning telling him that his wife has died and asking that he hasten home to attend to the funeral arrangements. It appears that everyone and everything is conspiring to prevent him from fulfilling his duties. The story tells of his aimless odyssey through the city streets on the weekend. Finally he escapes the conventions and his obligations by becoming a stowaway on a tramp ship bound for his Tír Tairngire, Boston! Such a summary tells little of the strange fantasy of this piece in which Ó Cadhain has presented skillfully and sensitively one view of the human condition.

These two pieces and others reveal what has been styled the lack of appreciation on the part of Ó Cadhain for the literary form known as the short story. One critic, Alan Titley, has studied the matter in a recent article, "Máirtín Ó Cadhain agus Foirm and Ghearrscéil."[3] He concedes that Ó Cadhain has taken liberties with the traditional form; however, the changes or developments he made in this departure from the canon were for flexibility and freedom to express himself.

Examples of the classical short story—the short piece illuminating some one significant event or action—abound in the collections: "Culaith le Cois," "An Bhliain 1912," "An Taoille Tuile," "Fios," "I mBus Catharach." There are other stories, usually long pieces like "An Strain-séara," "An Bóthar go dtí an Ghealchathair," "Ciréib," "An Ecohair," in which the illumination or epiphany does not depend upon one eye-opening flash but upon the accumulation of many minor revelations. Other items—fables, allegories, prose poems—resist neat classification. The reader does not find linear structure nor forward movement nor progressive plot development in pieces like "Cé Acu? . . . ," "Fuíoll," and "Fuíoll Fuine" (upwards of 50,000 words long).

The freedom Sterne, Joyce, and others found for the novel form, Ó Cadhain sought for the short story, the presenting of a view of life in other than neat patterns. Titley suggests that the remarks made by Ó Cadhain relative to the poetry of the eighteenth century might well apply to his own handling of the short story form: "Is féidir foirmeacha a chosaint ach ní féidir formulas . . . Ní foirm féin a d'fhan inti ach formula—formula ionann chomh tur le formula ailgéabair"[4] (forms can be defended but not formulae . . . what remained in it was but a formula, a formula as dry as an algebraic formula). The critical writings of Ó Cadhain do not reveal any set formulated literary theories. He gave full scope to his imagination; the view of the human condition he chose to portray dictated the form the story would take. His works should not be judged by any preconceived notions of literary conventions but on their own terms and the author's fidelity to his own vision of reality. For him, literature was to give more than a realistic representation of life, it was to be an extension of that life, describing not only what is but what might be.

Above all, he had a command of the language unequalled among modern Irish writers, an extensive vocabulary about which all marvel, and a strong robust style. His latest works reveal his great comic gift, the ability to sustain artful exaggeration with pure fantasy. He has assured himself a place in the long line of comic prose writers from Mac Conglinne down. Máirtín Ó Cadhain has shown, if it needed showing, that the Irish language is more than adequate as a literary medium.

Like Ó Cadhain, Liam Ó Flaithearta is also a native speaker. Early in his career he realized that his reading public would be an English-speaking one and so the bulk of his literary works, novels and short stories, were written in English. There is, however, one collection of short stories in Irish, *Dúil,* some eighteen stories mainly concerned with country people and with animals.[5]

The narrative skill of Ó Flaithearta seems instinctive: the ease and grace of his writing carry the reader beyond difficulties of language and dialect to sheer enjoyment in the mastery the author shows of his craft. Although *Dúil* might be read at one or two sittings, the stories are well above average and a few, "Teangabháil," "An Buille," "Díoltas," "An Culaith Nua," "Oifig an Phoist," excite the reader and awaken a response by reason of their fidelity to the aspects of the human condition portrayed. It is the measure of the author's ability that through the minute examination of the characters and actions of a few, Ó Flaithearta succeeds in conveying a sense of universality, a feeling tinged with understanding and humor, with pity and compassion.

Ó Flaithearta is attracted by the nature and mystery of life and living things, the cycle of birth, growth, decay, and death. His fascination and wonder are most evident in those stories which depict elemental instincts and reactions whether in man or animal. His imagination is captivated by the flight of a bird of prey in "An Seabhac" or by an examination of marine life on a half-submerged rock in "An Charraig Dhubh," or by the engaging innocence of childhood in "An Culaith Nua," or by the jealousy and malice of an old man in "Díoltas." So intense is his feeling that he seems to submerge his own personality as a writer in the nature of the things he chronicles. His descriptive powers are best seen in his treatment of nature in the raw, as it were, in the nature of birds, animals, and humans through their contrasting instinctual reactions to the opposing claims of love and violence, of strength and vulnerability.

In "An Seabhac" we see the fierce wild independence of the hawk, its concern and care for its mate, its triumphant return with its kill, and finally the grand and futile defense of its nest against the human intruder. In "Bás na Bó" the cow that plunges to her death seeking the remains of her dead calf is a symbol of protective motherhood, a symbol made more poignant by the grief and sympathy of the farmer's wife, herself a mother as the author reminds us. This illumination of an ordinary occurrence through its relationship with the human condition enhances the effectiveness of the symbol. In one of his most unusual short stories, "An Scáthán," the author presents a girl glorying in the beauty and mystery of her womanhood as she sees for the first time her own naked body reflected in a pool of seawater. This celebration of vibrant animal life, of corporal beauty is tinged with feelings of awe and fear on the part of the young girl. The vignette, however, does end with an affirmation of the acceptance of beauty and womanhood.

Young love is the theme of "An Teangabháil." Páidín Pheadair Réamoinn is determined that his daughter, Cáit, will marry someone other than the hired farmhand, Beartla. The tenderness of the young love has been expressed only through shy glances and an involuntary touch of the hands. In a harsh and brutal fashion, Páidín berates the young man for his lowly social status. Rather than show the manliness and courage expected by Cáit, Beartla meekly accepts the insults. It is a victory of the strong over the weak. Cáit realizes all too well that in the narrow circumscribed life destined for her the covert touch of the hands is all the love she will ever know and, also, that her father will make a match for her and sell her to the highest bidder.

This theme of the strong and the weak as evidenced in the relationship of a father and eleven-year-old son is the substance of one of the best of the stories, "An Buille." Éamonn Ó Floinn is a characteristic nineteenth-century gombeen man, successful, calculating, hard, aggressive, rough. He is disappointed in his only son, Neidín, a sensitive, dreamy, imaginative boy who appears to lack the father's ambition and drive to get ahead. When buying a litter of bonhams, Éamonn draws a parallel between the runt of the litter that seems unable to fight for its mother's milk and Neidín, who he says is spoiled by his mother. The boy protests and in a fit of anger the father strikes him. Neidín shows such silent, unflinching, terrible anger that the father is shamed and frightened. He is mollified, however, when Neidín expresses open admiration for the father's skill in bargaining. A new bond of affection has arisen between father and son, and although the former may still boast and brag, his voice is now respectful. This illustration of the blending of the tenderness and toughness of the Irish character is a triumph for Ó Flaithearta.

Few writers have projected the innocence of youth in as lively and touching a way as does Ó Flaithearta in "An Culaith Nua." Seven-year-old Seámaisín has been promised a new suit for Christmas; however, he must wait until the sheep are shorn, the wool carded and the suit made by the traveling tailor. The author portrays through this simple ordinary happening feelings the reader immediately recognizes as true—the direct singlemind-edness of youth, the inexhaustible patience of the mother, and the amused tolerance of age.

Admittedly the short stories of Ó Flaithearta lack the breadth and com-plexity of those of Ó Cadhain or of Seán Ó Faolain. The setting is the small farm and the seashore of the West; the people are farmers and fishermen. However, this simple world echoes the author's boyhood and is perfectly attuned to the passions and instincts he wishes to stress. He fashions images of a life that seems timeless. Readers regret that he has not written more in Irish. *Dúil* was enthusiastically received and has been consistently admired, so much so, that one critic labelled it the best collection of short stories in the language.[6]

Another writer whose reputation rests upon a slender output of short stories is Donncha Ó Céileachair. He grew up in the County Cork Gaeltacht but spent most of his adult life in Dublin. Part of his heritage from his father, a noted *seanchaí,* was a knowledge of folklore and story-telling. The most interesting portion of his literary work which includes essays, a travel journal, and biography, is a collection of short stories, *Bullaí Mhártain.*[7]

Ó Céileachair writes about change in post-war Ireland, particularly about changing life styles in the country. Other writers lamented the passing of olden ways and customs; Ó Céileachair is revealing what the passing meant to people who live in the changing times. When speaking of the men of the past he has Bullaí Mhártain, the principal in the title story, describe them thus: "Ba dhiabhail iad na seanbhuachaillí" (They were devils, the old boys). The pride, stubbornness, and aggressiveness of the old timers, traits often inherited by their sons, are the subject matter of the best of the stories: "Socraid Neil Chonchubhair Dhuibh," "Bullaí Mhártain," "Mac an Chait," "An Diúichín agus an Lady," and in an implied way in "Na Deartháireacha." The range of the stories is limited. Where Ó Cadhain will attempt to render moments of great human passion or suffering, Ó Céileachair remains, as it were, on the surface of things. He does, however, create a convincing atmosphere for the stories dealing with tradition and heritage, and writes with effortless ease.

In the rural society which Ó Céileachair describes, honor is paid to those who show superiority in natural endowments; in the case of the men, these qualities are strength, courage, and fighting ability. The action of the story "Socraid Neil Chonchubhair Dhuibh" takes place in the lives of people reared in the tradition of faction fighting but who had turned to peaceful ways at the urging of the clergy and of O'Connell. The uneasy peace between two opposing factions has been cemented by the marriage of Neil of

Na Loinnsigh and Muirtí Óg of Muintir Céileachair. When Neil dies in childbirth a dispute arises as to the place of burial, whether with her people or with those of her husband. Old enmities die hard and upon insisting on the right to inter her, Conchubhar Dubh precipitates a faction fight. Having won the fight and established the principle that might is right, Conchubhar yields to the counsels of peace and permits the burial with the husband's people. The glorification of violence is reminiscent of the heroic tale. It is interesting to see how Ó Céileachair uses some of the qualities of the folk tale: listing of details, the preparation for the fight, the use of compound adjectives in the descriptive passages. Through his detached ironic tone the author does succeed in revealing something of the people living in changing times.

Another character who does not understand the new ways and hence resists them is Bullaí Mhártain of the title story. He has inherited the pride and bravado of his father and grandfather, the latter a noted faction fighter. The story describes Bullaí attending a dance at the New Arcadia, Ballyduff. He despises the new-fangled behavior, the new style of dancing, the affected gentility of the dancers, and the cant words and phrases. He picks a fight, but in the struggle is struck from behind by a bottle wielded by a friend of his opponent. Bullaí is killed. The story concludes by having three observers discuss the incident dispassionately. The success of the story lies in the author's ability to create atmosphere, to describe realistically and vividly the dance hall and the fight. The characterization of Bullaí is superficial; indeed, the close identification of the author with his hero suggests an element of sentimentality despite the effort on the part of the author to maintain an ironic distance.

Another kind of reaction to change is suggested in ''Breathnach na Carraige.'' Breathnach, a farmer, has by his own industry and hard work turned a piece of bad land into a productive farm. He has been selected by the government to receive a farm of good land near Dublin city. The deep anguish he experiences in leaving the scene of his success, a farm that had been in his family for generations, is sharply contrasted with the unconcealed joy of the family, rejoicing in the prospect of living near the big city. Like most Irishmen he is unable or unwilling to express openly the soft side of his nature; anger is the only emotion he can show to conceal the heartbreak he feels.

This kind of psychological conflict is apparent in the story of two brothers, ''Na Deartháireacha.'' Páid, the older, has shed his rural background and has become, as he thinks, very urbanized. However, it takes but one evening of convivial camaraderie with his younger brother and some companions to reveal how very thin is the veneer of city life when confronted with memories of familial pride and boasting.

There is a strong vein of humor in Ó Céileachair, particularly when dealing with aspects of life associated with the city apartment, the office, the dance hall, the golf club. These pleasant little stories or anecdotes— "Pedro," "An Bráthair Seán," "Caitríona agus an Laoch," "An Grá Géar"—achieve their effect usually by some unexpected reversal occurring at the conclusion of the stories.

It is to be expected that Ó Céileachair would be influenced by the oral folk tradition of the Irish language. Writers and poets have drawn on the riches of folklore for characters and motifs. However, in a recent study of Ó Céileachair, Pádráigín Riggs has shown how Ó Céileachair has artistically woven the style and techniques of the oral folktale into the texture of his story-telling.[8] One significant theme she finds in many of the stories is what she styles *laochas,* translated variously as heroism, valor, boastfulness. There is a pattern in such stories as "Socraid Neil," "Bullaí Mhártain," "Mac an Chait," "An Diúichín agus an Lady": a series of happenings, stylized descriptions of the hero, his dress and behavior, a conflict, and authorial comment intruding upon the voice of the narrator. The mock-heroic element is pervasive; the echoes of the heroic style so skilfully introduced create an atmosphere that gives vitality and unity to the stories. And for those familiar with the oral tradition the range of the stories is extended and there is an added dimension of understanding and pleasure.

In view of the variety in the stories it would be unfair to characterize Ó Céileachair only as a lamenter of times past; what he does imply is that much is sacrificed if the past is too readily jettisoned for what appears to be improved modes of living.

The advance in the Irish economy since the sixties, the increased prosperity, the influence of the mass media, and the consequent influx of new ideas and life styles: all these developments have called in question and challenged many of the established religious, social, and national values. The short story writer has found new themes. The influence of Máirtín Ó Cadhain is strong on writers such as Pádraig Breathnach, many of whose stories deal with lonely and dissatisfied people at odds with life, who lack direction because they pursue wealth and worldly advancement to the neglect of those values that would enrich their lives. As is evident for the stories in his most recent collection, Breathnach is interested in the imaginative lives of his characters.[9] Their wishes, anxieties, and hopes are usually portrayed through the interior monologue as seen in "M'Ogbhean Ghleghorm,"

"Tráithníní," "Im-imní," and others. The title story, "Na Déithe Luachmhara Deiridh," is not unlike "Ciumhais an Chriathraigh" of Ó Cadhain
but Breathnach does not have the narrative skill of Ó Cadhain nor the latter's
control of image and metaphor.

There was no native tradition of the literary form we know as the novel
available for writers in Irish; their only model was that of the realistic novel
of the nineteenth century. The novel form itself was not static; twentieth-
century writers had shown the possibilities of development. It is significant
that the most important Irish novel, *Cré na Cille* (1949), by Máirtín Ó
Cadhain, should be influenced by the Joycean tradition. The *cill,* or cemetery, of the title is a small graveyard in Connemara and the characters of
the book are the corpses interred in the graveyard. The novel is written in
the form of conversations between the corpses and the action is advanced
by the arrival of fresh corpses with the latest news from the world above.
Identification among the characters is facilitated by the recurring
peculiarities in their speech patterns.

The style of life revealed is a narrow and harsh one: we are told about the
bitterness, jealousies, hates, and disputes among family members and
among neighbors. At the center of all the backbiting and revilement is
Caitríona Pháidín. All her thoughts and arguments with her companions are
colored by the deep consuming hatred she bears her sister, Nell (still living),
who stole the affections of the man she loved. Another principal is An
Máistir Mór, the local schoolmaster, whose marital problems continue after
his death when he learns that the smooth-talking Bileachaí an Phosta has
married his widow. The irony is compounded when she has Bileachaí
interred alongside her first love. More confusion is caused when malicious
arrivals deliberately supply false or inaccurate information. Without any
elaborate physical description Ó Cadhain has created a public that is credible, integral, and dynamic.

The strangeness of the form, a marked departure from the style of the
realistic novel, worried the reviewers. They recognized the novel as a major
literary achievement but deplored the biased description of the people—the
absence of any kindness or softness in their nature—and the lack of
psychological realism in that the characters remain static, as it were "frozen." However, recent criticism has adverted to the comic dimensions of the
work and stresses the need to examine its structure in the light of the
development of the novel form since Joyce. The most interesting critical
reading is that of Breandán Ó Doibhlin who views the work as a comedy.[10]
Accepting the novelist's premises—an imagined world of the dead which is
in sharp contrast to accepted beliefs of life after death—Ó Doibhlin sees the

possibilities of humor, irony, and comedy. The cultural tradition out of which *Cré na Cille* originates has nothing in common with such modern European concepts as advanced by the drama of the absurd such as the despair of reason and the tragic emptiness of life. The people Ó Cadhain creates do not manifest any loathing of the human condition, rather, they accept life's absurdities. Ó Doibhlin argues that to laugh at the meanness of life is more sensible than to cry, and that humor is a healthy restraint on over-seriousness or despair. These considerations lead him to see in *Cré na Cille* deeper and truer aspects of the Irish mind and character than had previously been shown either in Irish or English. Viewing the novel as a comedy of manners we can see why Ó Cadhain stressed the sordid side of life by holding up for ridicule personal weaknesses and faults so that the persons depicted become caricatures rather than characters.

Another writer interested in psychological probing of character is Eoghan Ó Tuairisc whose works include novels, short stories, drama, and poetry in Irish and English.[11] His first novel, *L'Attaque* (1962), deals with an incident in the ill-fated rebellion of 1798 when a French force under General Humber landed at Killala, County Mayo. The work lacks the wide scope, the plenitude of characters, and the plot development one expects in a historical novel. The pictorial language with its abundance of metaphor and the impressionistic style make it more a prose poem than a novel. The second work, *De Luain* (1966), is an imaginative reconstruction of the hours between midnight on Easter Saturday, 1916, and the reading of the Proclamation at noon on Easter Monday, and also of the thoughts and actions of the principals in the Rising. The consistency and accuracy of the historical portraits are convincing and they are sketched on a canvas sufficiently ample to allow the reader to visualize even minor details clearly. The literary method employed, the stream of consciousness, permits the author to illuminate motives and emotions. With Pearse and Plunkett the device is particularly successful, perhaps because Ó Tuairisc, himself a poet, discovered a certain affinity with these thinkers of the Rebellion. Movement in the novel is slow at times because of wordiness and diffuseness.

Writing about modern urban life in a language not ordinarily used as a medium of communication in the cities is a major problem facing the Irish writer. Not every writer has the linguistic resources which enabled Ó Cadhain to adapt traditional speech to modern forms. Diarmaid Ó Súilleabháin, brought up in an English-speaking environment, has made a conscious effort to depict contemporary life. Two of his novels deserve attention, *Caoin Tú Féin* (1966) and *An Uain Bheo* (1967).[12] There is a kind of story in the first-mentioned: Ian Ó Murchú, a schoolteacher, waking from a drunken sleep recalls the painful events of the night before, his wife's leaving him. In the cold light of the morning after Ian begins his ruminations, his self-examination, his introspective analysis. He reviews his boyhood, his adult years, his work, his marriage, his friends, and, above all, he wonders who and what Ian Ó Murchú is. *An Uain Bheo* is a more complex story dealing with one principal character, Louis Stein, a restless individual who feels estranged from life by reason of his self-consciousness as a Jew, his sense of loneliness, and his fear of death. His love for Orla gives some meaning to his life until the tragedy of her death in a car accident for which he feels responsible. Service to others does help to restore his ideals which, however, are based on feeling alone. The novel states that life is tragic, that the elements, such as love, which are supposed to give meaning to life are easily lost, and that one must have some ideals to survive.

The experimental modes of narration Ó Súilleabháin employs along with his untraditional use of the language have puzzled readers. He admits to a kind of missionary zeal in his effort to adapt the language to his purposes, an ambitious undertaking. While the interior monologue technique enables him to portray admirably the fragmentariness of life, his stylistic tricks—hyperbole, individualized syntax, use of capitals and parentheses—tend to distract the reader. To elect to write in Irish is a major commitment for writers such as Ó Súilleabháin who have grown up in the Galltacht (English-speaking) areas. Such a choice is one of the themes of Breandán Ó Doibhlin's one-character novel. *An Branar Gan Cur.* [13] The book describes a train journey from Dublin to Derry by Feargus MacGiolla Chalma, a young university lecturer. The trip is a sort of spiritual odyssey during which Feargus meditates on the history of the country through which he passes, on the people he meets, and on his own psychological problems. He illustrates well the disappointment and pain of the northern nationalist with the people of the South, their hypocrisy, and their rejection of the ideals of Gaelic Ireland. The book is more a dissertation than a novel, an examination of ideas such as love, freedom, service, ideas that the author enumerates but which are not imaginatively developed in the unfolding of the plot.

Story-telling, whether in the short story or novel form, has not been the only development in Irish prose; a sizable body of what might be styled factual literature—autobiography, memoir, biography, and academic writing—has been produced. Three autobiographies from the Blasket Is-lands published in the 1920s and 1930s were eminently successful. Their popularity has established the autobiography as a fashionable literary form. Among the many memoirs appearing since the 1940s have been the following most noteworthy ones: *Dialann Deoraí* (1960), by Dónall Mac Amhlaigh, who writes of life among Connemara navvies in post-war London; *Dialann Oilithrigh* (1955), by Donncha Ó Céileachair, who recounts a pilgrimage to Rome; and *Aisteoirí Faoi Dhá Sholas,* by Mícheál Mac Liammóir, the distinguished actor.

Many of those who played prominent parts in the struggle for national freedom and in the Gaelic League in the early decades of the century have written or dictated their memoirs. These books are an important and indispensable source of historical and sociological information about the beginnings of the modern Irish state. Many biographies have been published: those on Arthur Griffith, Eamonn de Valera, and other leaders are scholarly works and are the definitive histories of the lives they chronicle. Two biographies by Seán Ó Luing merit mention by reason of the thoroughness of the research and attractiveness of style: *Art Ó Gríofa* (1953) and *Ó Donnabháin Rossa I* (1970), *II* (1980). The most interesting and readable of the many biographies is *An Duinníneach,* [14] the life of Rev. Patrick Dineen, scholar, Gaelic Leaguer, lexicographer, and author. The joint authorship of this work has been a happy partnership. It is remarkable how skillfully the authors have presented the brilliant but eccentric scholar. It has been fashionable to write of the disintegration and decay of Irish cultural and national life at the beginning of the century. However, the essential links with the past were there. *An Duinníneach* captures the excitement and glamor of those decades in the lives of those who were consciously re-examining their cultural heritage and who were to establish a new Ireland.

The reading public for Irish literature is a largely urban intelligentsia. With the continual shrinking of the Irish-speaking areas there is the possibility that in the future, writers will not be the native speakers but learners who have acquired near native ability in the use of the language. It will be difficult for these latter to avoid an unwelcome division of mind, living, as they must, between the Gaelic world and the English-speaking world. Anglo-Irish literature by its choice of language is directed to a world audience. The writer of Irish has a smaller but more homogeneous public. It is regrettable that there is no satisfactory corpus of critical literature from which all writers would profit. Up to now there is no critical study of the most important author to date, Máirtín Ó Cadhain, who is likely to remain the model for writers of fiction in Irish, in particular for short story writers. The significant novels will only come with a greater degree of professionalism, a professionalism that comes from constant writing and total dedication.

Notes

1. Most of the collections of short stories as well as the novel *Cré na Cille* have been published by the Dublin firm, Sáirséal agus Dill; the two earliest collections were published by Oifig an tSoláthair and the pamphlet *Páipéir Bhána agus Páipéir Bhreaca* by An Clóchomhair Teo. A few of the short stories have been translated by Eoghan Ó Tuairisc, *The Road to Brightcity and Other Stories* (Dublin: Poolbeg Press, 1981).

2. Seán Ó Tuama, "Scríbhneoir Ionraic," *Feasta* (Samhain 1953), p. 13.

3. *Comhar* (Deire Fomhair 1980), pp. 34–40.

4. Ibid., p. 39.

5. Liam Ó Flaithearta, *Dúil* (Sáirséal agus Dill: Baile Átha Cliath, 1953). It is not easy to ascertain which stories Ó Flaithearta first wrote in Irish or first in English. Paul A. Doyle in *Liam O'Flaherty* (New York: Twayne Publishers, 1971), p. 133, suggests that about one-half of the stories in *Dúil* were first written in English.

6. Breandán Ó Buachalla, "Ó Cadhain, Ó Céileachair agus Ó Flaithearta," *Comhar* (Bealtaine 1967), p. 75.

7. Donncha Ó Céileachair, *Bullaí Mhártain* (Sáirséal agus Dill: Baile Átha Cliath, 1955).

8. Pádráigín Riggs, *Donncha Ó Céileachair: Anailís Stíleach* (Oifig an tSoláthair: Baile Átha Cliath, 1978), p. 153.

9. Pádraig Breathnach, *Na Déithe Luachmhara Deiridh* (Clódhanna Teoranta: Baile Átha Cliath, 1980).

10. Breandán Ó Doibhlin, "Athléamh ar *Chré na Cille*," *Léachtaí Cholm Chille* V (1974), pp. 40–53.

11. Eoghan Ó Tuairisc, *L'Attaque* (Allen Figgis agus a Chuid, Teo.: Baile Átha Cliath, 1962); *Dé Luain* was issued by the same publisher in 1966.

12. Diarmaid Ó Súilleabháin, *Caoin Tú Féin* (Sáirséal agus Dill: Baile Átha Cliath, 1967); *An Uain Bheo* by the same publisher appeared in 1968.

13. Breandán Ó Doibhlin, *An Branar gan Chur* (Gilbert Dalton: Baile Átha Cliath, 1979).

14. Proinsias Ó Conluain agus Donncha Ó Céileachair, *An Duinníneach* (Sáirséal agus Dill: Baile Átha Cliath, 1958).

Notes on Contributors

Anthony Bradley is a professor of English at the University of Vermont where he teaches Irish literature and is co-director of the Summer Program in Irish Studies. He holds degrees from Queen's University, Belfast (B.A.), and S.U.N.Y. at Buffalo (Ph.D.). He is author of *William Butler Yeats* (Frederick Ungar, 1979), *Contemporary Irish Poetry: an Anthology* (University of California Press, 1980), and various articles on modern Irish literature.

James D. Brophy has written the critical studies, *Edith Sitwell: The Symbolist Order* (Southern Illinois University Press, 1968) and *W. H. Auden* (Columbia University Press, 1970). He has edited (with Raymond Porter) and contributed to *Modern Irish Literature* (Iona/Twayne, 1972), a *festschrift* in honor of William York Tindall. A graduate of Amherst (B.A.) and Columbia (Ph.D.) and a former Fulbright Fellow, he is a professor of English at Iona College.

John Engle has been teaching American literature at the *Université de Provence*. He wrote a UCLA doctoral dissertation on contemporary Irish poetry.

Eamon Grennan is from Dublin. Educated at U.C.D. and Harvard, he teaches at Vassar College, and has published articles on Irish poetry in *Eire-Ireland, Studies,* and *Renascence.* He has also published poetry in Irish and American periodicals; he is working on a book-length study of Irish poetic identity after Yeats.

Eileen Kennedy is a professor of English at Kean College of New Jersey, where she directs a graduate program in the M.A. in Liberal Studies. She is the author of numerous scholarly articles which have appeared in the *James Joyce Quarterly, English Literature in Transition, Eire-Ireland, Victorian Poetry, A Wake Newsletter, English Language Notes,* and in *Modern Irish Literature.*

Daniel Leary teaches English and Irish drama at City College of New York. He has published articles on Shaw, Joyce, and Bridie. At present, he is the guest editor of *SHAW: The Annual of Bernard Shaw Studies for 1983.*

Maureen Murphy is Secretary of the American Committee for Irish Studies, Historiographer of the American Irish Historical Society, and Bibliographer of the International Association for the Study of Anglo-Irish Literature. She has written on Irish history, literature, folklore, and the Irish Servant Girl in America. She is an associate professor of English at Hofstra University.

Daniel O'Hara is an associate professor of English at Temple University and an assistant editor of *Boundary 2: A Journal of Postmodern Literature.* He is the author of *Tragic Knowledge: Yeats's Autobiography and Hermeneutics* (Columbia University Press, 1981) and many essays on contemporary literature and criticism.

Charles B. Quinn, C.F.C. is a professor of English at Iona College where he teaches courses in Irish literature, history, and language. Brother Quinn studied at

University College, Dublin, and has reviewed works in the Irish language for *Books Abroad*. He has recently completed an introduction to the Irish language entitled *Reading Irish*.

Robert E. Rhodes is a professor of English at S.U.N.Y. Cortland, where he teaches courses in Irish and Irish-American literature. A member of the executive committee of the American Committee for Irish Studies, he has served as guest editor of two numbers of *Eire-Ireland*. Together with Daniel Casey, he has co-edited *Views of the Irish Peasantry: 1800–1919* (Archon Books, 1977) and *Irish-American Fiction: Essays in Criticism* (AMS Publishers, 1979), the latter containing his essay on F. Scott Fitzgerald as an Irish-American novelist.

Raymond J. Porter is a professor of English at Iona College where he teaches courses in Irish literature. He has edited (with James Brophy) and contributed to *Modern Irish Literature* (Iona/Twayne, 1972), a *festschrift* in honor of William York Tindall. A graduate of Holy Cross (B.A.) and Columbia (Ph.D.), he is the author of books on Pearse and Behan and essays on Joyce and O'Casey.

DATE DUE

GAYLORD   PRINTED IN U.S.A.